To Alistair,

7/4/22 A 4·00

THE ME REVISITED

by

Nigel Bovey

7. XI. /0

If it is found to be well written and aptly composed, that is what I myself aimed at; if superficial and mediocre, it was the best I could do (2 Maccabees 15:38 *Revised English Bible*).

UNITED KINGDOM TERRITORY
101 Newington Causeway, London SE1 6BN

To
Maggie, Janine and Andrew
(God's generous gifts of mercy)

ISBN 978 0 85412 830 3

Major Nigel Bovey
was commissioned as a Salvation Army officer, with his wife Margaret, in 1979. They have two children, Janine and Andrew. Nigel previously taught Mathematics, Sociology and Economics in a comprehensive school. He served as a corps officer in Northern Ireland and England before being appointed to *The War Cry* staff in 1994. As well as contributing chapters to a number of books, he is the author of *Telling a Children's Story*, *The Mercy Seat*, *Christians in the House* and *God, The Big Bang and Bunsen-burning Issues*. He is also a published songwriter, lyricist and poet. He is the Editor of *The War Cry*.

Scriptural quotations from the Holy Bible, *New International Version*, copyright © 1973, 1978, 1984. Zondervan and Hodder & Stoughton Limited.

Design consultant Stephen Pearson
Cover picture of the William Booth College mercy seat by Nigel Bovey
Back cover picture of Sheffield Citadel mercy seat by Peter Longbottom

Printed by THQ Print and Design Unit

Contents

Chapter	Page
Acknowledgements	vii
Foreword	ix
Preface	xi
Introduction	xv
1. Square One	1
2. They Shall Come From The East	9
3. They Shall Come From The West	19
4. The Mercy Seat and William Booth	33
5. The Centre of Gravity	47
6. The Mercy Seat and Brengle	59
7. The Focal Point in Focus	63
8. All Over the World	75
9. The Holiness Table	85
10. Cue For A Song	95
11. The Mercy Seat In Verse	107
12. Personal Reflections	119
13. Around a Common Mercy Seat – the Mercy Seat and Other Denominations	135
14. Pitfalls of Free Fall	139

15. The Mercy Seat and Creative Response 1   149

16. The Mercy Seat and Creative Response 2   163

17. Refreshed and Fed?   173

18. A Place of Grace or a Means of Grace?   185

19. The Mercy Seat in The Old Testament   199

20. The Mercy Seat in The New Testament   205

21. Next?   215

Appendix A. 2009 UK Mercy Seat Survey   225

Appendix B. 2009 Mercy Seat Inscriptions by Corps   241

Appendix C. 2009 Mercy Seat Inscriptions with Frequency   251

Appendix D. 1994 UK Mercy Seat Survey   253

Appendix E. 1994 Mercy Seat Inscriptions by Corps   263

Appendix F. 1994 Mercy Seat Inscriptions with Frequency   273

Appendix G. Orders and Regulations   275

Appendix H. Bibliography   283

Acknowledgements

THE assertion that there is no 'I' in 'team' is not to help those who have trouble spelling but to remind team members that individually they are not as important as the collective – and collaborative – effort.

While there are two 'I's in *'The Mercy Seat Revisited'*, I gratefully and gladly acknowledge the contribution of hundreds of people who have responded to, and corresponded with, me over the years I have been researching the place and purpose of the mercy seat in The Salvation Army.

Many are mentioned in the text, many are not. Included in the latter group are my ultra-reliable *War Cry* team mates who have ensured our mainline ministry has continued on the occasions I have given focused attention to this book. They are Philip Halcrow, Stephen Pearson, Andrew Stone, Claire Brine, Gill Cox, Bruce Tulloch and my ever-efficient secretary Joanne Allcock.

One ever-present help throughout my research has been the gracious and generous Gordon Taylor, Historian and Associate Director for Historical Services, the International Heritage Centre, London.

I am also indebted to Christine Clement who as Editor-in-Chief and Publishing Secretary recognised the value in expanding the scope of the first edition of this book.

My thanks to my editor Philippa Smale, whose eagle eye and kind hand have rendered this volume fit for purpose.

Finally, I freely acknowledge the support and encouragement of my home team. I recognise the faith investment of my Salvationist parents, Ken and Jo, through whom I first met the mercy seat.

I am thankful for the ever-flowing love of my wife Maggie, whose questions and insights sharpen my thoughts and quicken my pen.

I never cease to thank God for the gift of our children – Janine and Andrew. To me they are living proof of a God who delights to deal in mercy.

NKJB

Foreword

I WAS delighted upon learning that Major Nigel Bovey was to conduct further investigations into the use of the mercy seat and publish a revised and expanded version of his 1994 book *The Mercy Seat*. This new text is timely and most helpful.

When leading worship I always invite members of a congregation to respond at the mercy seat. I have no doubt that sermons should be preached for a verdict and response – the most natural and immediate of which is surely a move to the mercy seat.

An obedient response to the prompting of the Holy Spirit that is manifested by proceeding to the mercy seat is powerful indeed. Adopting the posture of kneeling (where physically possible) helpfully inculcates a worshipful and reverent attitude of a seeker towards the Saviour.

At the mercy seat all distractions can be cast aside, as covenantal transactions take place between Creator and child. Definitive decisions can be reached while wrestling or reposing at this God-appointed space for grace. Skilful listening and appropriate pastoring can be offered, and an entire congregation can lovingly engage as intercessors.

The sight of an occupied mercy seat, the sound of gentle prayer and the sense that God is near will encourage and convict other members of the congregation. The typical question thus engendered is not 'What have they – the seeker – done?' but rather 'What should I now do?'

Any response to the mercy seat, therefore, while personal is also communal. Indeed, it can even become corporate as others are moved to seek the Lord in a significant way and discover that the mercy seat truly is crowned with glory.

This fine book offers encouragement to all as various recollections spanning the entire history of The Salvation Army affirm words of songwriter Edward Henry Joy:

All your anxiety, all your care,
Bring to the mercy seat, leave it there,
Never a burden he cannot bear,
Never a friend like Jesus.

And here we see the truth – the mercy seat is all about relationship with Jesus who offers salvation and sanctification in full measure.

Major Bovey – throughout this rigorously researched, cogently constructed and eloquently expressed book – clearly understands this fact. Evident also is his deep desire for people to meet Jesus and get saved. When can this happen? It can happen when the sermon is preached for a verdict, when an invitation is given, when the Holy Spirit's directing is obeyed and when the mercy seat is used.

Allow the words contained herein to edify you. More than that, ensure the Word of Life dwells within to save and sanctify you.

John Matear
Commissioner
Territorial Commander
United Kingdom Territory with the Republic of Ireland

Preface

AN Anglican friend once asked, 'We have Communion every week. What's the highlight of Salvation Army worship?' A good question, I thought to myself, and I suspect one's answer depends upon where one sits or stands on a Sunday. The musician may well regard the band or songster piece as the highlight. The preacher will like to think that the 'breaking of the Bread of Life' is the climax of all that precedes it. The lonely newcomer just loves the friendly welcome at the Army.

But what is the most sacred occasion in regular non-sacramental Salvationist worship? I say regular because moving occasions such as commissioning, love feasts and covenant days are (very) occasional events.

I suggest the most sacred moments in our worship are when people kneel or stand at the mercy seat. Some recount the days when the mercy seat was always 'lined'. There still exists the thought that the only 'good' meetings are when people have knelt at the mercy seat. Others wish the mercy seat was still roped off or that the gilt legend of 'Holiness unto the Lord' (or other text) hadn't been removed 20 years ago.

Not only is the use of the mercy seat the most sacred, it is arguably the only positive distinctive aspect of Salvationist worship. There are plenty of negatives – by which I mean things we don't do – which make Salvationist worship distinctive. We do not observe Communion, we do not baptise, we do not confirm. We do not use incense, anoint with oil, use the gift of tongues in public worship – with or without interpretation – or hold deliverance or healing services. There are few who worship like the Salvationist.

Over the years those once uniquely positive elements of Salvationist worship are becoming less distinctive. With churches of many denominations now boasting an orchestra or ensemble, the

Army's brass band is no longer the only alternative to the monopoly of the church organ. Handclapping, extempore prayer and personal testimony are just as likely to be found in a church as in a citadel.

'In the open air our Army we prepare', but with the likes of street theatre, the March for Jesus and personal contacting, many other denominations also take the gospel to the big outdoors. Even discounting those religious orders who insist on their members observing an ecclesiastical dress code, the Salvationist is not the only uniformed Christian on the streets. Members of the Northampton-based Jesus Fellowship church – also known as the Jesus Army – formed in 1985, choose to wear 'identifiable clothing', which consists of colourful jacket and T-shirt. The Jesus Army also has a motto – Love, Power and Sacrifice – evangelises the disadvantaged and produces a newspaper for distribution on the streets.

Salvationists may never let the old flag fall, but nor will Baptists, Methodists, Roman Catholics or Anglicans relinquish their patchwork banners. There are many who worship like the Salvationist!

Which leaves us with the mercy seat, although even that we share with some holiness churches.

While investigating past practices and present perceptions, it is my aim to look beyond conventional wisdom to investigate the scriptural teaching of the mercy seat. In so doing I hope that we shall gain a greater appreciation of the significance of the wooden bench which is not only the focal point of our hall design but is also central to our worship. And, thereby, to our mission.

NKJB 1996

'EVERY Salvationist needs to be instructed in the significance of Salvation Army ceremonies and the meaning behind our methods. The value of a public declaration of surrender to God at the mercy seat, the desirability of an open and joyous acceptance of the disciplines and privileges of soldiership in a public enrolment, the sacred obligations of parenthood faced and accepted in the dedication service are all matters that need defining from time to time if Salvationists are to avoid making too much or too little of them.'

So opens *The Sacraments: The Salvationist's Viewpoint*, a statement issued by the General in 1960. Published 36 years later, *The Mercy Seat* was my contribution to the defining of the mercy seat at that time. Whether I made 'too much or too little' of the mercy seat, I leave others to decide.

Since the publication of *The Mercy Seat* in 1996, there has been a number of significant changes within Salvationist worship in the UK. The widespread use of 'non-Army' songs and choruses (once considered radical and subversive) and the accompanying decline in the use of Salvationist-penned songs means that Salvationists and Christians in other denominations are literally singing from the same hymn sheet. One result is that Salvationist corporate singing is less obviously 'Army' than before.

Such openness to new influences has led to other developments in worship. In recent years, there has been a growth in inviting congregations to respond to God in ways other than by using the mercy seat. These 'creative responses' are used in other denominations. They are not elements that set Salvationist worship apart. They do, however, appear to be impacting the use of the mercy seat. To what extent is the mercy seat – a distinctive of our worship – under threat? Are we, Salvationists of the 21st century, making too much or too little of the mercy seat? These are some of the areas I explore in this book.

While *The Mercy Seat* contained insights from Salvationists in other territories, time and space did not allow a more formal presentation of mercy seat (and holiness table) use around the world. I am delighted to be able to include such findings of my international research in 2009 in this volume.

Part of the research for *The Mercy Seat* and this book was done by conducting UK territory-wide surveys of Salvationists in 1994 and 2009. The details of both surveys are found in the Appendix section of this book. In the text they are referred to as 'my 1994 survey' or 'my 2009 survey'.

Where quotes are not referenced, the quote has come from my personal correspondence with the contributor. The tag 'in correspondence' also indicates personal correspondence from the contributor.

This is the book it is because of the willingness of so many people to contribute. I am sincerely grateful for every contribution. Even those contributors who didn't make print informed my writing. Thank you.

All biblical references are from the *New International Version* unless otherwise noted.

NKJB 2010

Introduction

WILLIAM BOOTH knew exactly where he stood. On the eve of his visit to the USA in 1898, he stood on the Royal Albert Hall platform and told an expectant congregation: 'I am married to the penitent form.' More than 100 years on, the question is: How will history record our personal and corporate relationship with the mercy seat?

Staying with the marriage metaphor, let's look at four relationships. We start with divorce – the complete break-off of relationship.

In 1994 I conducted a UK territory-wide survey on the use of the mercy seat. These 'wedding snapshots' show that all of the 215 responding corps had a mercy seat and that all of them – to varying degrees – used it. There were no signs then that Salvationists were divorced from the idea of the mercy seat. But is that the case today? Are there individual Salvationists who would never darken the carpet at the mercy seat? People who just don't see the point?

The second relationship is a loveless marriage. Maybe in some corps the spark has gone. The mercy seat is still there. It is occasionally visited – wept on, even – but generally it is unappreciated, unused and taken for granted. Nobody actually suggests getting rid of it, but nobody much uses it either. This is a marriage in title only. There's no communication. Little commitment. No intimacy. No passion. No spiritual babies being born.

The third relationship is where, in the words of the late Diana, Princess of Wales, 'There are three people in this marriage.' Here the mercy seat is used but it is not regarded as the only – or even the main – way by which people make a public response to God. And, more importantly, where God meets his people.

One of the questions in my 1994 and 2009 surveys was: Are there suitable alternatives to the mercy seat? In both instances, the answer was 'yes'. The alternative responses included the raising of a hand, standing in one's place, the laying-on of hands and standing at the holiness table.

In recent years – as well as seeing people pray at the mercy seat – I have seen in Army meetings other invitations to respond to God, such as washing hands, picking up a stone, writing a prayer, lighting a candle, consuming bread and fruit juice and drawing in sand. (What I'm not sure I've seen is a follow-up mechanism for such responses in the way that officers were trained and expected to pay next-day pastoral visits to mercy-seat visitors in the days when mercy-seat visits were faithfully recorded in the seekers register.)

As well as what is known as 'creative worship' and 'creative response' (although Heaven only knows what was uncreative in, say, the ministry of Brengle, who in the first six months of 1919 saw 3,000 people respond to his preaching by kneeling at the mercy seat) there is another emerging, significant development in the spiritual life of the Army – the rediscovery of the prayer room.

Possibly inspired by the 24-7 prayer movement, a number of corps have introduced a permanent dedicated prayer room or prayer area. Depending on its location, it allows people to slip in unobserved and uninterrogated for a few moments' quiet prayer. For those seeking privacy and anonymity such a space is a much more attractive proposition than making their way to the mercy seat in full view of a congregation.

Finally, the fourth relationship – a happy marriage. It was this passionate commitment that Booth was describing to his Albert Hall audience. His own conversion came through the ministry of James Caughey, a visiting Irish-American preacher who called people to respond at the mercy seat.

Introduced to the mercy seat as a teenager, Booth later introduced the mercy seat to the Army, where over the years it has been the physical focal point of our halls and the spiritual focal point of our worship.

In 1998 the International Spiritual Life Commission called on Salvationists to 'recognise the wide understanding of the mercy seat that God has given to the Army; to rejoice that Christ uses this means of grace to confirm his presence; and to ensure that its spiritual benefits are fully explored in every corps and Army centre'.

The mercy seat – more specifically the spiritual truths of God's appearance, atonement and advice that it represents – has made the Army what it is. Today, though, how many of us are totally and faithfully committed to the place and purpose of the mercy seat in worship?

The Mercy Seat Revisited is a book for those who are looking for 'marriage guidance' on the mercy seat, those who want to renew their 'wedding vows' with the mercy seat, and those who are considering rejecting a monogamous relationship with the mercy seat. It is a book for all of us who live in sin.

Chapter 1

Square One

BEFORE we investigate what for many is, quite rightly, a very personal subject, this may be the place for me to state my starting point. As a child growing up in the Army, I can recall spending many hours in the young people's band room being taught the intricacies of the C scale in the learners' class.

I can remember how as a Sunday-school child I was expected to learn by heart week by week the simplified doctrine of the directory meeting. One's own investment of time, if you like. The responsive Bible readings and memory text of Sunday afternoons were similarly designed to sow the word of God into young minds. To this day I can recite Scripture so absorbed long ago: 'Even Solomon in all his glory was not arrayed like one of these.' Sad to say, that's it!

I recall the corps officer investing time in my education when as a teenager I attended recruits classes in preparation for senior soldiership. So many hours put in on my behalf by young people's workers, officers and, of course, my parents. But what I can't recall, although I may have been missing in spirit if not in body, is receiving any formal instruction about the splendidly polished dark wood, gilt-emblazoned mercy seat, which, with its crimson carpet, triple-twisted cords and shiny brass hooks, stretched nearly half way across the width of the hall.

What I can vividly picture, however, are Decision Sundays. Those afternoons characterised by not going to classes straight after the chorus-time but sitting uncomfortably while the corps officer exhorted us to admit our naughtiness and say sorry at the penitent form. If memory serves, such occasions usually ended with the singing of 'Just as I am' and, more often than not, a number of girls and boys (usually more girls than boys) sinking knee-deep into the plush-piled carpet to say sorry to Jesus. I must have sat through a dozen or so such meetings before, for the first time at the age of ten, I was on the carpet before God.

The unseemly delay may, in part, be due to the fact that I'd contrived a Decision Sunday survival strategy. I had a cunning plan. There was a lad in the YP band who was, how can I put it, a bit of a handful. He was always being told off for messing about. It would not be that unusual for him to spend part of the proceedings in a corner or expelled from his Sunday school class. Come Decision Sunday, I would wait to see if he was going to the mercy seat. Reckoning that I'd be spared the embarrassment of making my way forward, I'd strike a bargain with God. My terms were simple: 'If he goes, I'll go!'

The fact is, whether we're formally instructed or not, we all, young and old, work out a positional statement about the mercy seat for ourselves. Each of us has a Square One – a personal starting point. It is the aim of this book to accompany the reader from their Square One.

Since the early days of my officership, I have with the help of a trunk, a container of rice, two pieces of plywood and a golf club, presented congregations with the Bible's Square One on the mercy seat.

In house groups and one-to-one I have listened to personal Square Ones. I have watched as people have knelt at the mercy seat in response to the Holy Spirit and then have accompanied them to Square Two and beyond.

The notion to delve further into the subject came as the result of a casual remark made by my corps secretary, Jim Radcliff, while I was stationed at Liverpool Kensington in the early 1990s. In the weekly Bible study group we had been looking at the nature of sin and forgiveness. On many occasions the conversation drifted to the use of the corps mercy seat. Why people knelt there. Why people didn't. How could the stigma of kneeling there be removed?

At the end of yet another evening's lively discussion, Jim announced, 'Well, Captain, you'll just have to write about it.' It is the concern of ordinary, loyal Salvationists for the right use of their mercy seats that has driven me to the task. Thanks, Jim.

My Square One for this study is threefold. The mercy seat is special. Its use is sacramental. It is a concept that requires sensitivity.

A Special Place

The writer of *The Sacraments: The Salvationist's Viewpoint* states that:

'The Salvationist gives an honoured place in his meetings to the mercy seat.'

For Salvationists the world over, the mercy seat – whatever its physical appearance and composition – is an honoured and special place. It has no inherent power. It holds no magic or mystique. It is special only because of the sensitive nature of the business that is conducted there. Special always, magical never. It is not the place for the quick cure nor a short cut to cheap grace – or the platform. Special yes; superstition, no.

On one occasion I was due to enrol junior soldiers from a non-Army background. Shortly before the Sunday of the enrolment, I was approached by a local officer who told me these children couldn't possibly be Christians because she hadn't seen them kneel at the mercy seat. The children were enrolled, nevertheless.

That local officer was, as I gently pointed out to her, wrong. The mercy seat does not have the power to change a person's spiritual status. Nor does the act of moving towards the mercy seat. Nor does Salvation Army theology and thinking require a person to visit the mercy seat as a prerequisite to a spiritual transaction.

When God gave the Children of Israel a cure for snakebite (Numbers 21), the bronze snake which Moses made was the means by which God gave his children life. However, as time went by that replica reptile became more than a reminder of a spiritual truth, it became an object of adulation, an idol. Eventually Hezekiah destroyed it (2 Kings 18:4). May we never invest the Army mercy seat with power it does not possess in our enthusiasm to see it put to good use. The mercy seat cannot be regarded as a sacred snake or as a holy cow.

3

UK Salvationists are living at a time when society at large is recognising the value of special spaces and special places.

On the morning of Sunday 31 August 1997, when the UK awoke to the news that Diana, Princess of Wales, had been killed in a car crash, I was on my way to a *War Cry* appointment in central London. Crossing The Mall near Admiralty Arch at about 9.00 am, I spotted a young man carrying a single rose. He was heading towards Buckingham Palace. At the time I didn't realise the significance but he was one of the first to make a special journey, to a special place for a special reason. A few days later, I stood before the ocean of floral tributes in front of the palace.

It has also become increasingly common for roadside shrines of candles, flowers and cards to appear at the site of a fatal traffic accident or a murder. Celebrity deaths, such as those of Michael Jackson or Jade Goody, are also marked by people making a special journey to lay tributes at special places. The human need to want to make a statement – or memorial – at a special place, while as old as the proverbial hills, is now an everyday part of the British way of life.

Within Salvationist worship, the mercy seat gives us an opportunity to make a special journey, to a special place, for a special reason – to meet God.

A sacramental purpose

In many ways kneeling or standing at the mercy seat is an outward sign of an inner grace. *The Salvation Army Handbook of Doctrine* defines 'sacrament' in very similar terms:

'A sacrament has been described as "an outward and visible sign of inward and spiritual grace".'

Like a kiss, a sacrament is an outward demonstration that 'something's going on' inside a person. The New Testament word for 'worship' – *proskuneo* – literally means 'to kiss towards'. It is often accompanied by the idea of people falling on their knees, for example, the magi (Matthew 2:11), the soldiers (Mark 15:19), the disciples (Matthew 28:9) and Cornelius (Acts 10:25).

When a person kneels, however often, at the mercy seat, it is sacramental, in the sense that it is an outward sign of an inner grace – an indication that 'something's going on' in the person's life. As such it is the high point of Salvationist worship. As such it is not to be used lightly – not as a confessional in a superstitious way, nor as a bargaining agent: 'I'll go to the mercy seat instead of saying sorry to that person, Lord.'

If it is the use that sanctifies the seat, the Salvationist, without being fetishist, will want to uphold the specialness of the place. Perhaps the ropes of former days had their purpose. I know there's no intrinsic power in the bench of ash or beech, I know a simple chair will suffice, but it is hard to stomach the mercy seat being used as a jumble stall, a bench for the public address system, the repository for luncheon club cutlery, or a quick step up to the platform. Judging by the number of Sundays when nobody kneels at the mercy seat, it is not familiarity that breeds such contempt. Maybe if we used it more we would value it more and mistreat it less.

A sensitive procedure

The mercy seat is a sensitive area. We get upset about its maltreatment. Many people are also fearful of using it. They don't like the idea that the sign that 'something's going on' in their lives will become the subject of speculation and gossip. One reason why people are reluctant to use it is the insensitivity of others. They feel they are being judged by onlookers. Too many have been hurt by the real or imaginary musings of 'I wonder what she's done wrong', or worse still, 'Oh no, he's there again!'

In 2008 Adrian Maddern surveyed officers of the Anglia Division. One of his questions was: What holds people back from using the mercy seat? The commonest answer was 'what others will say'.

Sadly such a response is not confined to one division. In my 2009 survey I asked: Why is there sometimes a reluctance to use the mercy seat? The most likely reasons given were embarrassment, the perception that the mercy seat is a 'place for wrongdoers' and being assumed by the congregation that one has done something wrong.

Where such insensitivity exists, it is unlikely that the mercy seat will suffer from overuse.

Whenever I worship in an Anglican church, I notice a stark contrast between the ease with which communicants leave their seats and queue at the Communion rail and the awkwardness and embarrassment sometimes associated with someone leaving their seat and moving towards an Army mercy seat. At what is the focal point of a Communion service, the atmosphere invariably comes across as relaxed, unpressurised and non-threatening. (Maybe I just visit the right churches.) There is sensitive business going on, but people don't seem threatened that they're being called forward to receive from God. I'd like to think that the naturalness – the 'so-what-if-I'm-going-to-respond-ness' – is more than a case of safety in numbers.

(From Anglican communicants I also learn that while questions aren't asked of those who go forward, there is sometimes a 'wonder-what's-up-with-them' directed towards those who stay in their seats.)

It is time to get rid of the idea that the mercy seat is only a *penitent* form. I believe that one of the main reasons for the underuse of our place of prayer is that it has become part of ingrained Army culture that, 'That's where you go when you've done something wrong.' We even joke about it when we mockingly scold a fellow Salvationist, 'You need to go down the front, Sunday morning!' Some Salvationists think that they have to go to the mercy seat only once – to get saved. Once they are saved, the mercy seat's not for them.

Early Army writing, as we shall see, is full of references to the penitent form. In some corps there seems to have been a two-tier blessing system in operation: the penitent form for salvation, the holiness table for holiness. For other corps this twin approach was expressed by using the term 'mercy seat' for holiness seekers, and 'penitent form' for those seeking salvation.

In today's perception, however, I believe that the term 'penitent form' reinforces the notion that it's the place where others go. I (uniformed, educated, multi-generational Salvationist) don't need to go. After all, I've done nothing wrong!

I suggest that the very words 'penitent form' put the emphasis on the user or 'seeker'. If the person kneeling is a penitent natural curiosity demands to know, 'What've they done that they're penitent about?' With 'mercy seat' the emphasis is on God, the giver of mercy. We need his mercy for all sorts of reasons, not just when asking forgiveness.

When the time came for our daughter to be dedicated, we presented her to God not by handing her over to another officer but by kneeling with her at the mercy seat. We weren't penitent about being first-time parents, but did we need God's help and mercy! Two years later it seemed just as natural for us to dedicate our son likewise. When, at the age of seven, our daughter was enrolled as a junior soldier it was her unprompted idea to kneel by herself at the mercy seat to sign her promise card.

The mercy seat is not just a place for confessing sin. Not even when the insensitivity of others keeps many in their seats when the Lord has called them to his. Every worshipper in every Salvation Army meeting should feel at total liberty and comfort to use the mercy seat as the Spirit leads. Surely Salvationists can stain the mercy seat with tears of joy as well as with tears of remorse.

Chapter 2

They Shall Come From The East

WHILE Salvationists have their personal positional statements about the mercy seat, it is *The Salvation Army Year Book* which provides the nearest to an official view. It describes the mercy seat as: 'A bench provided as a place where people can kneel to pray, seeking salvation or sanctification, or making a special consecration to God's will and service. The mercy seat is usually situated between the platform and the main area of Army halls as a focal point to remind all of God's reconciling and redeeming presence.'

As a focal point the mercy seat is not only central to Salvation Army architecture but also to our building of the Kingdom.

'The mercy seat gives focus to our worship and our meetings,' writes General Paul Rader. 'The word of God preached and sung is intended to elicit a response, to result in a verdict. We expect people to get saved and sanctified in Army meetings... Confidence in the power of the gospel and the saving and sanctifying work of the Holy Spirit is central to our faith and worship. The visible and concrete presence of the mercy seat ensures that we confront that fact inescapably.

'Architecture so often reflects the nature of our worship and our understanding of its purpose. The high altar is central to those communions where the Eucharist is the central act of worship. In many Presbyterian churches the pulpit is large and often central, for the ministry of the word holds that central place in their worship tradition. Pentecostal churches not infrequently are constructed in the round, for what occurs in the pews is easily as important as what happens in the pulpit. The baptistery may be very visibly central in the Baptist tradition. In the Army, it is the mercy seat that holds the central place. That makes our worship intentional. If we neglect the mercy seat we are in danger of losing a distinctive of our faith and mission.'

The mercy seat as a Salvation Army distinctive is also a message contained in *The Salvation Army in the Body of Christ*, a 2008 statement from the office of the General. The statement's purpose is to 'clarify and consolidate present global thinking on our identity within the wider Body of Christ'. It outlines common beliefs shared by the Army and other denominations and points out distinctive characteristics of Salvationism. One of these is the mercy seat:

'The Army has been led of God to adopt... its tradition of inviting public response to the presentation of the gospel message, and its use of the mercy seat for this and other spiritual purposes.'

Despite being a distinctive feature of Salvation Army worship and outreach, the mercy seat is neither a unique nor an original Salvationist idea. Although its appearance and use has become developed and stylised over the years – and whenever and wherever there has been the Army, there has been the mercy seat – its roots, like other mainstays of Salvationist expression (for example female preaching, knee-drill and teetotalism) lie in our revivalist prehistory. If we are to gain a greater appreciation of its use in the future, we must first investigate its past.

The practice of individuals doing something as a mark of their spiritual intent can be traced to the earliest pages of Scripture.

Cain and Abel make the Bible's first offerings (Genesis 4:3-4). Saved from the Flood, Noah builds the Bible's first altar and offers the Bible's first recorded animal sacrifice (Genesis 8:20). Abraham makes the first substitutionary sacrifice – a sheep in place of his son – in Genesis 22. These instances are the sources from which major biblical themes such as redemption, forgiveness and salvation spring. They also suggest that the need for people to respond to – to connect with – their Creator is as old as human history itself.

The Mosaic Law contains a series of comprehensive codes regarding humankind's response to God through the giving of offerings, tithes and sacrifices. Under the Law, God's people were required to show their spiritual intent and strengthen their spiritual identity through doing something and a major part of 'doing something' was to offer a sacrifice.

Leviticus chapters 1 to 7, for example, outline five types of offering and sacrifice: burnt, cereal, peace, sin and guilt. They also describe what constitutes an acceptable sacrifice (for example, 'without blemish') and how it should be made. Other passages detail when sacrifices should be made.

The whole system of people making animal sacrifices to God under the old covenant is summarised in one verse: 'In fact, the law requires that nearly everything be cleansed with blood, and without the shedding of blood there is no forgiveness' (Hebrews 9:22).

Under the sacrificial system, provision was made for everyone – from pauper to High Priest – to meet the Law's requirements.

People expressing spiritual response by doing something is also a major theme of the prophets.

Prophetic giants such as Isaiah and Jeremiah warn God's wayward people to get their spiritual priorities straight, to destroy the false gods they are worshipping and to reconnect with the one, true God. If they do not, the kingdoms of Israel and Judah will be destroyed.

Joel calls for a response which is deeper, more meaningful, than mere symbolism:

'Rend your heart and not your garments. Return to the Lord your God...' (Joel 2:13).

Ezekiel looks forward to a time when people will have the inner spiritual resources to obey God's commands:

'I will remove from you your heart of stone and give you a heart of flesh. And I will put my Spirit in you and move you to follow my decrees and be careful to keep my laws' (Ezekiel 36:26-27).

Nevertheless, the overriding message of the prophets can be summed up in one word: Repent!

According to the *Hebrew and Chaldee Lexicon to the Old Testament Scriptures*, the Hebrew word for 'repent' – *nacham* – has its roots in 'to draw the breath forcibly' and 'to sigh'. But repentance is more

11

than sighing over sin. It is also more than a confessing of sins. Repentance is doing something about wrongdoing.

The Greek word – *metanoia* – literally means 'a change of mind'. The expectation is that when we change our minds about something we've done wrong we will also change our attitudes and actions regarding it.

John the Baptist not only cries 'Repent, for the kingdom of heaven is near' (Matthew 3:2), he also tells his listeners to 'Produce fruit in keeping with repentance' (Matthew 3:8). In other words, he is calling people to a spiritual exercise ('repentance') and for them to show evidence of that private spiritual exercise by doing something about it ('produce fruit'). He also challenges people to make a public statement of their changed life through baptism. Together, changed behaviour and baptism indicate an inner spiritual change.

Jesus, likewise, invites people to respond outwardly to his message of the possibility of a new relationship with God. He speaks of turning the other cheek, giving to those who ask and going the extra mile as signs that his followers are different from the world around them (Matthew 5:39-42). He tells the rich young ruler that if he is serious about getting right with God he should do something about it by giving his money away to the poor (Luke 18:22). He commends the cheating Zacchaeus, who shows the fruit of his repentance by promising to make amends for his sin (Luke 19:8-10).

In a number of healing miracles Jesus invites people to participate: to stretch out a hand, to stand up, to pick up a bed, to walk, to wash clay off the eyes. Jesus calls Peter out of the boat to walk with him on water. He instructs wedding servants to fill jars with water. He tells bystanders to release Lazarus from his grave clothes.

All of these, and more, are indications that God wants and expects his people to be involved with him. They are signs that, while faith in Christ is personal, it cannot be private. There is a public consequence to belief. It is called behaviour.

The practice of calling people to do something as a mark of spiritual intent continues through the very day the Church was born. In his Pentecost sermon, Peter – alive with the newly infused Holy

Spirit – preaches to a crowd (Acts 2). He explains who Jesus was and what his death and resurrection represent.

'When the people heard this, they were cut to the heart and said to Peter and the other apostles, "Brothers, what shall we do?" Peter replied, "Repent and be baptised, every one of you, in the name of Jesus Christ for the forgiveness of your sins. And you will receive the gift of the Holy Spirit"... Those who accepted his message were baptised, and about three thousand were added to their number that day' (Acts 2:37, 38, 41).

Likewise, the Ethiopian contacted by Philip (Acts 8) and Paul's Philippian jailer (Acts 16) want to respond to the gospel by doing something – and for them that something is to be baptised.

As the early Church develops, Christians sharing a meal together takes on a deeper significance. It becomes a time of worship, fellowship, learning from the Word and of remembering the Lord's death. Over time – and I leave it to ecclesiastical historians to recount in detail – Communion and baptism are formalised into the Sacraments observed today.

It was while tracing the history of personal response from the Old Testament to the present day that I discovered R. Alan Streett's book *The Effective Invitation*. I am grateful that it shares many of the waymarkers of my own research.

In his book Streett points out that Constantine's adoption of Christianity as the official religion of the Roman Empire in AD324 and the subsequent moving of his headquarters to Byzantium (AD330) led to the formation of the Roman Catholic Church. He writes:

'Under Roman Catholicism, sinners were saved by the church, not by the atoning death of Christ. Salvation was obtained by the observance of seven sacraments, and not through a relationship with the living God... For the next several centuries evangelism was relegated to a place of obscurity until the light of the Reformation shone through in the sixteenth century.'

Streett also notes that even before the Reformation there were preachers who believed that salvation comes through repentance of sin and faith in Christ, and that some of them continued the biblical practice of calling their listeners to make a physical response to the gospel.

In *The History of Christian Preaching*, Thomas Harwood Pattison describes a sermon of John Chrysostom of Antioch (347-407):

'As he advanced from exposition to illustration, from Scripture principle to practical appeals, his delivery became gradually more rapid, his countenance more animated, his voice more vivid and intense. The people began to hold their breath. The joints of their loins were loosened. A creeping sensation like that produced by a series of electric waves passed over the pulpit. They felt as if drawn forwards toward the pulpit by a sort of magnetic influence. Some of those who were sitting rose from their seats; others were overcome with a kind of faintness as if the preacher's mental force were sucking the life out of their bodies, and by the time the discourse came to an end the great mass of that spellbound audience could only hold their heads and give vent to their emotions in tears.'

Evangelistic Preaching by L. M. Perry and J. R. Strubhar refers to the ministry of Bernard of Clairvaux (1093-1153):

'The basic appeal of Bernard of Clairvaux was for people to repent of their sins. Often he would call for a show of hands from those who wished to be restored to fellowship with God or the Church.'

Twelfth-century Waldensians were known for travelling through Europe in pairs, preaching in public places and calling their listeners to repentance.

Pattison records the effects of the ministry of Antony of Padua (1195-1231):

'Shops were closed and thoroughfares deserted when he came to any town, and as many as thirty thousand persons would sometimes gather to hear him. His appeals must have been effective, for as he spoke men who came to attack him dropped the dagger and sought his embrace. Women cast off their ornaments and sold them for the benefit of the poor, and old and burdened sinners were brought to immediate confession.'

In the 15th and 16th centuries, Streett points out, the Anabaptists preached for a verdict. They called people to repent of their sins, commit themselves to Christ and to be baptised as an outward sign of their new relationship with God.

The Reformation, whose genesis is commonly attributed to Martin Luther posting his 95 theses to the door of All Saints' Church, Wittenberg, in 1517, produced preachers such as Zwingli and Calvin, who, like Luther, rejected salvation through the Church and preached salvation through repentance and personal faith in Christ.

One group who thought that the newly formed Church of England (1534) had not distanced itself enough from Roman Catholicism through the Reformation were the Puritans. Puritanism had a number of strands. Some remained in the Church of England and tried to 'purify' it from within. The Separating Puritans, or Separatists, however, believed that true Christians should break away from Anglicanism and form their own congregations.

The Separatists believed that salvation came through personal repentance from sin and faith in Christ. They advocated the priesthood of all believers. They invited converts to do something about their new relationship with God by being baptised.

In September 1620, under political pressure for their beliefs, a Separatist congregation led by John Robinson and William Bradford headed on the *Mayflower* from England to the New World.

In early 17th-century Scotland, meanwhile, the Presbyterian Church had devised a method of maintaining spiritual discipline among its flock. If a member of the congregation had been discovered committing an immoral act, they were required to sit during the service on a low stool in front of the pulpit. This was known as a 'stool of repentance' or 'cutty stool'.

Cobham Brewer's *Dictionary of Phrase and Fable* of 1894 describes its purpose:

'A low stool placed in front of the pulpit in Scotland, on which persons who had incurred an ecclesiastical censure were placed during divine service. When the service was over the "penitent" had to stand on the stool and receive the minister's rebuke. Even in the present century this method of rebuke has been repeated.'

Under the heading of 'Cuttie-stool' in his *Dictionary of Lowland Scotch* of 1888, Charles Mackay includes these observations by Dean Ramsay:

'A circumstance connected with Scottish church discipline has undergone a great change in my time – I mean the public censure from the pulpit of persons convicted of a breach of the seventh commandment... This was performed by the guilty person standing on a raised platform called the cutty-stool.'

He continues:

'The culprits did not always take the admonition patiently. It is recorded of one of them in Ayrshire, that when accused of adultery by the minister, he interrupted and corrected his reverend monitor by denying the imputation, and calling out, "Na! Na! Minister; it was simple *fornie* (fornication) and no *adultery* ava."'

Offences which required such public rebuke and penitence included acts of sexual immorality, adultery or having a child out of wedlock. If penitents showed sufficient remorse they were allowed back into full fellowship. If they did not, they were summoned to spend as many Sundays on the stool as it would take until they did.

In his book *The Cutty Stool*, Murdoch Lothian calculates that the first mention of the stool in St Giles' Cathedral, Edinburgh, was by King James VI in 1603. It is difficult, however, to be as precise as to when the practice of using cutty stools died out. Lothian writes:

'There is no record of when the stool was last used but Rev. George Tyack wrote in 1898: "The repentance-stool has maintained its place in scattered instances down to modern times, one of the latest instances of its use being in 1884, when a man stood on the stool to be publicly rebuked in the Free Kirk at Lochcarron."'

Another Edinburgh church, Greyfriars Tolbooth and Highland Kirk ('Old Greyfriars'), also used a stool of repentance. There is no precise record of when it was introduced nor when it was withdrawn from service. However, in correspondence, church worker Bert Hutchings writes:

'We are quite certain, from the known characters of our ministers, that the original stool would not have been used in this building after 1840, and possibly not for some time before that. However, in country districts, and especially in the North and in the Hebrides, I surmise that the custom is likely to have persisted for much longer, possibly even into the early 20th century.'

The Presbyterians were not the only ones to use such measures. St Michan's Church of Ireland parish church in Dublin has a penitent's desk. Here, parishioners 'who were open and notorious naughty livers' did public penance. It dates from the 18th century.

In correspondence, former curate of St Michan's, the Rev Roy Byrne, writes:

'This strange piece of furniture, known as "the penitent's desk", was originally called "the oak moving desk". It was used by the clergy during baptismal services and other occasional offices. It was commissioned in 1724, like the pulpit, from Christopher Stevens and cost one pound, three shillings.

'The desk was also used for restoring penitents into communion with the church, following public confession. The penitent knelt in the desk in the centre aisle and after confession and absolution from the priest was given the sacrament. Records recall how Christopher Pell was led into the church by the churchwardens for public confession. He had argued with the clergy over his child's funeral and was summoned to appear before the Archbishop of Dublin. The archbishop ordered that he make his confession in St Michan's in front of the whole congregation and receive absolution for his objectionable behaviour.'

What Byrne describes as a 'penitent's desk', is also described today as a 'penitent's pew' (*The Rough Guide to Dublin*) and a 'stool of repentance' (*Irish Churches and Monasteries*).

Right from the beginnings of Scripture, people have sensed a need – a divine requirement, even – to do something in response to God. Throughout church history there have been those who have emphasised the need to make a personal response. Salvationist worship follows in the line of such verdict preaching – presenting the claims of the gospel, emphasising the need for personal salvation and giving people the opportunity to do something about it by going forward to meet God at the mercy seat.

Like those Puritan Separatists, Scottish Presbyterians and Irish churchmen and women of many denominations, it is to the New World that we now turn as we continue to trace the source of the Army mercy seat.

Chapter 3

They Shall Come From The West

ENGLISH emigration to the New World started with the arrival of a three-ship, all-male expedition from the London Company, which had set off from Blackwall in December 1606. On landing at what would become known as Jamestown on 26 April 1607, Anglican chaplain Robert Hunt offered a prayer of thanksgiving and a cross was erected.

Over the next 100 years or so, various Protestant groups, many of them facing religious persecution in homeland Europe, arrived in America. Puritan Separatists (who would later be known as Congregationalists), Quakers (most famously through William Penn, the founder of Pennsylvania), Huguenots, Mennonites, Moravians, Amish, Anabaptists and Lutherans were among the nonconformists who headed west.

It is from these New World settlers and their descendants that we can continue to trace the beginnings of the spiritual practices familiar to today's Salvationists the world over – an appeal (or 'altar call') and a public response at the mercy seat.

In *The Altar Call: Its Origins and Present Usage*, David Bennett records that Dutch Reformed pietists in New Jersey experienced revival in the 1720s.

'Whilst revival should not be equated with the altar call,' he notes, 'is it possible that the pietists, with their intensely personal religion, first used the public invitation, or set in place the foundation for its use? Pietism was born in 17th-century Germany, and subsequent German immigration to America was considerable... So if, as seems probable, the public appeal was born in America, some pietistic influence in its birth is possible.'

R. Alan Streett in *The Effective Invitation* documents that two of the prominent preachers associated with the New World's religious revival of the 1730s (known as the Great Awakening) were Connecticut-born Jonathan Edwards and Gloucester's George Whitefield. In what Streett describes as 'the standard procedure during the early eighteenth century' Edwards and Whitefield ended their sermons with an invitation not for seekers to go forward to the front of the church but rather to speak with them privately after the service.

Streett notes that 'it is estimated that 40,000 colonists, or 25 per cent of the population of America, were won to Christ' during the Great Awakening. While the evangelists would have rejoiced at such a moving of the Spirit, the physical and emotional demands on them of so much personal counselling were enormous.

The England of the late 1700s was also going through a revival under the ministrations of John Wesley. Unlike Edwards or Whitefield, Wesley was comfortable with the idea of calling people to make a public there-and-then response to the sermon. Sometimes he invited seekers to step forward and present themselves for church membership. Sometimes he used a mourner's bench or anxious seat.

Streett records:

'In each meeting house there was reserved a pew where those convicted of their sins and anxious about their soul's salvation could come to receive prayer and spiritual counsel. As the mourner's bench was located at the front of the church, those desiring help needed to make their way forward.

'Wesley's use of the mourner's bench predated Finney by more than fifty years. It seems likely that he was the first to practise the use of a mourner's bench. Charles Wesley supposedly uttered, "Oh, that blessed anxious seat" – the first traceable use of the phrase in church history.'

What is as yet untraced, though, is the context and occasion of Wesley's alleged utterance. For anyone hoping to map a definitive history of the mercy seat this is very frustrating. According to the Wesley Centre, Oxford, it is not a line from one of his many hymns.

In a series of lectures in 1868, which were published as *Lectures on Revivals* eight years later, Edward Kirk also quotes the line. Outlining the benefits of the anxious seat, Kirk says:

'It has often proved a most efficient means of fixing the mind in that momentous decision by which the dividing-line between life and death is crossed. (Charles Wesley says, "Oh that blessed anxious seat!" &c.) It operates on the same principle, in many cases, as the pledge.'

As we shall see later in this chapter, Kirk himself may be something of a linguistic pioneer. I suggest he is the first (so far discovered) to use the term 'mercy seat' in a decision-making context.

In 18th-century America the practice of calling seekers forward was gaining ground. According to Bennett, on 1 November 1741 Congregationalist minister Eleazar Wheelock was preaching at a church in Taunton, Massachusetts. As he did so, he kept being interrupted by the 'distress and outcry' of the congregation. The minister of the Taunton church, Josiah Crocker, records the following:

'The distress and outcry spreading and increasing, his voice was at length so drowned that he could not be heard. Wherefore, not being able to finish his sermon, with great apparent serenity and calmness of soul, he called to the distressed, and desired that they gather themselves together in the body of the seats below. This he did, that he might the more conveniently converse with them, counsel, direct, exhort them, etc.'

Bennett also chronicles that the Great Awakening caused a split in the Congregational Church in New England. One group – the 'Separates' – were 'out and out revivalists'.

'The Separates,' writes Bennett, 'desired a pure church, which contained only those who had been born again, and often excommunicated those who did not measure up.'

In keeping with 2 Corinthians 6:17, the Separates expected Christians to 'come out from among them and be ye separate'.

'Many of them,' says Bennett, 'eventually became Baptists, and these Separate Baptists definitely were amongst the first to use the public invitation, and may have been the first to systemise it.'

From R. I. Devin's *History of Grassy Creek Baptist Church* Bennett quotes an event which 'appears to have occurred some time towards the end of the 18th century in that North Carolina Separate Baptist Church':

'At the close of the sermon, the minister would come down from the pulpit and while singing a suitable hymn would go around among the brethren shaking hands. The hymn being sung, he would then extend an invitation to such persons as felt themselves to be poor guilty sinners, and were anxiously inquiring the way of salvation, to come forward and kneel near the stand or... kneel at their seats, proffering to unite with them in prayer or their conversion.'

Bennett concludes that, while there is argument about the precise date, 'some of the Separate Baptists regularly used a specific form of the public invitation with some frequency and prior consideration, and thus by the 1770s had systemised it.'

By the late 1790s the United States of America was seeing an expansion not only of frontiers but also of the reaching of the common man with the gospel. The Second Great Awakening (1795-1835) was a time when revivals were commonplace as itinerant preachers campaigned throughout the New World. Their enthusiasm linked with the power of the Spirit not only brought new converts but also challenged old churches. No denomination was unaffected. Episcopalian, Roman Catholic, Presbyterian, Unitarian, Lutheran, Baptist and Methodist had to respond to the original 'old-time religion'.

By now the Edwards and Whitefield post-service method of dealing with seekers was a thing of the past. One of the main features of revivalism was the call to come forward in response to the word of God. In *The Origin of the Altar Call in American Methodism*, Robert Coleman suggests the first public invitation to come forward for prayer may have been in a Methodist church in Maryland in 1798. Jesse Lee, one of the leaders, that night records in his diary:

'The preacher then requested all that were under conviction to come together. Several men and women came, and fell upon their knees; and the preachers, for some time, kept singing, and exhorting the mourners to expect a blessing from the Lord, till the cries of the mourners became truly awful. Then prayer was made on behalf of the mourners, and two or three found peace.'

Streett, however, states that:

'The first recorded use of the altar in connection with a public invitation occurred in 1799. At a Methodist camp meeting at Red River, Kentucky, an altar was erected in front of the pulpit "designed as a place for penitents, where they might be collected together for prayer and instruction."'

As the reader may be becoming aware, the Army mercy seat does not have a straight-line family tree. If the mercy seat is a conduit for the river of divine grace, then that conduit itself has many tributaries. If this is frustrating, it must be borne in mind that spiritual revival – people coming to faith (and renewed faith) in their hundreds or thousands – is a hectic process. Revival resembles a messy, noisy maternity ward, not a quiet and orderly mortuary. The main participants – those who could provide authoritative first-hand details – are often too involved in soul-saving to analyse and record the events taking place. In the greater scheme of things, this is the way it should be.

It was an American, one Lorenzo Dow, who is credited with what Bennett calls 'the first definite usage of the public invitation in the British Isles, so far uncovered'.

On 27 November 1799 Dow arrived in Larne, Co Antrim. In his journal, *History of Cosmopolite*, he records the events of 29 November:

'After preaching, said I to the people, as many of you as will pray for yourselves twice in twenty four hours for two weeks, I will endeavour to remember you thrice, God being our helper: and you that will come forward, that I may take your names in writing, lest that I forget. A few came forward that night, some the more next day, and so on.'

(When Dow revisited Ireland in 1806, he preached in Mount Melick and 'invited up the mourners to be prayed for; several found peace, and we had a refreshing season from the presence of God.' In November that year he visited Congleton, Cheshire and noted:

'At the close of the meeting I invited the mourners to come forward: about fifty distinguished themselves. I prayed with them; several professed to find deliverance. I retired, leaving a number of mourners with those who were helping.')

Meanwhile back in the States, the first use of the mourners' bench, according to Coleman, was in 1800. He cites the experience of Henry Boehm in evidence:

'Henry Boehm, venerated pioneer Methodist preacher, witnessed the use of this technique in the early part of the year 1800 during a great revival at Cecil Circuit, Maryland, where William P. Chandler was the preacher in charge. Commenting upon the effectiveness of this new method of gathering souls, he said, "It was a great advantage because, with the seekers scattered all through the congregation, it was difficult to give them suitable attention. By bringing them together they were accessible to those who desired to instruct and encourage them. In the early part of the revival I saw 12 men kneel at the mourners' bench, and they were all quickly converted."'

Richard Carwardine in *Transatlantic Revivalism 1790-1865* cites the earliest church-based example of calling seekers to public decision as 1801 when Richard Sneath, in St George's Methodist Church, Philadelphia, invited all the mourners 'to come to the Communion table'. The date was 25 January. Robert Coleman records a letter Sneath subsequently wrote describing the experience:

'After Mr Cooper had done preaching, I invited all the mourners to come to the Communion table, that we might pray particularly for them. This I found to be useful, as it removed that shame which often hinders souls from coming to Christ, and excited them to the exercise of faith. About 30 professed to be converted, and 26 joined the society.' Coleman adds, 'The altar call soon became a common observance in the church, and among the Methodists, at least, it became virtually a universal practice.'

The *Dictionary of Christianity in America* states that, although 'possibly originating in the eighteenth century, the term [mourners' bench] is common only from 1800'. It also cites 1801 as an occasion when the bench was in use: 'The Cane Ridge, Kentucky, meeting in the summer of 1801 was attended by thousands and set the stage for the camp-meeting approach with its emotional appeals, use of the mourners' bench and the holding of periodic meetings at which the Spirit moved.'

(The Cane Ridge camp referred to was hosted by Presbyterian minister Barton W. Stone. It began on Friday 8 August 1801 and attracted 25,000 people.)

According to *The Encyclopedia of World Methodism*'s treatment of the term mourners' bench, 'It is difficult to say when or where this arrangement or term first originated. It seems to have been used very early in the history of camp meetings, which began around 1800.'

However, the encyclopaedia is clear as to what is meant by mourners' bench:

'A term used in camp meetings and early revivals referring to a certain number of benches directly in front of the speaker's stand or pulpit, which were enclosed by low rails on three sides... Persons seeking salvation were invited to come within the enclosure to kneel by or sit on the benches where they were made objects of prayer by the preacher and the congregation. Here they "mourned" for their sins until they were transformed by the "joy of salvation". Sometimes the enclosed space was referred to as the "altar" or, by the irreverent, as "the pen"... The men were usually separated from the women in the mourners' benches of the early camp meetings... The "mourners' tent" in early camp meetings was an outgrowth of the mourners' bench... It was kept lighted all night so that at any hour of the day or night the "mourners" or "anxious ones" might come in for prayer. A curtain was hung to separate the men from the women.'

In 1806 Aaron Hunt, the minister of Forsyte Street Methodist Church, New York, received word of a scheme used in camp meetings where there was, according to Carwardine:

'A space in front of the stand, called an altar, where mourners and those who were considered capable of instructing and praying with them were invited to meet, apart from the great congregation.'

Bennett notes the growing formal use of the mourners' bench:

'As early as 1810, Francis Asbury, the American Methodist leader, was trying to ensure that new Methodist meeting houses included "as much as one seat space left before the pulpit for mourners", clearly indicating that the public invitation was a common part of American Methodist worship by that time.'

A different approach emerged in the ministry of Ashael Nettleton, a Calvinist preacher who worked in the Congregational churches of the east coast from 1811. Rather than call to public decision at an altar rail, he invited those seeking salvation to a separate 'inquiry' or 'anxious' meeting. However, some Calvinists were prepared to experiment. During the 1822 Washington revival it was noted:

'They are introducing all the habits and hymns of the Methodists into our Presbyterian churches. After the regular service is closed by the clergyman, the congregation rise, and strike up a Methodist hymn... then [the minister] calls on the mourners to come forward, and he and others pray over them, as they loudly vent their sorrows.'

Five years later, it was recorded that similar practices had spread south to Georgia:

'Penitents at the altar, sudden conversions, and sudden admissions into the church, formerly the anomalies of Methodism, are no longer uncommon incidents with our brethren, especially the Presbyterians.'

In England, meanwhile, Methodists of the Primitive persuasion were adopting some of the revivalist practices of their American cousins. In Staffordshire, Hugh Bourne and others started holding all-day prayer meetings and in 1807 introduced the first American-style camp meeting.

Such methods did not go down well with the wider Methodist Church, and Bourne left the church and in 1811 with William Clowse formed the Primitive Methodist Connexion. They continued to hold camp meetings.

Bennett suggests that:

'It is probable... that the Primitives were using some form of the public invitation between Dow's two visits to England [in 1806]. Certainly, they knew of such a method through Dow's writings, and presumably, his practice. Though Bourne does not date it clearly, the first known use of the public invitation by the Primitives was about 1820.'

The story so far, on both sides of the Atlantic, is one of an emerging practice. Some preachers are calling for a here-and-now public decision, others prefer to counsel seekers in private after the service. Some responses are at church altars, some at makeshift chairs, some at specially designated mourners' benches. Until now, what today's Salvationist would recognise as mercy-seat use has been sporadic and spontaneous. The haphazard technology needed a coherent methodology. Former lawyer Charles Grandison Finney was just the man to provide it.

Finney liked the altar-call style of the Methodists, but in 1830, while conducting a campaign in Rochester, USA, the Presbyterian evangelist decided to use the 'anxious seat' as the climax to his appeal. Recalling the work in Rochester, he writes:

'I made a call, I think for the first time, upon all that class of persons whose convictions were so ripe that they were willing to renounce their sins and give themselves to God, to come forward to certain seats, which I requested to be vacated, while we made them subjects of prayer.'

As is often the case, the introduction of a new idea was met with criticism. In *Lectures on Revivals of Religion*, published in 1835, Finney addresses his anxious seat critics:

'By [the anxious seat] I mean the appointment of some particular seat in the place of meeting, where the anxious may come and be addressed particularly, and be made subjects of prayer, and sometimes conversed with individually. Of late this measure has met with more opposition than any of the others. What is the great objection? I cannot see it. The design of the anxious seat is undoubtedly philosophical, and according to the laws of mind. It has two bearings:

'When a person is seriously troubled in mind every body knows that there is a powerful tendency to try to keep it private that he is so, and it is a great thing to get the individual willing to have the fact known to others. And as soon as you can get him willing to make known his feelings, you have accomplished a great deal. When a

27

person is borne down with a sense of his condition, if you can get him willing to have it known, if you can get him to break away from the chains of pride, you have gained an important point towards his conversion. This is agreeable to the philosophy of the human mind. How many thousands are there who will bless God to eternity, that when pressed by the truth they were brought to take this step, by which they threw off the idea that it was a dreadful thing to have any body know that they were serious about their souls.

'Another bearing of the anxious seat is to detect deception and delusion, and thus prevent false hopes. It has been opposed on this ground, that it was calculated to create delusion and false hopes. But this objection is unreasonable. The truth is the other way. Suppose I were preaching on the subject of temperance, and that I should first show the evils of intemperance, and bring up the drunkard and his family, and show the various evils produced, till every heart is beating with emotion. Then I portray the great danger of moderate drinking, and show how it leads to intoxication and ruin, and there is no safety but in total abstinence, till a hundred hearts are ready to say, "I will never drink another drop of ardent spirit in the world; if I do, I shall expect to find a drunkard's grave." Now if I stop short, and let the pledge be circulated, and every one that is fully resolved, is ready to sign it. But how many will begin to draw back and hesitate, when you begin to call on them to sign a pledge of total abstinence. One says to himself, "Shall I sign it, or not? I thought my mind was made up, but this signing a pledge never to drink again, I do not know about that." Thus you see that when a person is called upon to give a pledge, if he is found not to be decided, he makes it manifest that he was not sincere. That is, he never came to that resolution on the subject, which could be relied on to control his future life. Just so with the awakened sinner. Preach to him, and at the moment he thinks he is willing to do anything, he thinks he is determined to serve the Lord, but bring him to the test, call on him to do one thing, to take one step, that shall identify him with the people of God, or cross his pride – his pride comes up, and he refuses; his delusion is brought out and he finds himself a lost sinner still; whereas, if you had not done it, he might

28

have gone away flattering himself that he was a Christian. If you say to him, "There is the anxious seat, come out and avow your determination to be on the Lord's side," and if he is not willing to do such a small thing as that, then he is not willing to do any thing, and there he is, brought out before his own conscience. It uncovers the delusion of the human heart, and prevents many spurious conversions, by showing those who might otherwise imagine themselves willing to do any thing for Christ, that in fact they are willing to do nothing.'

However, Finney, the great methods-analyst of his day, did not allow himself to be tied exclusively to one method of helping the unconverted into the Kingdom. Carwardine notes that:

'When working with Methodists he used the Communion rail; in Manchester and Huntingdonshire he held separate "meetings for anxious inquirers"; in Scotland he challenged the prevailing antipathy toward public decision by encouraging the anxious to stand or raise their hands.'

However:

'In addition to the more reputable inquiry meetings, the "anxious seat" was employed. This was a pew set aside at the front of the congregation where those in a state of concern over their souls could go to be exhorted and prayed for by the minister and where a public commitment might be expected. Here, and in his work generally, the minister was helped by a "Holy Band", a close-knit group that included laymen dedicated to bringing waverers to salvation.'

By the time Finney campaigned in England for the first time, in 1849, the anxious seat had already received widespread publicity and gained increasing acceptance. Carwardine observes that:

'Even amongst the Primitive Methodists, more receptive than most to innovations in revivals, the "mourners' ring" (in which members encircled penitents) was far more common than the "penitents' form" in the 1830s; only in the 1840s did the latter become commonplace.'

Finney's way in England had been prepared in the 1830s by Calvin Colton. Colton, one of a number of revivalists to cross the Atlantic, arrived to raise money for the work in the States and evangelical awareness of revival methods.

In 1832, in his *History and Character of American Revivals of Religion*, Colton outlines his use of the anxious seat, on which the inquirer sat, rather than knelt:

'It is not considered prudent to employ it except when there is manifestly a special degree of feeling in the congregation. On such occasions, and ordinarily towards the close of the meeting, a challenge is formally made on all who are willing publicly to signify their anxiety to secure an interest in the great salvation – to separate themselves from the congregation and come forward and be seated by themselves, that public prayer may be offered on their behalf and that they may receive advice and exhortation...

'The individual who rises for such a purpose is apt to be so overwhelmed as to be unable to reach the place without the guidance and support of a second person; and immediately the sympathies of the whole congregation, except those who are hardened and resolved in sin, are roused to unwonted energy... And now the offer is suspended and fervent importunate prayers are offered up on behalf of those anxious souls, who kneel weeping before the altar of God. And the congregation weep with them. And they are counselled, exhorted and dismissed... and the effect of this step on them ordinarily is a speedy conversion. The same amazing power of the circumstances, instrumentally, seems to bring out their feelings, to enforce them to the crisis of submission to God.'

Colton was not slow to recognise the emotional side to an appeal to the anxious seat. The modern-day concern that people respond out of over-emotionalism or through undue pressure is one that seems to have accompanied the use of the mercy seat ever since its inception. Carwardine notes:

'Methods like the anxious seat stirred in the individual fear of the community and anxiety to conform to its standards and aspirations. Fear of parents, and a desire to conform to their will and gain their approval was also involved, as well as the subtler pressures of contemporaries.'

In his *Lectures on Revivals*, published in 1875, Edward Kirk also considers the uses and abuses of the anxious seat. He writes:

'The anxious seat. The title was peculiarly unhappy. It can easily and properly be made ridiculous: it easily becomes cant. It is peculiarly offensive to certain persons just awakened from spiritual torpor, to be classified thus by their tenderest, profoundest feelings, and to hear that term associated with the business-like talk into which people easily slide when the reverential regard of the Holy Spirit's operations has passed away, as it so often does.

'But we are now to deal with the thing itself. Its essential feature is calling persons who have become solicitous about their spiritual condition, and desire to receive suitable instructions, to separate themselves from the congregation, and take seats apart, where prayers will be offered specifically for them, and counsel be given them.

'Is it a desirable practice? In certain cases it seems to be precisely the step that enlightened zeal in a pastor would take. But as soon as it is used mechanically or superstitiously, as a part of a Revival-routine or machinery, it becomes decidedly mischievous. Instead, therefore, of attempting to decide in the abstract when and where it may be safely employed, I will set before you its advantages and its perils.

'THE ADVANTAGES.

a. It has often proved a most efficient means of fixing the mind in that momentous decision by which the dividing-line between life and death is crossed. (Charles Wesley says, "Oh that blessed anxious seat!" &c.) It operates on the same principle, in many cases, as the pledge.

b. Its effect on the wavering, to see others so definitely expressing decision, is powerful.

c. Its effect on a church is, for a time, very beneficial. But in this it shows itself to be a human device. Unlike the divinely-ordained instruments of good, it wears out.

d. It encourages the inquirer to find the sympathy which his case requires.

'EVILS AND DANGERS.

a. Inquirers easily substitute the mechanical act for the spiritual step that leads to the Saviour. I have known leaders to become so earnest in urging to this bodily exercise, that it seemed to me certain some of those thus urged would lose sight of the spiritual objects

31

which are the only real magnet to draw the life into new channels, while their attention was engrossed with the outward.

b. And, when they yield to this urgency, there is some danger they may substitute the outward act for the faith which saves, depending on the measure instead of Christ.

c. The leader is often placed in a very undesirable position. He has undertaken a public contest with the inquirers; and I have seen one become angry because he was foiled in it. This can be avoided, however, by simply making the offer, and not undertaking to urge the step.

d. The inquirer sometimes is hardened by his resistance to the minister; so that he the more easily resists the Spirit of God. His success in the contest with God's servant emboldens him.

e. The attention of the Church becomes diverted from the mercy-seat, to watch the success of this measure, with mixed emotions of true zeal, curiosity, and a party spirit.

'I have known an evangelist who seemed to be conscious of considerable tact in manipulating an audience. His aim seemed to be to get his hearers on their feet, for any one of twenty objects.'

Some 140 years later, Kirk's analysis is still pertinent to response within Salvation Army worship, whether at the mercy seat or elsewhere.

Chapter 4

The Mercy Seat and William Booth

USING the mercy seat as a place of response and decision had its shortcomings before it became an integral part of Salvationist culture. It has always been open to abuse. We did not inherit an immaculate concept. So how did the mercy seat pass into Army hands?

The man responsible is Irish-American preacher James Caughey. Caughey, born in Northern Ireland in 1810, emigrated with his family to America while he was still a boy. After he was converted during the Second Great Awakening, he became a Methodist minister. In the 1840s he campaigned in the industrial heartland of England. It is reckoned that during this time tens of thousands were converted or 'entirely sanctified'. One of whom was a teenage William Booth. Cyril Barnes in *Words of William Booth* records:

'As a boy, in 1844, William Booth knelt on the floor in the middle of a downstairs room of the Wesley Chapel, Broad Street, Nottingham. That spot became his penitent form because there he confessed his sins, met with God, received his forgiveness and became converted.'

Robert Sandall in *The History of The Salvation Army* records a later event in young William's life:

'When the Rev James Caughey visited Nottingham in 1846, his red-hot revival oratory set aflame the fire that laid in the boy's heart, and William Booth determined that "God should have all there was" of him.'

From that day there were to be no half-measures for the Founder.

Booth himself, in *Twenty-one Years Salvation Army*, describes the mark Caughey made on his life:

'Two events, which transpired soon after my conversion, had, I have no doubt, a very powerful influence in moulding my religious character and shaping my after life. The first of these was a remarkable religious awakening that came to the society and congregation of which I was a member, and which extended for miles around the town. At that time the Reverend James Caughey, an American minister, was making an evangelistic tour through the country. He was an extraordinary preacher, filling up his sermons with thrilling anecdotes and vivid illustrations, and for the straightforward declaration of scriptural truth and striking appeals to the conscience, I had up to that time never heard his equal; I do not know that I have since... There were wonderful meetings, wonderful influences, and wonderful conversions. Multitudes were saved, many of whom became the most useful members of the society. All this had a powerful effect upon my young heart... I saw as clearly, as if a revelation had been made to me from Heaven, that success in spiritual work, as in natural operations, was to be accounted for, not on any mere abstract theory of Divine sovereignty, or favouritism, or accident, but on the employment of such methods as were dictated by common sense, the Holy Spirit, and the word of God.'

Richard Carwardine records that early in his ministry Booth incorporated some of those 'such methods':

'In the mid-1850s as a young man he had achieved remarkable results as a Methodist New Connexion evangelist in Guernsey, the West Country, the Midlands, and the North, employing special services modelled on Caughey's methods. The New Connexion Conference at first approved of his itinerancies, but in 1857 those critical of his emotionalism, "penitent-form revivalism", and challenge to connexional order managed to persuade Conference that he should be given a regular circuit.'

The seeds of conflict between leadership within Methodism and William Booth on the subject of 'penitent form revivalism' were sown some years earlier. The penitent form was the focus of Booth's soul-saving endeavours right from the beginning. He was still a teenager when, as St John Ervine records in *God's Soldier: General William Booth*, he led one of Nottingham's well-known sinners to Christ at the penitent form of the Wesleyan Chapel to which he belonged.

'About this time, he made what probably was his first sensational conversion: he brought a notorious drunkard and wife-beater, known as "Besom Jack", to the penitent form, and kept him in a decent and honest life. The whole of Nottingham, apparently, talked, mostly in derision, of the event, and the deacons, already worried, became more perturbed; for they dare not think what other unusual acts the ardent young man might perform.'

In *Twenty-One Years Salvation Army*, Booth describes how, shortly after his awakening under Caughey, he joined those who were evangelising the poor. He was not yet 17 years old.

'Our plan of operation was simplicity itself. We obtained the loan of cottages and in these held meetings every night, always commencing with an open-air address, fine weather or foul, all the year round, inviting the people indoors for another meeting. Here again we had lively songs, short and sharp exhortations insisting upon decision for Christ upon the spot, which was to be signified by coming out and kneeling at the round table that stood in the middle of the room.'

From his earliest days as an evangelist Booth called for public decision. Arguably, none of his campaigns was as foundational as the one he undertook with Catherine in Hayle, Cornwall, in August 1861. At the time Booth had not long left the Methodist New Connexion.

In *William Booth: Soup, Soap, and Salvation*, Janet and Geoff Benge describe the background:

'The Reverend Stone [one of Booth's previous converts] wrote a letter inviting William and Catherine to preach in his chapel, though he warned that his congregation was small and elderly and that the chapel could afford to offer him only a few shillings' remuneration for his efforts. It was the only offer William had, and he gladly accepted. In August 1861 the Booths left their children with the Mumfords [Catherine's parents] and travelled to Cornwall.

'Since he had last seen John Stone, William had been experimenting with a new format for his revival meetings. This new format involved inviting members of the audience who wanted to repent of their sins and become Christians to come to the front of the church. There they publicly stood at the "penitent rail", confessed their sins, and asked Jesus to come into their lives. The New Connexion leaders had opposed this way of doing things because they felt it made too much of a show over sin, that it was better for such matters to be dealt with in a private manner. Thankfully, the Reverend Stone agreed with William's approach and gave him permission to use a penitent rail in the chapel.

'The results of the meetings in Hayle were astounding, even to William and Catherine.'

Booth wrote a report of the events in Hayle for the *Connexion Magazine*, which is quoted by George Scott Railton in *General Booth*.

'We arrived here on the 10th inst. and commenced labour on the following Sabbath. The chapel was crowded. Gracious influences accompanied the word. Many appeared to be deeply convicted of sin, but no decided cases of conviction took place that day.

'On Monday afternoon we had a service for Christians, and spoke on the hindrances to Christian labour and Christian joy. Evening, chapel crowded. Very solemn season. Nearly all the congregation stayed to the prayer meeting that followed, and many appeared deeply affected, but refused to seek the mercy of God.

'A strong prejudice prevails here against the custom of inviting anxious inquirers to any particular part of the building. The friends told me that this plan never had succeeded in Cornwall; but I thought it the best, considering the crowded state of the chapel, and therefore determined to try it. I gave a short address, and again invited those who wished to decide for Christ to come forward.

'After waiting a minute or two, the solemn silence was broken by the cries of a woman who at once left her pew and fell down at the mercy seat, and became the first-fruits of what I trust will be a glorious harvest of immortal souls. She was quickly followed by others, when a scene ensued beyond description. The cries and groans were piercing in the extreme; and when the stricken spirits apprehended Jesus as their Saviour, the shouts of praise and thanksgiving were in proportion to the previous sorrow.'

The new format was a spiritual success. Booth was convinced.

'When he conducted revival services in churches he invited seekers to kneel at the Communion rail,' chronicles Sandall. 'He put the penitent form into use in the earliest days of The East London Christian Mission. Peter Monk knelt at a penitent form at one of the first Tent meetings. In his own accounts of the first meetings held in the Dancing Academy [1865], William Booth wrote of having led seekers "up the room" and "to the other end of the room".'

In *Twenty-one Years Salvation Army*, Railton outlines Booth's nomadic East End ministry in those pre-Salvation Army days. The following extracts illustrate how pivotal the calling of people to make a public decision was to Booth and also demonstrate his willingness to adapt methods according to circumstance.

Referring to the days when Booth used a dancing room for Sunday services, Railton writes:

'We had no place for our week-night meetings except the open air on the Mile End Waste, and here we carried on till nine and after, then inviting those who were anxious to remain and seek salvation on the spot on which they stood.'

Some time later:

'We went to a covered skittle alley in Whitechapel, where they bowled and gambled, and drank and swore, on a week-day. A temporary platform was constructed over the square upon which the pins stood, and on that platform, or in front of it, I have seen as many as twenty people at once kneeling and weeping as they sought salvation.'

Later Booth used the old Effingham Theatre 'on the stage of which there regularly mounted forty, fifty, and sixty sinners on Sunday night seeking mercy'.

By 1879, the use of the mercy seat was a tried and tested method of soul-saving. Not that seekers went forward with the reserved reverence so characteristic of today's meetings, as a reporter from the *Newcastle Daily Chronicle* discovered. He spent a week of May 1879 recording the Tyneside activities of General Booth and his Hallelujah lasses. His assignments included a night of prayer at Handyside's Hall, Gateshead. The meeting, which had started quietly enough, had been going for a couple of hours when the reporter joined it at two in the morning.

'If ever I go to an all night prayer meeting again,' he writes, 'I shall take something to steady the nerves. Such a terrifying gathering as that which was held last night, has, I should think, never been seen before – not in the wildest excesses of Primitive Methodism... The people present, taken as a whole, were the roughest lot I have seen at any of these meetings... The close-cropped bullet-headed youth in the muffler was the rule and not the exception...

'On Monday night – rather, I should say, on Tuesday morning – the General requested his audience to sit still and sing when the "witnessing" was concluded. He gave out these lines: "I need thee every hour, Most gracious Lord!" The words were taken up by the whole audience; the chorus was rolled out to a rattling tune, and was no sooner finished than it was commenced again with additional vigour. This chorus might have been sung perhaps a dozen times when there was a shrill scream, a bustle around the platform, and a general rise of the audience. Seats were mounted; hands were waved in the air; the singing was mingled with loud "Hallelujahs", bursts of vociferous prayer, shouting and hysterical laughter. To add to the commotion four of the forms fell backwards, and threw their occupants into a common heap on the floor. So great was the commotion in the centre of the room, so terrifying was the din, that this incident, which would have thrown an ordinary congregation into uproar, passed almost unnoticed. Sinners were creeping to the penitent form; The Salvation Army was rejoicing; fully one third of those present acted as if they were more or less insane... Several figures are bent double near the platform, groaning and wringing their hands.'

Attempting to 'describe the indescribable', he continues:

'Until penitents "throw themselves at the feet of Jesus", as it is called, a meeting of The Salvation Army is a tolerably sane affair. The fat is at once in the fire, however, when penitents come forward. Let me endeavour to recall some details of the fearfully confused scene which was to be witnessed at half-past three o'clock on Tuesday morning. By dint of climbing as high as the forms will allow, I can see over the heads of a large part of the audience… a little of what is going on round the platform. One can only take it in piecemeal. Half-a-dozen crop-headed… youths are praying vociferously, with their faces towards me. Did I say praying? I only suppose they were. It was vociferous shouting, with closed eyes. Their bodies sway to and fro; their hands are lifted, and brought down again with a thump on the form; they contort themselves as if they were in agony…

'I watched the proceedings for some time from my point of vantage on a back form; and then struggled through the crowd to get a look at the penitents. They had fainted away. Here lay a woman in a dead swoon, with six "Hallelujah lasses" singing round her, and not one of them trying to bring her round even by so much as sprinkling water on her face. On the other side of the platform was a man lying full length, his limbs twitching, his lips foaming, totally unregarded… the "General" was leading the singing, whilst the people were praying or shouting as the whim took them, the penitents whose repentance had been the cause of so much rejoicing were lying unconscious.'

Just three years before those remarkable events the very future of the mercy seat within the ministry of The Christian Mission lay in the balance. Some members wanted to abolish it. It was Catherine Booth who rose to its defence at the annual conference of The Christian Mission in June 1876.

'I just want to mention one matter which has long been upon my heart,' she said. 'I refer to the important subject of selecting the right kind of people to seek out the anxious and induce them to come to the penitent form. I am sure that much harm is done by injudiciously pressing people to come forward who are not really deeply convicted… I believe in the penitent form, and have insisted on the use of it, in spite of people's prejudices. When holding services outside the Mission, friends have sometimes persuaded me to give way in this matter: but I never did so without spoiling my prayer-meetings. And friends sometimes say to me now, "The people here strongly object to a penitent form; they are too respectable; they will be offended. You had better ask them into the ante-room." But I reply, "No; I have tried it;

and whomsoever it may offend or please, I am going to have a penitent form."'

For Catherine, like William, this was not mere theology, this was spiritual reality. She knew for herself the effect of calling the penitent to a public show of repentance. Sandall records the events at the opening of the People's Mission Hall, Whitechapel, in April 1870. William, although in attendance, was too ill to preach. Catherine took his place.

'The "Communion rail" (penitent form) was crowded, first by persons who responded to Mrs Booth's appeal that the occasion of the dedication of the building should be made one of personal reconsecration, and later by unconverted persons seeking salvation. The number of these was estimated to be 150, in addition to many seekers who knelt in other parts of the hall.'

In his Easter Monday address the following year in that same hall, the Founder was fit enough to state his view:

'Our cry is still, "Souls, souls, souls!" We are still a penitent-form people; we believe in getting sinners to the penitent form. The penitent form is the focal point of all Salvationist endeavour.'

(In *The Officer* November/December 2009, Stephen Grinsted refers to this quote when considering Booth's 'Passion for the Penitent Form'. He then remarks:

'I feel it is important to stress that we do not become Salvation Army officers to "make a difference". We become officers to get people to the penitent form. If the penitent form was William Booth's passion, should it not be ours too?')

Booth's Cornish hope of a 'glorious harvest of immortal souls', did, in the estimation of Railton, come to pass. In *General Booth*, he writes, 'He probably led more souls to the penitent form than any man who has ever lived.'

In the same book, Railton explains the Founder's commitment to the public response at the penitent form.

'From the first beginnings of his cottage meetings as a lad in Nottingham, he always aimed at leading every sinner to repentance, and he always required that repentance should be openly manifested by the penitent coming out in the presence of others, to kneel before God, to confess to him, and to seek his pardon.

'This is merely in accordance with the ancient customs practised by the Jews in their Temple, to which practice Jesus Christ so strikingly calls attention in his parable of the publican who cried, "God be merciful to me a sinner." The psalms of David abound with just such cries for deliverance, and with declarations that God heard and answered all those who so cried to him in the anguish of their guilt.

'The General was never blind to the fact that open acts of contrition like this may be feigned or produced by a mere passing excitement; but having seen so much of the indifference with which men generally continue in sin, even when they admit their consciousness of guilt and danger, he always thought the risk of undue excitement, or too hasty, comparatively small.'

Railton also explains the purpose of the mercy seat to the uninitiated.

'The penitent form of The Salvation Army is simply a form or row of seats, immediately in front of the platform, at which all who wish to seek salvation are invited to kneel, as a public demonstration of their resolution to abandon their sins and to live henceforth to please God. Those who kneel there are urged to pray for God's forgiveness, and when they believe that he does forgive them to thank him for doing so. Whilst kneeling there they are spoken to by persons who, having passed through the same experience, can point out to them the evils and dangers they must henceforth avoid, and the first duties which a true repentance must demand of them.

'There are many cases, for example, in which the penitent is urged to give up at once some worldly habit or companionship, or to make confession of, and restitution for, some wrong done to others. An officer or soldier accompanied the penitent to his home or to his or her employer, should such a course appear likely to help him to effect any reconciliation, or take any other step to which his conscience calls him. The names and addresses of all penitents are recorded, so that they may be afterwards visited and helped to carry out the promises they have made to God.

41

'For convenience sake, in very large meetings, such as those the General himself held, where hundreds at a time come to the penitent form, a room called the registration room is used for the making of the necessary inquiries and records. In this room those who decide to join the Army have a small piece of ribbon of the Army's colours at once attached to their coats. But this registration room must in no way be confused with an inquiry room, where seeking souls can go aside unseen. The General was always extremely opposed to the use of any plan, other than that of the penitent form lest there should be any distinction made between one class and another, or an easier path contrived for those who wish to avoid a bold avowal of Christ.'

As well as Booth not liking the idea of inquiry rooms, Railton records that he was wary of how counsellors used the Bible with seekers:

'He always refused to allow any such use of the Bible in connection with penitents as has been usual in inquiry rooms, where the people have been taught that if they only believed the words of some text, all would be well with them. The faith to which the General desired all who came to the penitent form to be led is not the mere belief of some statement, but that confidence in God's faithfulness to all his promises, which brings peace to the soul.'

Addressing critics of the mercy seat, Railton continues:

'Nothing could be more unjust than the representation that by the use of the penitent form an attempt is made to work up excitement or emotion. Experience has proved, everywhere, that nothing tends so rapidly to allay the painful anxiety of a soul, hesitating before the great decision, as the opportunity to take at once, and publicly, a decisive step...

'But the penitent form is no modern invention, nor can it be claimed as the speciality of any set of religionists. Even heathen people in past ages have provided similar opportunities for those who felt a special need either to thank their God for blessings received, or to seek his help in any specific case, to come forward in an open way, and confess their wants, their confidence, or their gratitude, at some altar or shrine.

'Shame upon us all that objection should ever be made to equally public avowals of penitence, of submission, of faith, or of devotion to the Saviour of the world. The General, at any rate, never wavered in demanding the most speedy and decisive action of this kind, and he probably led more souls to the penitent form than any man who has ever lived.'

On the question of terminology, Booth himself was bilingual. He used the terms 'mercy seat' and 'penitent form' unsystematically and indiscriminately. Thus setting the pattern for successive generations of Salvationists! In *The Founder Speaks* Booth records:

'In a remarkable meeting I held in one of the large cities of Japan, during my visit to that country, a dear woman came to the mercy seat. She found forgiveness for herself, and went straight from the registration room to the place where she had been sitting, brought her two children to the penitent form, and, kneeling between them, pointed them to the Saviour, whom she had just found.'

On the subject of backsliders in *The War Cry* of 10 January 1885, he writes:

'Many of these have been at our penitent forms, borne their testimony with streaming eyes and joyful hearts in our free-and-easys, marched in our ranks, worn our badges, and sung with rapture our songs. What can we do for them?... We shouted and laughed and rejoiced when we first got them to the mercy seat.'

He starts a letter to young Christians, which is included in the anthology *With Colours Waving*, with:

'Dear Young Friends, you have been to the mercy seat, confessed your sins, promised to follow Jesus Christ and believed that God has forgiven you.'

On one occasion he exhorted:

'Go on begging men and women to kneel at the drum, or come to the mercy seat, or in some other form to seek forgiveness, so entering the family of the great Father, and finishing up in Heaven.'

The mercy seat was getting the Army noticed in high places. In December 1897 William Booth spent time in private discussion with the Prime Minister, William Gladstone. One of the topics of conversation was the Army's use of the penitent form. (How many Prime Ministers since then have heard about the mercy seat?)

On the eve of Booth's visit to the United States in January 1898, 7,000 Salvationists packed London's Royal Albert Hall. Towards the end of a rousing address, the Founder made an appeal. *The War Cry* (15 January 1898) picks up the story:

'"I declare to you," he said. "I delight in it. I am married to the penitent form." Without any confusion a dozen rows or so of the area chairs were vacated and turned into the Army's latest penitent form. Steadily seekers stepped into the pool – officers, soldiers, backsliders. Those who could not get there stood up in the stall box or gallery and joined their kneeling comrades in a covenant of submission and consecration.

'Then Commissioner Coombs invited a general pledge to capture at least one soul for God in the General's absence and got a magnificent standing response, on which he asked God to set his seal.'

Four years later, in June 1902, Booth was in Berlin when he heard that King Edward VII had been taken to hospital for an emergency appendectomy, just two days before his coronation. At a time of national crisis – survival rates for the surgery were not good – Booth's response was to turn to the mercy seat. He wrote:

'The whole city has been startled, and no one more so than myself, with the news that the King is ill, has had an operation, and the coronation is indefinitely postponed. What my feelings are it is impossible to describe. The German nation has been feeling very strongly against Great Britain on account of the South African War, and has been at no pains to conceal her bitterness. Any deep sympathy is not to be expected now. I have wired IHQ to call for prayer for His Majesty the world over. I have no doubt about the response.

'[At the beginning of the meeting] I asked for prayer from my own people, and all who feared God, and then led the audience to the mercy seat, a great hush seemed to come down on all present.'

The mercy seat was becoming more widely known throughout the nation. In *The Great Idea*, Arnold White describes a meeting for vagrants at London's Blackfriars hostel in 1909 during which 40 people knelt at the mercy seat, declaring that 'The penitent form is a national asset in the hands of such men as Brigadier Playle.'

On his 80th birthday, 10 April 1909, Booth wrote to his officers. His letter reveals the lasting impression his first visit to the mercy seat made upon him:

'When that lad of 15 walked out unsolicited and unnoticed to the mercy seat, and made a full consecration of his little all to the service of his King, who would have thought that God had such a wonderful future in store for him? That boy certainly at that time entertained no higher notions of his own powers than to have the privilege of leading a cottage prayer meeting... And yet, see the honour that God has conferred upon him by making him the General of The Salvation Army!'

In *The Officer* (May/June 2010) David Hammond highlights the profound importance of the mercy seat to the Founder, when he writes:

'William Booth once said of it: "I began there and I intend to die there; and if there is anything to be put in my coffin as an emblem of my heart's delight, let it be a mercy seat."'

Booth's last appearance in the Royal Albert Hall was on 9 May 1912. In *Words of William Booth* Cyril Barnes records the scene:

'Colonel John Lawley, faithful attendant and helper, took the General's arm to lead him from the platform, but was stopped as William Booth looked toward the congregation. "I'm not satisfied," he said, "I want to see the penitent form."'

Three months later he died. That the mercy seat did not die with him is due to the fact that William had long-since encouraged his son Bramwell and others to see the mercy seat as an essential method of soul-saving.

In August 1876 William had written to Christian Missioners:

'In dealing with the anxious let no one be urged to go forward to the penitent form who is not deeply convinced of sin and thoroughly earnest for salvation. The more thoroughly persons are awakened and broken down before God the more readily will they exercise faith in Christ and enter into rest, and the more stable will they become afterwards.'

Twenty-nine years and countless mercy seat users later, William wrote to Bramwell about his visit to Jerusalem's Wailing Wall:

'We have seen the Jews wailing on what remains of the foundations of the walls of the city. It is one of the most pathetic scenes I have ever witnessed. It is like one long penitent form, with the people standing instead of kneeling, with broken hearts and overflowing eyes.'

William's efforts were not lost on his son, as Joseph Pugmire records in *The Officer*, July 1924, when he describes his experience of working with Bramwell:

'I have found invariably that, "Just as I am, thy love I own", is as powerful a verse as any. During the last three years, when travelling as ADC to the General, I have seen many hundreds weep their way to the mercy seat while this has been sung... The rule in the General's meetings now is that the person who deals with a soul at the penitent form should also accompany him to the registration room.'

Bramwell shared his father's enthusiasm for the mercy seat and his indiscriminate labelling of it. Neither stumbled over terminology. With typical familial pragmatism what counted was that those who stumbled in sin should find redemption there.

In *Echoes and Memories* Bramwell uses both terms with no obvious distinction. Describing a visit to the hall at the Hadleigh farm colony by Cecil Rhodes he writes:

'I shall never forget the expression on Rhodes's face as he stood and looked down at the penitent form. "Ah!" he said, "I see. This is the dividing line between the old life and the new."'

A few pages later he recalls 'a man of very striking religious experience who suffered from the most awful lisp I have ever had the agony to listen to. He was a convert of the Mission, and had come one day to the mercy seat in Whitechapel. I was delegated to speak to him. I found that he was seeking the power of God to witness for Christ'.

Like runners passing on a baton in a relay race, a transatlantic preacher handed William the idea of the mercy seat. William in turn not only convinced his own generation about its validity but also enthused the next. By the time William passed it on to Bramwell, the mercy seat had already become part of the furniture.

Chapter 5

The Centre of Gravity

IN March 1877, Bradford's Ted Irons found salvation at the Eastbrook Wesleyan Chapel. By the following October, Captain Ted Irons was leading others to the Saviour through the mission of The Salvation Army. A mission gathered round one mercy seat.

In *Captain Ted,* Irons recalls events of 1878 in Coventry:

'Inside the Factory [a 'Salvation Factory' opened by the Founder in 1878] were packed 2,000 people, whilst in the cellar Mr Railton, I, and some others had about 400 people, out of which we got about 12 to the penitent form...

'Yesterday morning we began our prayer meeting by 7.10. Whilst I was giving out the hymn, a big drunkard came and fell down at my feet at the penitent form and began to pray for mercy. We went on singing the hymn, and in less than two minutes another followed, and then another, and so on, until we had finished the hymn, no less than five big sinners were crying to God for mercy.'

Irons describes the conversion of Tom Shirley, a backslidden drunkard who had come near to suicide:

'Upon the Sunday when the Factory was opened, this man listened in the open-air, but kept away from Christ till late in the evening. He had gone home under deep conviction and had lit his pipe... but he could not smoke, and at length he returned to the Factory, and walking right up to the penitent form, fell at the feet of Jesus.'

Not many weeks later Shirley's wife was converted:

'I remember', writes Captain Ted, 'leading her to the penitent form. At first she had a struggle, but soon jumped up, praising God for his saving grace. Next to her, at the penitent form, knelt a young man whom she knew, and as soon as she had got through herself, she turned to him, and, thumping him on the back, said, "Now Tom, roll it all on Jesus, same as I have done; now then, he'll bear it; roll it on him." And so, before she was five minutes old in grace, she pointed another poor soul to Jesus.'

Tom Shirley, his wife and the many others who knelt at the mercy seat under the guidance of Captain Ted in 1878 were, according to *Twenty-one Years Salvation Army,* published around 1886, part of a far larger picture:

'More than 10,000 anxious inquirers' names had been recorded at the penitent forms in the course of the year.'

The newly-formed Army press was quick to pass on word of mercy-seat victories. The first edition of *The Salvationist,* 1 January 1879, carried this report from Bolton:

'A cock fighter came to a meeting under the influence of drink, but he was very soon under the influence of the Spirit. He was convinced of sin, came to the penitent form, gave his heart to God, and is now rejoicing.'

Bolton was still witnessing mercy-seat miracles some months later, as this April report confirms:

'Another man, known as the greatest drunkard in Bolton, came several times to our meetings. At last the scales were removed from his eyes, he saw the blood that was spilt for him, and rushing to the penitent form cried aloud for mercy. I went and told his wife her husband was at the penitent form. She jumped to her feet, went down the hall, fell by his side, and was soon enabled to sing, "The precious blood of Jesus, it cleanses from all sin." Since then their daughter has been saved, and she says their home is the happiest home in Bolton.'

Likewise the first edition of *The War Cry,* 27 December 1879, carried two reports of mercy-seat happenings. The first quotes the *Northern Echo*'s coverage of the Darlington council of war.

'Ticket holders went to the Central Hall, where a crowded audience heard Miss Booth sing and preach. The General was again in charge at the Livingstone Hall, and they had a very excellent meeting. After both services the usual prayer meeting was held. About 20 persons came forward to the penitent form.'

On the following page is this report from Newcastle upon Tyne:

'On Sunday God was with us in mighty power, processions larger, theatre packed, and a good many in the Varieties. Four souls, one had just served five years' penal servitude. Last night we had a man saved in the mud in the open air. Our congregations are large in the hall since the weather has changed. Last Thursday night we had 10 fallen women in the hall; seven at the penitent form; three good cases. Fearful unexampled cold weather. The water was frozen in the glass on the Hall of Varieties' table the other night. One man when asked to give God his heart, said he was too cold to do so. Dreadfully cold.'

It was not only the established press that was taking note of the mercy seat. The Honiton-based *The Skeleton* – the paper of the Skeleton Army – had a clear mission:

'The real object of this paper is to stamp out the fanaticism and blasphemy of the Salvation Army, which is doing so much to bring Christian religion into ridicule.'

In *The Salvation Army Origins and Early Days: 1865-1900* Glenn Horridge highlights extracts from the issue of 16 December 1882. *The Skeleton* includes this report on a *War Cry* story:

'To judge from the "Captain's" address and the manner in which he murders the English language... it causes us to suppose that he knows as much about the Bible as the Bible knows about him. And yet on looking through the columns of the *War Cry* "novelty", the man who lately conducted the services here appears in comparison with many other Salvation officers, a perfect gem, a pearl without price, an archangel! We read of a music hall clog dancer who, having been "saved", got on the so-called "penitent form" and enlightened the wicked "unsaved" ones before him by saying that he used to clog dance to such as them but, in future, he'd clog dance to Jesus!

'We are afraid if our Redeemer were to descend now there would be a greater clearance than the occasion on which he cast out the buyers and sellers from the Temple.'

Centred as Salvationists were on the public conversion of the likes of clog dancers and on 'fishing' – leaving their seats to persuade those who looked troubled in spirit to kneel at the mercy seat – it is fitting that *Twenty-one Years Salvation Army* records the salvation tactics employed at the opening of the 700th UK corps in a Cornish fishing town. The year is 1885.

'The rush of what appears to be the entire male population old and young, to see the new sight; the turning of every eye upon the new comers whenever and wherever they appear; the discussion in every home... the taking up of our simple choruses by every child in the street... the dense crowd surrounding the speakers in the open air... the open-mouthed astonishment with which every song and testimony seems to be drunk in... the fall, night after night, of rows of penitents at the mercy seat, and the rise, day after day, of rows of real soldiers of Christ, ready to march to the rescue of others; such is the story of every advance of The Salvation Army.'

As the mercy seat was in some respects an American import, it seems only right that it should be re-exported by the advancing new Army to the New World. Again, *Twenty-one Years Salvation Army* reports:

'Some four or five years ago in the United States there was a saloon keeper in Bridgeport, Connecticut, outside whose door an aged Christian woman stood alone to preach. The man was ashamed, as he saw others mocking her, that he could not go and take his stand by her side. He went into the cellar to weep and pray, but although he became so miserable as to sell out his business, for two years afterwards he remained a wretched wanderer without God, often on the brink of suicide.'

This man made his way to New York, the report continues, where he met an Army open-air meeting. Although under conviction, he preferred rye to repentance. The next Sunday finds him alone:

'Passing along the street in a partially intoxicated state he seemed to be irresistibly drawn into the barracks. In the course of the meeting he was somewhat sobered, and at 10.30 pm he rose from the penitent form praising God for salvation.'

Eventually he became 'a glorious worker for the salvation of souls'.

Like their founders, early-day Salvationists were discovering the spiritual reality of the penitent form. Here hardened men were softened. Here wayward women were put straight. Here was the place for the lifting of burdens.

The Salvation War of 1885 contains further evidence of lives changed at the mercy seat. A Canadian convert recounts his impression of his first visit to an Army Saturday night meeting:

'I was astounded at their earnestness, and the joy they evidently had in serving God. I had never heard such palpable earnestness in God's service... That night I prayed to God. I returned to the barracks twice next day, and I continued attending for many evenings, feeling myself being drawn closer by the earnestness of these people. At last I could resist no longer, and, in answer to the repeated solicitations, went forward to their "penitent form" and publicly prayed God to forgive the sins of my past life... And now I sent the good news to my sister... an educated lady, and a splendid specimen of the Church formalist in England. After a few weeks she also had to come down to the low and degraded penitent form, and there God spoke peace to her heart.'

Another battle, another victory, this time in Tunstall, this time a bull-baiting, dog-fighting, drunken gambler in his seventies:

'The nephew, who was very anxious for his old uncle's salvation, got him to the barracks, where he sat, shaking in his seat, from the beginning of the meeting. The spirit of God laid hold of the old man. He was helped to the penitent form, and in a few minutes a wonderful change took place, and he was shouting and praising God as if he would have had the roof of the barracks off.'

Another battleground, the same battle:

'Ben Wingfield was rolling drunk throughout the streets of Northwich one evening when the sound of the Army's drum struck his ears and roused his morbid senses. He followed to the Bull Ring, where an open-air meeting was being held, and there stood making drunken exclamations, which so aroused the attention of the soldiers to his presence that two of them took him between them in the procession and marched him to the barracks, where, in his shameful drunkard's rags and a pair of old clogs, he was helped to the penitent form and got savingly converted to God. He became the drummer of the corps, and for four years did his best for God and the salvation of souls.'

For early-day Salvationists the term 'penitent form' came quite naturally to the lips. Not only did it speak of revivalist roots but also it ably described the purpose for which most people knelt, that of seeking salvation.

In *The History of The Salvation Army* Robert Sandall records that 250,000 people knelt at Army penitent forms in the period 1881-1885, a result which more than vindicates Catherine's 1876 insistence on its use. By contrast, first-time seekers (those recorded as seeking salvation) in the British Territory 1981-1985 totalled 10,688. In 2001, the number of first-time seekers in the United Kingdom Territory was 695. In 2008, the figure was 261.

During the First World War, Salvationists serving in the British Army not only held meetings in the trenches, but also called their hearers to kneel at the mercy seat – made of army greatcoats, as this *War Cry* report of 20 February 1915, from Gunner Tom Troke, RFA, records:

'One very cold, dark, sleety night, when the big guns were booming and shells were constantly exploding near by, God drew very near to the faithful six as they pleaded with their comrades to turn to him. Regardless of the cold they took off their overcoats and of them made a penitent form, at which they invited the men to kneel and seek mercy. Three responded and at this strange penitent form cried aloud for salvation.'

The report's headline of 'Mercy seat behind the guns – comrades seek salvation at penitent form made of overcoats' shows both Salvationist ingenuity in practice and terminological indecision in prose.

Although interchangeable in Army parlance, the terms 'penitent form' and 'mercy seat' suggest a difference of emphasis. It is difficult to be certain when this sea change took place, especially as people's use of language is itself imprecise.

Both terms were in use in the early 1900s, as the following glossary entries in *The Salvation Army Year Book 1906* – the first year book – show:

'Penitent-Form: It is an almost invariable practice of The Army to set apart a seat near the front of the platform in its meetings for those persons to kneel at who desire publicly to declare their sorrow for having lived a godless life, and their desire to submit themselves to Christ and to begin a new course. It has been found everywhere pre-eminently useful to give everyone this opportunity to take a decided stand in the presence of others. The Army never teaches that the mere coming to this form, or any prayers or professions made there, necessarily prove a person to be changed. But the general experience has been that the very large majority of these penitents manifest even afterwards that a deep inward impression has been made upon them. The names and addresses of those who come to the form are taken, so that they may be visited, and every effort is made to help and encourage them in carrying out the promises there made.'

And

'Mercy-Seat: A familiar Army term for the penitent-form to which all seeking Salvation are invited, thus making a public renunciation of sin.'

With the mercy seat/penitent form not mentioned in *Orders and Regulations* until 1917, these entries may well be the first published official definitions.

The first *War Cry* use of the term 'mercy seat' appeared in this report from Willenhall in the 12 January 1882 edition:

'This week the work has been glorious. Several poor drunkards rose to their feet and walked boldly to the penitent form, where, after some severe struggling, they laid hold of Christ by faith... In the Theatre we had a glorious time, 14 souls found their way to the mercy seat.'

Forty years on, two articles from *The War Cry,* 18 November 1922, underline the continuing uncertainty of terminology. The first is entitled 'Penitents' Mats'.

'All diligent readers of *The War Cry* will have been struck by the increasing number of people of all classes who seek salvation in the open air. As many as 30 at one time knelt in the street at Barrow-in-

Furness not many weeks ago and confessed their sins. Four more did the same in Hyde Park on Tuesday night last.

'In the majority of cases penitents in the open air have nothing upon which to kneel, unless some comrade takes off his coat and spreads it on the ground.

'Mrs Booth, the British Commissioner, has recognised this disadvantage, and in order that it may be overcome has arranged for the use of a specially constructed mat which officers can obtain at small cost from Salvationist Publishing and Supplies, Ltd. It is already in use in some places. This is a significant sign of the times!'

On the same page a corps report notes:

'A drunkards' raid at Seaham Harbour, led by Lieut-Colonel and Mrs Brown on Saturday night, finished with 17 penitents kneeling at the mercy seat.'

Incidentally, the penitent's mat did prove useful in open-air meetings, as this *War Cry* report reveals:

'A young woman under the influence of spirit-drinking attracted to the meeting by the singing, a young married woman who was present through the invitation of a Christian companion, and a young man, all knelt at the penitent's mat at Hyde Park.'

The Mrs Booth of that article, Florence, Bramwell's wife, is quoted in *With Colours Waving,* as observing that:

'Many a sinning and conscience-stricken soul comes to the mercy seat under the pretence of wanting power. If you heal the hurt of such a one lightly, he had better never have knelt there.'

On the subject of mercy seat prayer mats, Sven-Erik Ljungholm, in correspondence, writes:

'I have a prayer rug that was woven by officers in Russia around 1922 from remnants of sweaters, skirts, etc, which was collected from the soldiers, officers and cadets. They tried to use Army colours and it became a secret mercy seat when the Communist ban on the Army became imminent. It was carried from home to home of the soldiers by my grandparents. Eventually it was taken back to my homeland of Sweden and used there among the Sami people. My grandparents carried it in their backpack as they skied from village to village.'

A different kind of penitent mat appears in *Salvationist* 3 April 2010. Reporting the gift of a mercy seat kneeler at Exeter Temple, Laurie Bovey writes:

'Artist and tapestry creator Pat Johns undertook a commission to make a kneeler to accompany the new mercy seat in the community hall. As part of their [Mobilise] award work, the junior soldiers visited Pat to see how the work was progressing. She provided a loom so the children could have a go at weaving and see how much time and effort were going into the kneeler. Pat explained the design and, in a devotional time, the children looked at the idea that their Christian lives could often seem like a tapestry seen from the reverse side, with God's perspective being very different from their own.'

In the July 1924 *Officer*, Joseph Pugmire suggests some methods of leading a prayer meeting. He begins:

'Upon entering the prayer meeting the leader should announce plainly that no movement should be made before singing, except to the penitent form. Silence is power in a prayer meeting... A move to the penitent form will create interest and hold the people as well as inspire the comrades of the corps. A good start means a great deal.'

He continues:

'Work at the mercy seat must not be hurried. Seekers must be made to confess to God all wrong and then give an assurance that everything is right before they leave. It is not the business of the penitent-form worker to say whether a seeker is right with God. The Holy Spirit himself will reveal this.'

The Army's third General, Edward Higgins, like his predecessors was also convinced of the need to be a penitent-form people. While Chief of the Staff under Bramwell Booth, he wrote in the same edition of *The Officer*:

'We must be true to the principle of penitent form, demanding from sinners a public acknowledgment of their need of salvation, and urging them to come out and declare before all men their determination to give up sin and to serve the Lord Jesus Christ. We must endeavour to make all our meetings point to the penitent form.'

If people would not come to the mercy seat, the mercy seat in the shape of a drum would be taken to people.

In his book *The Salvation War in the West,* Abram Davey describes an early-day instance of such use:

'One evening, while holding an open-air service on the Quay, in Exeter, an invitation was given to those who wanted salvation to come out, and kneel at the drum. Seven accepted the invitation, amongst the number was Mrs Routley, who, with her husband and family, had been living anything but righteous lives.

'Not long after her conversion, she persuaded her husband to accompany her to The Salvation Army; he accepted her invitation, after which he continued to come, until at length he surrendered himself to God. One of the worst Skeletons that we had to contend with was their eldest son; but the dear lad soon followed his father's example, and gave his heart to God; and now the family may be seen at any of our Exeter open-air engagements – the father carrying the colours, the son beating a drum, and the mother playing a tambourine.'

A *War Cry* report of 19 April 1947 entitled 'Drumhead Harvest' also notes the benefits of this alfresco altar:

'Cadets of the Warriors Session being trained in Atlanta, Southern US Territory, are enjoying a "drumhead" harvest. By the middle of February they had seen 192 people kneel at the drumhead in their open-air meetings in the city and 229 seekers in other meetings. During recent out-of-town weekend campaigns another 121 decisions were secured. On one occasion there were 22 seekers kneeling at three drums. "It was one of the most powerful meetings I have ever seen at a street corner," states Brigadier R. B. Fitton, the training principal. For the launching of the "Fighting Faith" campaign, the cadets led a noonday street meeting from a truck which transported the 18-ton bulldozer they had borrowed to symbolise the "Bulldozers of Religion" which they are striving to be.'

By comparison, the British Army has had a drumhead service for years, where upturned drums are used as a battlefield altar. Today, the drumhead service is a ceremonial occasion.

'The drumhead service is used for the consecration of regimental colours,' writes Staff Chaplain, the Rev Mike Parker in correspondence. 'This usually takes place within barracks but sometimes, as with the Royal Highland Fusiliers in Afghanistan in 2008, it occurs in theatre. On these occasions the colours are laid on the drumhead before being presented to the regiment. The drumhead altar and field service can also be held on Regimental Days, especially if they coincide with a special occasion such as St George's Day.

'Perhaps the best known occasion is at the Royal British Legion Annual Festival of Remembrance at the Royal Albert Hall, where as part of the act of remembrance, a book of remembrance is place on the drumhead.'

As we have seen from the notion of percussion and penitent mats, Salvationists have long been adaptable in presenting both the gospel and an opportunity to respond. Charley Morey recalls his childhood days on the Isle of Wight:

'On Sunday mornings in August 1939 two boys would dig long sandcastles for the open-air meetings later that day on the beach at Ryde. These boys were paid a penny each. One pile of sand was shaped into a mercy seat. The CO, Captain Pratt, always invited people to come and kneel there at the end of the meeting, because, in his words, "Jesus saves". I knelt there and gave my heart to Jesus that year. The tide has washed those mercy seats away many times. Likewise, my sins have been washed by Jesus' blood. PS. I was one of the boys who was paid a penny.'

The writer of this editorial in the Australian *War Cry*, 3 January 1959, had building of a more permanent nature in mind when he wrote:

'The whole structure of The Salvation Army is built on the penitent form, and there was never a time when we needed to do more building than now. The only justification for the Army's existence is its success in getting people saved. We were not raised up to bless saints but to save sinners... Finance, manpower, property and other factors of the Army's warfare are certainly all of vital importance, but if the mercy seat is the centre of our greatest concern and our busiest action, "all these things will be added".'

Whether the writer realised it or not, his 'centre of our greatest concern' echoed a fellow *War Cry* reporter's assessment from 61 years earlier. The *War Cry* reporter who recorded the Founder's Royal Albert Hall farewell meeting before leaving for the United States in 1898 described the mercy seat like this:

'The penitent form which, so to speak, is the beautiful centre of gravitation round which all the Army's efforts arrange themselves.'

Over the years the mercy seat has become the centre of gravity of Salvationist identity. Millions of people have gravitated to the mercy seat and found salvation. Millions more have sensed a divine pull to the mercy seat and there discovered help, healing and holiness. The mercy seat has appeared in different guises – a bench, a chair, a drum, a mat, a pile of coats, a tapestry of sweater wool, a sand sculpture and (at the school-based outreach centre at which I worship) a gym bench. But whatever form it takes, the significance of using the penitent form remains unchanged and undiminished.

Chapter 6

The Mercy Seat and Brengle

ARGUABLY the greatest mercy-seat exponent and front-line fighter was Samuel Logan Brengle. For Brengle, the penitent form was the birthplace of the movement. In *Love-Slaves* he writes: 'The Salvation Army was born, not in a cloister, nor in a drawing-room, but on a spiritual battlefield – at the penitent form.'

In *Samuel Logan Brengle: Portrait of a Prophet,* Clarence Hall recognises that:

'The penitent form was the immediate goal, the focal spot, toward which Brengle's every point in his meeting technique turned.

'Besides being the place to which he drew tens of thousands during the active years of his service, it was also within the penitent form's sacred precincts that he learned much that he knew of the peculiar impulses and passions of the human heart. Here, kneeling beside penitents in the throes of conviction and confession, he met and battled with the stark forces that move men to all manner of deeds of evil. Here, among the tangled and baffling cross-weaves of the heart, he made contact with the spitework of human tongues, the inordinate animus of those eager not for purity but position, the unforgiving hatreds showing dull and hard in the eyes of persons wronged and waiting for a day of revenge, the shifty look of the guilty, the frightened stare of those with sins threatening to find them out.'

In *Ancient Prophets* Brengle admits to his passion for the penitent:

'In the old days, when my hearing was more acute, I seldom let anyone leave my penitent form without dealing with him myself. It was a great tax upon my time and strength, but my heart would not rest in peace until I had done my utmost to lead each one into light, and into the sweet and assured rest of faith. I felt I must make full proof of my ministry, and I judged of its acceptance with God and its harmony with his truth, his principles and Spirit, by its fruits in joyously saved and sanctified souls.'

He rejoiced when others discovered Jesus, as he describes in *Love-Slaves*:

'And as I talked she saw Jesus; the sin of the other man faded from her sight and her own sin grew big before her eyes, until she was in tears; then rising, she rushed, sobbing, to the penitent form to confess her own sin to the Lord, and, I trust, to be restored once more to his favour.'

Brengle was not distracted by knowing that not all of those who found salvation would find a place in the Army but was thankful that he had played his part. In *Resurrection Life and Power* he writes:

'Everywhere and always he [a brilliant young minister] testifies how he, a young, struggling, ambitious preacher, found Christ in all fullness at a Salvation Army penitent form with an old drunken "bum" kneeling on one side and a woman of the street on the other.'

Such a convinced practitioner was keen to share his skill with others. When advising a fellow-officer in the art of mercy-seat counselling he wrote:

'Permit me to suggest that, when people have reached the penitent form, they be allowed to kneel in silence before the Lord for a time without having two or three people come to question them and pour advice into their ears... We must not hurry people into the Kingdom at the penitent form. Give God a chance to deal with them... If we help souls too much at the penitent form, we may do them more harm than good.'

An early rationale of the Army was that if people didn't go to church then the church must go to the people. Brengle was happy to extend this concept to win souls who had come to church. If the people won't come to the penitent form, then the penitent form must go to the people. He describes one such occasion:

'Unable to get anyone to the penitent form in one meeting, I finally got a man on his knees at the door just as he was going out. So I suggested that we move the penitent form to the other end of the hall, which was done, the soldiers flocking down *en masse*. When that man got through, we turned our attention to a backslider in the rear, and soon the new convert and the rest of us were down around him – and he got through. Then a young lad near the door gave in and got beautifully saved. Finally there was only one unsaved person left in the hall – the backslidden wife of the sergeant-major. We all turned our attention to her and soon she was on her knees in the middle of the hall, where she got saved. So we ended with every sinner in the hall converted. It was a blessed time. It is most interesting to turn the whole hall into a penitent form!'

Perseverance became the hallmark of Brengle's approach. His success was not instant even if it were to seem constant. He describes the events at one of his early-day meetings, following a time of personal soul-searching:

'The next Saturday and Sunday I saw about 50 souls at the penitent form for salvation and holiness, and from that hour God has blessed me and given me souls everywhere.'

Despite the success, Brengle never lost sight of his own need. He practised what he preached:

'I have carried a penitent form around in my heart for half a century or more. And if there is ever any need, I constantly fly there.'

On his 59th birthday, 1 June 1919, he recollected in *Love-Slaves* that:

'This past year has been wonderful. Since the first of January considerably over 3,000 souls have knelt at the penitent form in my meetings, seeking pardon and purity. Seldom have I seen such manifestations of God's presence and power as during these months.'

Whereas Booth used the terms penitent form and mercy seat seemingly indiscriminately, Brengle was singular in his terminology. Whether used for holiness or salvation, it was always 'penitent form'. Whereas some invited holiness seekers to kneel at the holiness table, Brengle directed their search to the penitent form.

In *Helps to Holiness*, he asks:

'Were you at the holiness meeting? Did you come out to the penitent form? Did Jesus make your heart clean? And did you receive the Holy Ghost?'

Describing one night in Australia in *Resurrection Life and Power,* he writes:

'That night we had a great meeting. Thirty souls were at the penitent form – sinners, backsliders, Christians seeking clean hearts, were all kneeling and seeking together.'

In 'An Open Letter to a Young Man Seeking Spiritual Help', he asks:

'Did you come to the penitent form seeking a clean heart?'

Recounting a meeting in Boston, Massachusetts, in *Helps to Holiness* he writes:

'I attended an "all-night of prayer." It was a blessed time, and scores of people sought the blessing of a clean heart... Just before the meeting closed, Commissioner Dowdle, speaking to those who had been to the penitent form, said, "Remember, if you want to retain a clean heart, don't argue!"'

He inspired other officers to so direct their efforts to penitent-form decisions. In *Love-Slaves* he records:

'An officer, who had lost the blessing, attended one of my officers' meetings on the Continent and went away with her heart breaking after God... Sunday morning came, and she was again wrestling with God, when suddenly the great deep of her soul was broken up and she was melted and flooded with light and love and peace and joy. The Holy Ghost had come... She went to the holiness meeting that morning and told her experience. The Spirit fell on her soldiers and they flocked to the penitent form and sought and found.'

Little wonder then that his biographer Clarence Hall concludes:

'If one would take the full measure of Brengle's genius and heart as a soul-winner, he must look here... Brengle on the platform was mighty. But Brengle at the penitent form was mightier.'

It may have been Booth who brought the penitent form to the Army, but it was Brengle who brought the Army to the penitent form.

Chapter 7

The Focal Point In Focus

FOR Brengle and the early-day Salvationists the role of the mercy seat was clear cut. As Brengle wrote in his diary, 'Since the first of January considerably more than 3,000 souls have knelt at the penitent form in my meetings, seeking pardon and purity.' This was the place where the two great spiritual crises – salvation and sanctification – were resolved.

Today's mercy-seat use covers a multitude of purposes, if not sins.

In his *Historical Dictionary of The Salvation Army*, John Merritt defines a 'seeker' as:

'A person who kneels at a Salvation Army mercy seat/penitent form to pursue the solution to or to pray about a particular spiritual need. He or she may be a Christian or an unconverted person. If unconverted, the individual may be expressing an interest in the new birth for the first time and may not necessarily be making the faith commitment that is necessary to receive the inward witness of the Holy Spirit that authenticates a sound conversion.

'Hence, Salvationists prefer the more comprehensive, yet less specific, term "seeker" to that of "convert" in designating an individual who kneels at the mercy seat.'

Mercy-seat inscriptions along the lines of 'Pardon, peace, power' could be described as mercy seat mission statements. Those responsible for the inscriptions had a clear idea of the purpose of the penitent form. (A list of inscriptions can be found in Appendices B and E.)

General Albert Orsborn also had a clear view of the significance of the mercy seat. It is reported in the Australian *War Cry*, 8 August 1936:

'There are those who tell us that the hope of The Salvation Army for the future is in its young people. I do not agree with that. The hope of the Army is in the penitent form. As soon as that goes out of use we go out. The sign of the finger of God on the mercy seat is the crowning glory of God's favour on The Salvation Army.'

The editorial of the 3 January 1959 issue of the Australian *War Cry* firmly states:

'The primary aim of Salvationists again this year must be the bringing of sinners to the mercy seat. Every meeting held, every programme presented, every contact made must be a means to this end – the salvation of souls.'

But are we as clear about the role and function of the mercy seat today?

The stipulation in *Orders and Regulations* is that 'a penitent form must be available for use in all Salvation Army meetings'. What does not appear, however, is an exhaustive list of the purposes to which it should be put.

Since those clear-cut days of Brengle it seems that our collective focus on the focal-point bench has become hazy. Maybe as the Army's got older (some would say, matured) a form of cataract has grown, clouding our vision of, and for, the mercy seat. A natural part of the ageing process, some might say. After all, the Movement's not as mobile as it once was. Let's grow old gracefully.

We cannot avoid the issue, however, because how we see the purpose of the mercy seat is how we see the purpose of the Army. A highly-polished-but-seldom-used mercy seat is indicative of its corps. The mercy seat, highly polished or not, reflects the Army. It is the beginning and end of the search for identity – both individually and corporately.

Wesley Harris, in *Battle Lines,* writes:

'The mercy seat is central to Salvationism and without it all our Army activities must be as wheels without hubs. The mercy seat represents a saving encounter between sinful man and almighty God and nothing can be more important than that.'

General George Carpenter saw the mercy seat functioning as a guest room:

'The mercy seat ought to be like a guest room, with everything joyfully and thoughtfully prepared, and those who come there ought to be as carefully and thoughtfully received as the guest, for guests they are – prodigals coming home!'

While for Alfred Cunningham it is a labour ward: 'The place of the coming to birth of the new life.'

In *Community in Mission*, Phil Needham outlines the Army's place in the Church Universal. Here he describes the mercy seat as a place of salvation:

'The Salvationist fellowship has its own rites of public witness to conversion. When the gospel is preached in Salvation Army meetings (services of worship), persons are invited to respond by coming forward and kneeling at a mercy seat (a place of prayer), thereby signifying their penitence, desire for conversion, and personal resolve. The symbolism of this action is reminiscent of Jesus' frequent call for would-be disciples to step out, leave what they have and follow him. The kneeling at the mercy seat points to the true humility of those who see the inadequacy and shame of their life outside discipleship, and the longing to be converted to true discipleship through spiritual death and resurrection. Through faith the seeker rises from the mercy seat a new person in Jesus Christ.'

Lest his readers get the impression that a journey to the mercy seat is essential to a step of faith in Christ, Needham points out:

'There is, of course, no guarantee of conversion by virtue of the act of coming to the mercy seat, nor is this regarded as an essential precondition of membership. The coming forward is only a sign that a search is in progress and conversion is contemplated. As such, it strengthens the seeker and elicits the support of the congregation in concerned prayer.'

So, coming to the mercy seat is a sign. 'Handle with care' might be an appropriate one. Maybe if we wore L-plates on our uniforms we might be less full of ourselves and more sensitive to others. Come to think of it, didn't those who found salvation at the mercy seat in Booth's day wear the sign 'Under new management'? But we digress.

Although expressed in different ways – prodigals coming home, people coming to new birth, a sign that a search is in progress – the mercy seat is still being linked with salvation.

While in his book Needham explains the use of the mercy seat in terms of salvation, he also believes it has value in a wider spiritual context. In correspondence he writes:

'I think the mercy seat should be utilised for any purpose involving prayer. I think it is quite useful for Salvationists to be invited to come together for prayer at the mercy seat for any number of purposes. Unfortunately, in too many corps coming to the mercy seat means that there is something wrong or there has been a distressing defeat in the person's life. Having Salvationists come together in positive prayer around the mercy seat can help to remove some of the unfortunate barriers.'

The booklet *How to Counsel Seekers* offers a number of suggestions as to what constitutes purposes involving prayer:

'The counsellor should be aware that seekers kneel at the mercy seat for a variety of reasons. These cannot always be specifically allocated to either salvation or sanctification. They may go forward as a special act of prayer or rededication, or as an offering for special service, locally or perhaps as an officer.'

It enlarges on the 'variety of reasons':

'Described by General Bramwell Booth as "the scene of The Salvation Army's miracle", the penitent form, or mercy seat, has no virtue of itself, but kneeling there is a public confession of spiritual need and desire after God; in many instances it expresses decision, confession, seeking and always provides a place where spiritual guidance can be given. To kneel at the mercy seat is a public confession of Christ.'

In *Battle Lines,* Wesley Harris, describing the mercy seat as 'a place of grace not disgrace', offers a number of other valid uses:

'We may kneel to give thanks, to intercede for others, to dedicate ourselves, and to share spiritual communion with Christ, and whatever our need we can be assured that God can meet it.'

Using the mercy seat as a place of intercession for others is common. Kneeling at the mercy seat in somebody else's place is less so. General Frederick Coutts, in *In Good Company,* cites the vicarious use of the mercy seat:

'Remember Molly Weir, now a television personality, who described in *Shoes are for Sundays* how she went to the penitent form at Springburn for her grandma who couldn't come herself because she couldn't leave the house.'

Decision, confession, seeking, guidance, offering for service, rededication, thanksgiving, communion, these are elements that have a wider context than just salvation or sanctification. These are reasons for using the mercy seat with which today's Salvationists identify. It is to ask for help, to say sorry, to be reassured, to pray for ourselves and others that we keep coming back to the mercy seat. This is why we value the opportunity of responding to God there.

But this is by no means exhaustive. In 1994, I conducted a survey of UK corps officers on the subject of the mercy seat (see Appendix D). In answer to, 'Why do you give the invitation to come to the mercy seat and what do you expect will happen there?' Bryony Stimpson summarises the wide-ranging complexities in mercy-seat usage:

'I offer kneeling at the mercy seat as one of a number of options for response. The call might be to receive forgiveness, to commit to follow Jesus for the first time, to receive his grace for a particular need, or his healing touch. It may be to register availability for service and ask for an anointing of Holy Spirit power to fulfil it. It could be to request a first-time or a subsequent infilling of the Spirit, or whatever he suggests. I might ask people to raise their hand, stand where they are, stand at the front, come and kneel or come aside for prayer and counsel after the meeting is over. I try to do whatever God is asking at the time.'

In 1994 other meeting leaders also found that trying to do 'whatever God is asking at the time' required not only making a variety of appeals but occasionally offering a variety of ways to respond. Although for some it was only one of a number of options, the main way of responding to God was to come forward to the mercy seat.

(My similar survey of 2009 reveals that other response options have become more widespread. We shall take a closer look at this in the next chapter.)

In 1996 the International Spiritual Life Commission convened to 'review the ways in which The Salvation Army cultivates and sustains the spiritual life of its people'. One of the areas reviewed was 'the place of the mercy seat', which, in the words of the report *Called to be God's People*, the commission 'confirmed as integral to the Army's life'.

Among the twelve spiritual calls the commission issued to the worldwide movement was a 'Call to the Mercy Seat.' It reads as follows:

'We call Salvationists worldwide to recognise the wide understanding of the mercy seat that God has given to the Army; to rejoice that Christ uses this means of grace to confirm his presence; and to ensure that its spiritual benefits are fully explored in every corps and Army centre.

'We affirm that the mercy seat in our meetings symbolises God's unremitting call to his people to meet with him. It is not only a place for repentance and forgiveness, but also a place for communion and commitment. Here we may experience a deep awareness of God's abundant grace and claim his boundless salvation. The mercy seat may be used by anyone, at any time, and particularly in Army meetings when, in response to the proclaimed word, all are invited to share loving and humble communion with the Lord.'

In 2008 one of the commission members, Commissioner Linda Bond, reflected on this call. In the November edition of *Pipeline* she writes about the mercy seat. Inviting the reader to imagine that she is a tour guide showing a party around an Army hall, she continues:

'The climax of my presentation would take place in front of the mercy seat. My explanation would go something like this:

'"Ladies and gentlemen, you are looking at a simple piece of furniture that has deep meaning for Salvationists. We call it the mercy seat or penitent form. The first name recalls the mercy seat of the Old Testament that symbolised for Israel that God was present, calling his people to meet with him, offering to them his grace. Salvationists see this place in the same way, a place to come and meet with God, to receive his mercy.

'"When we call it a penitent form we are putting the emphasis on the one who comes in repentance, confession and submission. The two

68

terms are used interchangeably but always with the understanding that one who comes humbly before God never fails to receive from him.

'"Salvation Army mercy seats have taken many forms; a drum in the streets, a chair, or just a space set apart. It is symbolic of our meeting with God and as you know, that can happen anywhere, anytime. This piece of furniture has no special power or grace in itself. It is a place of prayer, a place of decision. Going to the mercy seat is an outward expression of the inward leading of the Holy Spirit...

'"The elements of a Salvation Army meeting include robust or reflective singing, prayer, Scripture reading, testimonies, a ministry of music, and giving of our monetary gifts. But the whole meeting leads to a climax with the proclamation of the Word of God and an invitation to respond. So the mercy seat offers a place for visible, intentional response to God's gracious invitation. It may be a response to his offer of salvation or sanctification (holiness) or a commitment to his special calling on your life. It is most often associated with a significant decision. But the use of the mercy seat has widened and now many would see it as a place of prayer, of bringing before our gracious Lord our personal needs or the needs of others, or for dedicating or rededicating of our lives to his service.

'"Let's move closer to the mercy seat. What generally happens is that following the sermon, we have a time of prayer when an invitation is given to come and kneel. A song or chorus carefully suited to the message is selected. To see people come in humility before the Lord is the most moving part of any Army meeting. It is the highest point of worship.

'"Another aspect of kneeling at the mercy seat that needs to be mentioned is this: it is done in the presence of God's people. Now that very fact is the reason many would not come. They do not want to be a public spectacle, having people wonder what great sin they committed. But from my experience, the very opposite is true. The congregation moves to a higher level of participation as they support the seeker in love with prayer and often tears. Wise counsellors are available to come alongside the one who kneels at the mercy seat, to offer a listening ear, to share an appropriate verse from the Bible, to pray on their behalf and then invite the one who kneels to pray personally. But a desire to pray alone is always respected.

'"I have some wonderful stories I could tell. I think of my father's return to the Lord. Our whole family was marked by his transformation. I remember Sandra, a heroin addict who knelt at the mercy seat believing for the first time in her life that she could be different. A most vivid recollection was seeing a godly retired Salvation Army commissioner move forward to receive God's provision. I recall the mercy seat scene in the Democratic Republic of Congo when it seemed two-thirds of the congregation moved in a wave so they could kneel before the Lord. Many other stories could be told of backsliders returning to Christ, sinners being saved, saints seeking God and Salvationists coming together to meet with God.

'"Would The Salvation Army still exist if we removed these simple pieces of furniture from our buildings? No doubt it would. But I believe it is one of the most basic and profound symbols of all that we are – a salvation people.

'"No Salvation Army hall can be without one and every Army worship service should reach its climax with an appeal to meet with God, before his people, at the mercy seat."'

Writing in *Salvationist* (5 March 2005) as UK Territorial Commander, Commissioner Shaw Clifton also speaks about the centrality of the mercy seat in Salvationist worship:

'Is it my imagination or are our mercy seats shrinking? I seem to notice smaller and smaller mercy seats on my travels. The focal point of every Army hall is the mercy seat. It is also the central architectural symbol of our mission – to facilitate an encounter by a child or an adult with their Maker and Saviour.

'Salvationists are taught – are they not? – that each of us carries a ready-made mercy seat in our heart, and that therefore we can meet with God in any place and at any time. This is a precious truth. The mercy seat in our hall is thus not the only place where we can encounter the Lord. Yet it is a place set aside for response. It is a place to which a person can be lovingly invited. There we can pray with a special intentionality, or be prayed with helpfully.

'The mercy seat must be a welcoming place. It needs to be freely accessible, not cluttered by tables, flower stands or collection plates. Also, it needs to be of a size that will allow more than just one or two to kneel. Perhaps the trend away from a large, fixed platform in favour of a smaller, more flexible, moveable dais has inadvertently left some of our mercy seats too small.

'We need to be on guard. Let us be aware. The mercy seat and all it represents is our pulse, our heartbeat as an Army of God. This Scripture-based symbol of our mission (see Exodus 25:1–22) cannot ever be allowed to become but a token feature in our halls. We must keep it welcoming, open, accessible and accommodating.

'Still today people will use it. The invitation can be made, gently but clearly. The meeting planner must provide time for this and for an unhurried, thoughtful response. The prayer meeting and response time is still hated in Hell. The unsaved person will still come, seeking forgiveness and newness of life in Christ as Saviour. The saved person, wanting to express deep love for the Lord or to make a self-offering in rededication, will also still come. Sinners and saints will kneel side by side.

'I thank God for his gift to us of the mercy seat. If we neglect it, marginalise it, tokenise it, we do so at our peril. Salvationists are at their best when on their knees in prayer. It is then that Satan trembles.'

Many present-day Salvationists are also thankful for the gift of the mercy seat, for it was here that as children they first gave their hearts to the Lord. Although the quarterly Decision Sundays are no longer a fixture on the UK territorial calendar, many corps make provision for children to make a commitment to Jesus at the mercy seat. Sometimes this is in a dedicated children's meeting – either on Sunday or midweek – sometimes it is within an all-age Sunday meeting. The keyword seems to be 'flexibility'.

In response to my 2009 poll across the territory, one divisional children's officer writes:

'We provide opportunity for children to use the mercy seat as and when they wish, however, there is a lot of prayer and discussion around the table as it were and we see this as time for children to deal with issues of life and faith.'

Another says:

'While more than half of corps in the division give opportunity for children to make a decision for Jesus, a number of corps do not have dedicated children's programmes. Others say they have community-driven programmes where the opportunity for children to make decisions would be inappropriate.'

A children's worker writes:

'Children at our corps have an opportunity to make a decision for Jesus at the end of the junior soldier preparation course. If children are not taking this course, there is no formal opportunity, rather we hope that a child wishing to make a decision will speak to a member of the YP workers team.'

Another children's worker explains the set-up at her corps:

'We choose an appropriate time in the year to have Decision Sunday, for example, when we know the children have expressed an interest. We often join Decision Sunday and Junior Soldier Day of Renewal together and give children the opportunity to use the mercy seat to sign their promise or make a commitment.'

On the subject of Junior Soldier Day of Renewal, it seems that while some corps hold a separate opportunity within a senior Sunday meeting, others incorporate this with senior soldiers' Commitment Sunday and junior soldiers are invited to sign their promise cards at the mercy seat along with the adults.

A children's worker writes:

'At our corps we have a full day for Junior Soldier Renewal. The morning meeting (all-age family worship) is led by the junior soldier sergeant and junior soldiers. The children have control over the organisation, theme, Bible readings, thoughts, etc, and the junior soldier sergeant simply co-ordinates it into a running order. The children respond well to this.

'In the evening we have the promises renewed. While contemporary worship music is played in background, all names are read out in turn and the children are invited to sign their promise at the mercy seat. The lead-up to this involves reading the promise together and thinking about what it means today, making it up to date and relevant. Children are not forced but all are encouraged and they are all aware in advance of what will happen – those who are hesitant are spoken with individually.

'We use the mercy seat so that children understand it to be a place of personal prayer and because it has a central place in our church.'

From Potton, Sarah-Jane Gregory describes what took place during a midweek children's meeting in November 2009:

'At Kids Club a small group of children were kneeling near the mercy seat in the young people's hall, having their drink and biscuits. We took the opportunity to talk to the whole group, all of them from non-Salvationist families, about the mercy seat.

'Some of the children likened it to the "friendship bench" in the school playground where someone sits when they are lonely and want someone to play with.

'We then invited the children to pray at the mercy seat if they wanted. A number did so. Two boys prayed for their friend who wasn't able to be in club that night because he had been grounded by his parents. They prayed that God would help him to be good so he would be allowed to come next week.'

The mercy seat as the immoveable physical centrality of a corps hall is also gradually becoming a thing of the past. The move towards multi-purpose worship halls and the moveable dais has for some corps resulted in a foldaway or moveable mercy seat which is less imposing than the grander designs of old. Some people even feel that when the old mercy seat went the blessing went with it.

As well as adapting to the practicalities of a multi-purpose hall, since 1995 the mercy seat in the UK has been subject to legislation. Since that year, 24 new or refurbished corps halls have been built. Each of them has a mercy seat which complies with the Disability Discrimination Act 1995. The requirements are that a wheelchair user should be able to gain easy access to the mercy seat, that those who have difficulty in kneeling should be able to lean on the mercy seat while standing and that there should be easy access, including a tonal difference between mercy seat carpet and surround, for people with visual impairment. The mercy seat at Stockton, for instance, complies with these statutory requirements and comprises sections at different levels.

Sheffield Citadel's mercy seat (pictured on back cover) is carpeted in a contrasting colour to the rest of the hall and is augmented with a table and chairs at either end for those who find it difficult to kneel.

All of these mercy seats are made of ash, are free-standing, inscription-free and, at a minimum of three metres wide, are wide enough to accommodate four people.

Another external influence on mercy-seat use is health and safety legislation. This applies to hiring a public venue for Salvation Army worship.

For example, at the UK's 2010 Roots conference – a four-day gathering for spiritual renewal – organiser Mark Sawyer had to give consideration to health and safety protocols when it came to public response.

'Under health and safety requirements, the host theatre couldn't allow large groups of people spontaneously going forward to the mercy seat in subdued lighting,' he says. 'To enable this to happen we had to post stewards at every junction and on the steps so members of the congregation could be safely guided forward.

'This meant that, just after the sermon, before calling people forward in response to the word of God, I had to give detailed instructions about which route people should take. Such requirements, while understandable, run the risk of spoiling a sensitive moment. In the event, hundreds of people made their way forward in a special act of commitment.'

The mercy seat in the UK, in all its forms, was the subject under discussion when the Territorial Advisory Council met in April 2009. The issue for this group of representative local officers was 'not the mercy seat as it stands but our understanding of its use, its purpose and its meaning'. The recommendation to territorial leadership was that 'we need to increase the number of people coming to our meetings to see the mercy seat used as a place of salvation. We need to refocus our mission and remember that we are called to save souls, grow saints and serve suffering humanity.'

Chapter 8

All Over The World

MUCH of the discussion so far has centred on mercy-seat use in the United Kingdom. If, however, the mercy seat is – as *The Salvation Army in The Body of Christ* points out – a distinctive characteristic of Salvationist worship, then seeing how the mercy seat is used in other territories could prove beneficial and inspirational.

In 1998 the mercy seat was one of five integral elements of The Salvation Army discussed by the International Spiritual Life Commission. One of the commission's members, Commissioner Robert Street, writes in correspondence:

'The mercy seat is part of the Army's DNA. It is not possible to answer whether the mercy seat has been used more widely since the International Spiritual Life Commission issued a call to the mercy seat. What is evident is that mercy-seat use varies widely from country to country and territory to territory.

'In some territories it is used extensively and constantly. Some, like the UK, have a more reserved culture. Some, like the USA, still use the holiness table in places, and differentiate between reasons for coming forward.

'A wider use of the mercy seat seems to have developed in the sense that it is used for many kinds of prayer – not just as a penitent form. Internationally, the mercy seat remains a focal point for response and public expression of commitment.'

As one of my 2009 survey respondents puts it, 'Although it is not its original intention, the mercy seat helps bind thousands of corps in all territories around the world.'

To gain a more global view, I sent via IHQ a short questionnaire to every territory. I also invited response via a letter in *The Officer*. I asked:

75

What is the mercy seat used for? What is the purpose of the holiness table? What other response mechanisms are used? This chapter covers the question of mercy-seat use. The other two areas are covered later.

Brian Peddle writes of the mercy seat in his home country:

'The mercy seat in the Canada and Bermuda Territory retains its place as a central focus in the design of buildings and prescribed usage during public worship. It would be my evaluation that the traditional reference to the mercy seat as a place of seeking salvation has been increased to include group prayer, a place to bring the hurt and pain of the daily journey and a place of deep personal conversation and communion.'

Based in Atlanta, Georgia, Jude Gotrich is Territorial Director for Worship Development and Prayer Initiative in the USA Southern Territory. As well as serving in the United Kingdom, she has served in all four American territories, in the Canada and Bermuda Territory, in the Australia Southern Territory and in various European headquarters. What is her wide-ranging view of mercy-seat use?

'The mercy seat has had multiple functions but primarily it is an altar for prayer. It is a place of penitence – for salvation and rededication – in response to the word of God. It is a place of dedication in response to a vow or covenant (such as soldiership or marital vows) declared before all the assembled.

'The mercy seat marks a furnishing in the sanctuary that is designated as a place of meeting between the petitioner and Christ the Mediator. It is a place of agreement between believers; an altar to place petitions for intercession. It is a private place for the express purpose of meditation, confession, intercession, adoration, thanksgiving and praise.'

The following insights give an idea of how widespread these mercy-seat functions are.

'In the USA,' writes David Jeffrey, 'every adult rehabilitation centre and corps sanctuary has a mercy seat/altar directly in front of the platform. It is used as a place of prayer. Sinners are invited to receive Christ there, Christians are invited to receive sanctification. There are invitations given to come and pray for others, and for one's own needs.

'At divisional camping events for adults and youth the mercy seat is the focal point, as campers are invited to accept Christ, restore broken fellowship or to lay their burdens before the Lord.'

This echo of the pre-Army use of the mourner's bench at American revivalist camp meetings in the early 1800s also resonates in the USA Eastern Territory.

Howard Burr writes:

'Every summer camp has a chapel where all the campers are invited to accept Jesus Christ as their Saviour some time during the week of the camp.'

Regarding the territory, he continues, 'Whenever a corps building is being used throughout the week, the chapel is often open for prayer. Some corps invite people to pray at the mercy seat alone or as a family before the holiness meeting begins. Many corps have an invitation to pray for salvation or holiness after the sermon.

'There is a tradition in many corps for junior and senior solders to sign their covenants at the mercy seat. The mercy seat is also occasionally used during weddings.'

In the USA Southern Territory the mercy seat is, as Suzanne Haupt puts it, 'regarded with respect and is a place of honour and reverence'. It is used for salvation, holiness, commitment, the dedication of new soldiers, officers signing Covenant cards, dedication for special service, pre-meeting prayer, conflict resolution.

In the USA Western Territory, says Lee Lescano in California, people are invited to 'pray at the mercy seat at the end of the meetings. Invitations are given for salvation and holiness, as well as a general invitation to pray for any need'.

In Alaska, the mercy seat is used for 'repentance, forgiveness, peace, spiritual counsel, surrender, blessing, intercession, healing, calling, offering, receiving grace... any kind of meeting with God', says Sheryl Tollerud.

While in Hawaii: 'The mercy seat is used for personal prayer, particularly during altar calls but also for individual private prayer during the week. We often have new soldiers sign their Soldier's Covenant at the mercy seat. When we commission a local officer we pray with them at the mercy seat, asking other Pastoral Care Council members to join them,' writes Brian Saunders.

The mercy seat is used in San Francisco as 'a place for intercessory prayer, prayers of thanksgiving, prayers for salvation and forgiveness,' says Jack Phillips. 'It is a place for spiritual counsel and a place to make a commitment.'

The same is true in Spokane, from where Lisa Smith writes:

'The mercy seat is a place of prayer and commitment to the Lord for first-time seekers or for prayer for special concerns or needs. People can pray in groups or individually. It is a place for spiritual counselling but if in-depth counselling is needed seekers are often taken to a private room. Seekers sometimes use the mercy seat at the invitation of the preacher but also kneel there without invitation. Sometimes a family will gather at the mercy seat to pray together.'

In Mexico, the primary use of the mercy seat, according to Victor Valdes, is to 'permit the repentant to take a public step in faith to dedicate their life to their Lord and Saviour, Jesus Christ. Some corps are in the habit of inviting their soldiers to pray very early, so they make use of the mercy seat.

'I have also seen the mercy seat used for weddings, children's dedication, dedication of celebration of a 15-year-old – especially in Latino countries – in graduation thanksgiving services, special services for Sunbeams and Girl Guards.'

Olin Hogan adds the following to the list: 'restoration of health, prayer for family members, renewal of holy vows, personal development of spiritual values and renovation.'

In the Caribbean, the mercy seat is used in similar ways. Sherma Evelyn writes:

'The mercy seat is used as a place of prayer, of forgiveness, of restoration, of healing, of holiness, of salvation, and as a place to pray before signing covenant cards.'

Sonia Bouzigues writes from the headquarters of the South America East Territory, a territory that covers Argentina, Paraguay and Uruguay:

'The mercy seat is used for seekers looking for salvation and sanctification; for prayer for different needs and on special occasions such as cadets' Covenant Days, the commissioning of new officers and the installation of a new divisional commander or territorial leaders.'

From Malawi, Diane Payne writes:

'In Africa, the mercy seat is a central part of worship. It is integral to the spiritual life of Salvationists. A call to the mercy seat is given in almost every meeting. The mercy seat is seen as a special place to meet with God for whatever reason. It could be financial difficulties, work, food or health problems, as well as a place to seek salvation, sanctification and spiritual gifts and power through the Holy Spirit.

'People also come forward simply to praise and thank God for the likes of healing, protection while travelling or through childbirth or because they have had enough to carry them through the week. There may even be a mercy-seat call at a funeral.'

From Namibia, Lenah Jwilli writes:

'In South Africa the mercy seat is a place for having effective communication and communion with God. It is a place for building a relationship with God by seeking forgiveness through the confession of sins.'

From Goodwood, Western Cape, Graham Brooke-Smith adds:

'The mercy seat is a place for seeking salvation, claiming holiness, personal prayer and limited counselling.'

According to Marieke Venter, the mercy seat in South Africa is also used for intercession, signing of promises, rededication and specific calls to prayer.

'In St Helena the mercy seat is greatly revered,' writes Coral Yon from that remote South Atlantic island. 'It is mainly used as a place of prayer, either by people seeking Christ for the first time or by soldiers and adherent members making recommitments. It is a place where people know they can draw close to God for help in any circumstance of their lives.'

Commissioner Stuart Mungate notes that in the Democratic Republic of Congo the mercy seat is used 'for meeting with the Lord the first time by new seekers as we invite them to make a public declaration to give up sin and accept to follow Christ.

'An opportunity is given in nearly every public meeting for Salvationists to consecrate their lives to Christ by coming forward to the mercy seat and the response is always overwhelming.

'My soul rejoices and praises the Lord when I see God's people responding by coming forward to kneel at the mercy seat in search of God's touch.'

Commissioner Kenneth Hodder records that in Kenya 'the mercy seat is used for all kinds of things. Beyond salvation and holiness, Salvationists feel free to offer prayers of thanksgiving and every kind of need. There is a tremendous sense of freedom in the use of the mercy seat, and virtually every meeting will find the altar lined with seekers.'

Frequent mercy-seat use is also a feature of Salvationist worship in India.

From Tirunelveli, Commissioner M. C. James writes:

'The India South Eastern Territory gives great importance to the mercy seat in all our corps. After every sermon an invitation is given to use the mercy seat for prayer and rededication. Usually we see people making new decisions at the mercy seat.'

From Mizoram, Samuel Charan writes:

'In the India Eastern Territory we use the mercy seat for altar call after the message. It is a place for rededication, spiritual renewal, repentance and prayer.'

From Thiruvananthapuram, Jayapaul Devarapalli writes:

'In the India South Western Territory we use the mercy seat in every meeting. It is used for those who want to speak with God about any need and for those who want to dedicate their lives to serving the Lord. The mercy seat is also used as a place of repentance and confessing of sin. We also ask people to raise their hands as a way of indicating that they are making a decision instead of going to the mercy seat.'

From IHQ, Commissioner Lalkiamlova confirms that 'in India the mercy seat is used for salvation, rededication and a place of prayer at any time and for any reason'.

Similarly in Brazil, 'At most corps the mercy seat is often lined with seekers every Sunday evening,' says former Brazil-based John White.

From Brazil, a correspondent writes:

'The Portuguese for "mercy seat" roughly translates as "bench for penitents". It generally consists of a series of kneeling pads on the floor at the foot of the platform. Sometimes there is a more substantial structure with a railing. Most halls do not have a modesty rail on the front of the platform, so the elevation of the platform functions as the railing of the mercy seat.

'As the structure may be a by-product of the size and shape of the halls, which generally are not purpose-built, in most halls the mercy seat is not a visually important furnishing.

'It is used as a place of prayer, usually at the conclusion of the meeting.'

From Portuguese-speaking Brazil to Portugal, where Alberto Serém says the mercy seat is used for 'salvation, sanctification, consecration, forgiveness and thanksgiving'.

Anne-Florence Tursi has served in Italy, Switzerland and Germany for more than 25 years. In regards to these countries, she writes:

'As far as I know, the mercy seat is used only for a first-time response to the call to salvation or for dedicating one's life to God in holiness and consecration.'

In Sweden, writes Helena Andersson, the mercy seat is used for 'a search for holiness, taking new steps, salvation, intercession, time to be with God, listening to God'. Fellow corps officer Anne-Li Marthinussen also observes that 'small children enjoy spending time there walking and crawling'.

In neighbouring Finland, says Johnny Kleman, the mercy seat is used for 'all kinds of prayer needs and pastoral care'.

From Tallinn, Estonia, Evelyn and Tim Clark write:

'The mercy seat is used for all sorts of prayer requests – to receive salvation and sanctification, for guidance in making a decision, for strength to overcome temptation, for commitment and recommitment.'

The Eastern Europe Territory comprises the countries of Georgia, Moldova, Romania, Russian Federation and Ukraine. The mercy seat is used, says one correspondent, as 'a place of prayer for salvation and holiness, a place to pray for others, a place to sign covenants for soldiers and cadets'.

Another correspondent writes: 'In the Eastern Europe Territory the mercy seat is used by seekers of salvation and holiness, by people to pray for or with their family, by cadets at their commissioning and by some couples during their wedding ceremony. There is often an open prayer in the middle of the worship for anyone preparing their heart for the meeting.'

One of those involved in reopening the work in Eastern Europe in the post-Communist era was Sven-Erik Ljungholm. He writes:

'My wife, Kathie, and I were appointed to Leningrad in 1991, where chairs and benches were used as mercy seats. Some months later we "opened fire" in Moscow. During our time there we enrolled more than 450 junior and senior soldiers. Many Baptist churches in Leningrad and Moscow sing "Ring the Bells of Heaven" when a seeker stands to their feet at the mercy seat. The seeker is then expected to testify. This process is repeated regardless of the number of seekers.

'I'm told it is a custom that was carried over from the time when the Army was banished in 1923 and Salvationists joined in fellowship with Baptists.

'In 1993 we opened in Kiev, Ukraine. There was no mercy seat as such, just a sort of railing. Every Sunday morning 60 or 70 people would come forward to the front. As there were no other officers or soldiers apart from my wife and myself, we couldn't offer counselling. People would stand at the railing while we said a prayer, followed by an invitation to attend recruits classes. Of the Kiev enrollees, 30 were hearing impaired so a signer translated my penitent-form prayer for them. The signer and her husband are now officers in Ukraine.'

'In some Asian corps,' writes Barbara Jeffrey, 'those wishing to come to the mercy seat use a pillow on which to kneel.'

A feature of mercy-seat use in one Singaporean corps in the past was the provision of a bucket.

'Converts from Buddhism used to induce vomiting as they knelt at the mercy seat as a way of indicating that they were getting rid of the spirits of the past, so a bucket was provided for this purpose,' offers a correspondent.

Regarding the Singapore, Malaysia and Myanmar Territory, another correspondent writes:

'The mercy seat is used as a place of prayer and on special occasions as a place of commitment. Often there is a move towards the mercy seat at the end of meetings conducted by Westerners. I am told this happens because people think this is what Westerners want to see happening, which makes mercy-seat use in this case something of a duty.'

New Zealander Ross Gower says, 'In Indonesia, the mercy seat is not so much a form but a big area at the front of the hall. It is primarily a place of prayer, not a place of penitence.

'When an appeal is made it is the first ones who respond who get to kneel at the mercy seat, others kneel and pray in the space behind them. After an appropriate time, the meeting leader prays. When the prayer is over, those who have been kneeling stand up and resume their seats and a second wave of seekers comes forward. Generally there are only two shifts.

'People pray out loud. Sometimes people are left to pray by themselves and sometimes they are asked if they would like someone to pray with them. The whole thing is very ordered, very intense and very emotional.'

Regarding New Zealand, Canadian Brian Peddle writes:

'Our time in the New Zealand, Fiji and Tonga Territory taught us that with the unique design of buildings and new generations of seekers the mercy seat can become a well established prayer room, a reserved space in the sanctuary appropriately arranged, or standing in circles with focused prayers. In the corps we attended a cross on one side created an appropriate atmosphere while a garden of Gethsemane was arranged on the opposite side. When people knelt the mercy-seat experience was very real.'

In Australia, writes Mal Davies, the mercy seat is used for 'first-time commitments and recommitments, the signing of pledges and covenants, a place for displays that support the sermon, a place to sit to deliver the children's story and a place of counselling and prayer after the conclusion of the meeting.'

Also from Australia, Stephen Court writes:

'The mercy seat and holiness table are important and effective. Their use during a prayer meeting or appeal constitutes the most important part of any Salvation Army meeting. Likewise, any decrease in their use is probably indicative of a wandering from our theology and mission.'

Chapter 9

The Holiness Table

IT is a well-documented fact that the Army mercy seat started out as the revivalist's anxious seat, on which the seeker sat, rather than at which the seeker knelt. What is far less clear is the origin of the table as the dispensary for holiness. As we have seen, Brengle invited seekers of salvation and sanctification exclusively to the penitent form.

Robert Sandall in *The History of The Salvation Army, Volume Two* notes:

'Another point sometimes lost sight of is that there was from the first a vital distinction between a "penitent form" and a "holiness table". The configuration of modern buildings is often such that it is difficult to place a table at the front as was done in holiness meetings of earlier days, and the penitent form has to do duty for both. But for those seeking the higher life it is *figuratively* an "altar" or "mercy seat" and not a penitent form.'

What is puzzling, however, is the relatively few references to holiness seekers kneeling at the table. In *Spiritual Breakthrough* John Larsson includes a testimony from Julius Horskins:

'Our captain announced a night of prayer to be led by the General at 272 Whitechapel Road. How I longed for this night. A whole night for prayer! The time went all too slowly; I not only counted the days but the hours as the time grew nearer. The anticipated night came and I hastened to the hall. The crowd! The singing! The preaching! Everything held me. At 3 am I was at the holiness table, giving my heart, my life, my all to God and the Army for officership. Oh, what a flood-tide came! That night's consecration decided my life-work for God.'

In *The Officer*, October 1924, Frank Field writes of his concern for the lack of holiness among Salvationists. One of the problems he addresses is the lack of sufficient time on Sunday mornings. (And we think we've got problems 80-odd years later.) He writes of:

'The distance many of our people live from the hall, and the need for the bandsmen to return in time for the open-air meeting and the company guards for the company meeting. Special care has had to be exercised in the holiness meeting so that the leading of our people to the holiness table would not be hurried or neglected entirely.'

Mrs Elsie Bradshaw of Bolton would be among those who recognise the situation to which the adjutant referred. In correspondence, she writes:

'I was dedicated to God at the holiness table in March 1912. I took my daughter to be dedicated there in 1944. In more recent years I have seen people take their wedding vows at the holiness table. I have seen many people seek the blessing of a clean heart at the table.'

Orders and Regulations for Officers (1925) acknowledges what was common practice:

'"Seekers" include all who come to the penitent form or holiness altar.'

It is worth noting that from 1925 to 1950 *Orders and Regulations* referred to the 'holiness altar' rather than the 'holiness table'. For more details see Appendix G.

Even though in more recent years the holiness table is used less frequently, the 2003 edition of *Orders and Regulations for Officers* includes the following:

'The mercy seat or penitent form (and where used, the holiness table) is the central place in Salvation Army worship.'

We have already seen the provision of penitent's mats for use in open-air meetings. We know of the drum being used as an outdoor mercy seat.

Again, in *Spiritual Breakthrough*, John Larsson includes an example of an unusual holiness table. Mrs Booth Davey describes the difference the blessing of holiness had made to her life. She recalls:

86

'My love for sinners changed. It became a passion, so that everything in my life must bend to it. I shall never forget an incident at Sherburn Hill. I was wedged in amongst a lot of "drunks" in a billiard room. The power of God fell, and 10 of them made a penitent form of the billiard table. We were so packed together that to deal with them our faces nearly touched, and we had the full benefit of the spray of their drunken spluttering.'

Even in recent times the holiness table remains something of an enigma. In my 1994 survey 31% of respondents said that they had seen the table used as a focal point for public decision, while 69% said they had not. One can reasonably assume that almost everyone questioned has seen or has used the table as a repository for offerings, altar service gifts and commitment cards. Only a small proportion of the 31% said the table was used for its original purpose, to receive the blessing of holiness. One person offered it as a place for prayer for physical healing.

Some people use the holiness table as a place of decision on special occasions such as Commitment Sunday or New Year. Some use it for the signing of articles of war, junior soldier's promise, or junior soldier renewal cards.

Some use the table as a practical alternative to the mercy seat where, for instance, the seeker is physically unable to kneel at the mercy seat or when the mercy seat is full.

One officer has used the table as a place of reconciliation for soldiers who had become estranged from fellow Salvationists, while others used it as the centrepiece of a love feast.

Paul and Lorna Doust are among those who have put the holiness table to wider use. They write:

'We have used the holiness table as a point of asking people to come and pray. Whilst we would suggest that they could either sit or kneel at the mercy seat, the invitation is given to those who are committed Christians to realise that they come to a place of prayer, a place of communion, a place of fellowship with the Lord. We have used the holiness table in the context of signing the Soldier's Covenant, or covenants at the beginning of the New Year or phased within people's Christian experience. Here people sat at the table to sign.

'On the first Sunday of one new year, we used the table as a focal point of prayer. We placed it in the centre of the congregation which was sat round in a semicircle, facing the mercy seat. We prayed for everyone associated with the corps. At the end of the prayer time we held a love feast around the table.'

A number of respondents voiced concern not only over the use or non-use of the table as a place of spiritual decision, but also its very existence.

'I would actively discourage any separate use of a holiness table,' writes David Taylor. 'It smacks of being a superior act. I dislike the distinction between "seeking holiness" and "penitence". Are they not ultimately the same thing?'

Robert Lake recalls seeing the table used by those seeking holiness. 'But,' he writes, 'I could never see the relevance of bypassing the mercy seat to do so.'

It is, perhaps, Cecil Waters who expresses the thoughts of a large number of weekly mercy-seat practitioners when he writes:

'The holiness table is an anomaly. The mercy seat is a suitable place for all seeking. I have rarely encountered any use of the holiness table as a special place.'

Cyril Halstead expresses a typical reservation from the UK when he writes:

'I recall instances many years ago when we had officers who made special mention of the holiness table and encouraged people to kneel there on a Sunday morning only. My feelings were, and still are, that this tended to create a first- and second-class seeker. Throughout my officership, I have encouraged people to use only the mercy seat as a place of prayer. I find that, when Salvationists kneel there, the way opens for newcomers to kneel and seek the Lord's forgiveness.'

Phil Needham echoes this sentiment when he comments: 'I must confess that I am uncomfortable with this [use of the holiness table] since it tends to create a two-tier approach – ie, if you come forward to the holiness table, you are obviously more spiritually advanced –

you are seeking a "higher experience".' Needham further feels that he 'cannot support a view where the leader of the meeting would say, "Now if you need salvation come and kneel at the mercy seat, and if you are seeking after the experience of holiness kneel at the holiness table".'

General Jarl Wahlström shares Needham's two-tier concern. 'As far as I can remember,' he writes, 'I have seen a holiness table in use only once – at a North American Training College. In Scandinavia the idea of having a special holiness table has not gained ground. I would not recommend that it be introduced on a local or territorial level.

'The use of a mercy seat and the holiness table could easily create an impression that there are believers of two distinct levels in the congregation. The truth is, of course, that all have need of salvation, mercy and divine grace, and that all Christians are called to a life of holiness. Lady Beatrice in the musical *Glory!* knelt at the mercy seat next to the tramp. They were "both seeking the same Saviour".'

General Eva Burrows contends that the mercy seat and holiness table are in frequent use by Salvationists in Australia. A view confirmed by Commissioner Wesley Harris when he writes:

'The holiness table is still a feature of many corps in Australasia. Often there is a red tablecloth bearing the words, "Holiness unto the Lord". But in more-recently-built halls this is not always found.'

However, when it comes to explaining the growing non-use of the holiness table, he also has *Glory!* in mind. 'The use of the holiness table may have diminished as the sharp distinction between holiness and salvation has become less clear,' he writes. 'The thought that we are "all seeking the same Saviour" may also have had an effect.'

The holiness table in Australia, writes Stephen Court, 'seems to be as open as the mercy seat. It is used for consecration and holiness.' This, though, is not the experience of fellow Australian Mal Davies, who says, 'The holiness table is rarely used and an increasing number of corps don't have one.' He adds: 'The purpose of the holiness table is unclear, especially to those who have joined the Army in the past 20 years.'

In Indonesia, say Ross and Annette Gower, the holiness table is not used as a place to receive the blessing of holiness but as an overspill area from the mercy seat and a place to display an open Bible.

'Virtually every corps in the USA has a holiness table,' writes General Paul Rader. 'I have often seen it used and have, myself, invited seekers to come and pray there when seeking the blessing of a clean heart.'

However, he also expresses some concern about the holiness table:

'I have some difficulty with it as a concept from a theological point of view. Salvation is all of a piece, although we have long believed, taught and testified to two works of grace. I believe in the sanctifying work of the Spirit in a crisis of cleansing. But it is certainly on the grounds of that same atoning work and wrought in the heart by that same Holy Spirit through whom we first come to new life in Christ. Having said that, one would not want to do anything to diminish our heart holiness and the purifying and empowering work of the Spirit.'

'The presence of the holiness table,' General Rader concludes, 'is a constant reminder of the central importance of holiness of heart in the life of our Movement – a reminder that we are and must be a holiness movement. Ours is a gospel of blood and fire!'

Today, what is the place of the holiness table in our international Movement? My 2009 survey suggests that holiness-table use is on the increase in the UK. In 1994, 31% of respondents said they had seen the holiness table used as a focal point for spiritual decision. In 2009 the figure was 49% (see Appendix A for more details).

There is little evidence, though, to suggest that Salvationists in the UK are increasingly using the holiness table in connection with sanctification. However, some corps are putting the holiness table to imaginative use.

From Exeter Temple, Ken Bovey writes:

'One Sunday prayer request cards were handed to people as they entered the hall. During the singing of a song those who wished to placed their cards on the holiness table for the officer to include in the prayer time. Some of those who took cards to the table then knelt at the mercy seat.'

The holiness table seems to be more of a feature of Salvationist worship in the USA than in the UK.

Among its uses in the States are the claiming of holiness, as a focused worship centre, for the signing of soldiers' covenants, dedications, to stand photographs and the ashes of the deceased at memorial services and for the standing of unity candles at weddings.

Writing from Indiana, USA, in 1974, Will Roberts records:

'It has only been in comparatively recent years that the holiness table has appeared in Army halls in the USA... Nearly every corps we visit now has a holiness table and it is used extensively in the holiness meeting and at times of reconsecration. I cannot remember seeing any corps which has a table where there has not been a cover with the words "Holiness unto the Lord".'

In 2009, from Virginia, Mark Israel writes:

'We seem to have lost the distinction between the holiness table and the mercy seat. Unfortunately, the holiness table is used for worship centres and displays more than as a place of prayer.'

Commissioner Eva Gaither writes:

'I believe that where the holiness table has traditionally been used it has lost its purpose – used as a worship centre rather than as an extension of the altar for seeking holiness.

'I have used the holiness table in seeking a deeper relationship with the Lord and believe the symbolism is extremely important.'

From Hawaii, Brian Saunders writes:

'We were taught in training school that the holiness table is a place of private prayer and dedication, but unfortunately it seems most often to be used as a table to hold flowers or offering plates. If someone comes to the altar [mercy seat] a counsellor often goes to pray with them. If someone goes to the holiness table they are signifying that they do not want anyone to pray with them. This is, though, a rare distinction many people will not have heard about.'

This is a sentiment Kelly Igleheart shares:

'The holiness table is a place where the saved person can commune with God or seek holiness. Unfortunately, it is sometimes decorated to highlight a meeting theme or the season in the church calendar.'

From San Francisco, Jack Phillips writes:

'The holiness table is used regularly in the many corps where we have a weekly holiness meeting. It is used by Christians who wish to go forward for prayer but who are not praying for salvation. It is used in adult rehabilitation centres less frequently. However, we teach holiness in the ARCs and once this is taught those at ARCs use the holiness table after their conversion.'

James Lee ministers at the Sunnyvale Grace Korean Corps in California. He writes:

'At the corps we have a 6.00 am prayer meeting five or six days a week. Shortly after we start I encourage people to kneel at the mercy seat to pray. I kneel at the front of the holiness table for 40-60 minutes. I intimate with God fully and feel the Holy Spirit's blessing and gain God's will and vision. It is a great opportunity to have a deep relationship with God.'

From Alexandria, Virginia, Suzanne Haupt writes:

'As I enter the chapel for worship I see the words of the holiness table "Holiness unto the Lord". These words are a reminder of what the Lord expects from me as a believer and a child of God.'

From Mexico, Olin Hogan writes:

'The holiness table is used when there is a special call to holiness. It is not completely understood nor fully utilised.'

Also from Mexico, Victor Valdes seems to back up this point:

'For some territories it is not a problem to place a crucifix or the statue of a saint or the Virgin Mary on the holiness table. For the Latinos who have been rescued from idolatry this is offensive.'

Joan Canning has served in the Canada and Bermuda Territory, at IHQ and at USA National Headquarters. Hers is a succinct view:

'In some cases there was no holiness table. In some cases, I'm not sure if the purpose was ever articulated to the congregation. My experience is that in places where it is available it is not frequently used.'

From Canada, Merriell Hanks reports that while at her corps the holiness table is not in use, its future within corps worship is being discussed.

In Brazil, says one correspondent, 'holiness tables are not part of the furnishings in a corps hall'.

In Argentina, Paraguay and Uruguay, says Sonia Bouzigues, 'the majority of corps have a holiness table covered with a cloth with the words "Holiness unto the Lord". However, the holiness table is not used as a place of prayer for sanctification.'

In the Caribbean, reports Sherma Evelyn, the holiness table is usually 'used only when the mercy seat is full'. However, when in June 2009, Commissioners Raymond and Judith Houghton farewelled as territorial leaders the Caribbean *War Cry* reported that:

'In his final appeal, Commissioner Raymond Houghton called for committed persons to stand with him at the holiness table and there was a healthy response.'

Holiness-table use in South Africa is generally similar to that within the UK. It is used less often than the mercy seat, when it is used it is for prayer for sanctification. It is often used as the repository for flowers and collection plates, for the signing of dedication and marriage registers, a place of challenge to officership and an alternative to the mercy seat for people who cannot kneel.

There are, says one correspondent, only a few holiness tables in the Eastern Europe Territory as the Army does not own much property, also many places of worship are small and cannot contain a holiness table and a mercy seat.

'The few corps that have a holiness table use it to place a Bible, perhaps a candle and sometimes the offering plates,' she says. 'I don't think people consider it as a place to seek holiness but I have seen people kneel there where there's been no room at the mercy seat.'

In Portugal, Alberto Serém reports, the holiness table is used only on very special occasions for holiness and consecration.

In the Singapore, Malaysia and Myanmar Territory, writes a correspondent, 'there seems very little purpose for the holiness table. It is rarely used other than as a place to set the flowers.'

In Italy, writes Anne-Florence Tursi, the holiness table is 'used during self-denial altar services to receive gifts, but not in ordinary holiness meetings'.

Corps in Nordic countries such as Sweden and Finland, and Baltic states such as Latvia and Estonia do not have holiness tables. Nor do corps in Malawi or Kenya East, where, says Commissioner Kenneth Hodder, 'Most Salvationists here would regard it as obstructing their access to the mercy seat!'

Chapter 10

Cue For A Song

GENERATIONS of Salvationists have long had a source of mercy-seat perception to hand and, in some cases, in their handbags. Since its first appearance in 1899, The Salvation Army's Song Book has contained hymns, songs and choruses drawn from a wide spectrum of the Christian Church. The 1953 edition contains 983 songs. Fifty-three are the work of anonymous lyricists. Of the 930 attributed songs, only around 255 were written by Salvationist songwriters.

Similarly, the 1986 edition contains 962 songs, some 365 of which were written by Salvationists. The balance is the work of writers from other denominations. Methodist, Baptist, Anglican, Roman Catholic, Congregational, Presbyterian, Moravian and Quaker are among the congregations represented.

The Song Book, and *The Christian Mission Hymn Book* before it, has always contained a number of songs referring to the mercy seat from the pen of non-Salvationist writers.

Nicolaus von Zinzendorf's 1739 'Jesus, Thy Blood and Righteousness,' has been in Army hands since Christian Mission days. Alluding to the Old Testament use of the mercy seat on the Day of Atonement, its fourth verse refers to the atoning qualities of Jesus' blood:

> Lord, I believe thy precious blood,
> Which, at the mercy seat of God,
> For ever doth for sinners plead,
> For me, e'en for my soul, was shed.

William Cowper, whose work has been regularly published in our Movement since *The Christian Mission Hymn Book*, wrote 'Jesus,

95

Where'er Thy People Meet' for a prayer meeting conducted by John Newton in 1769. Its opening lines remind the reader of the Old Testament promise of God to meet with his people at the mercy seat and the New Testament promise of Jesus that, where two or three gather in his name, he will meet with them:

> JESUS, where'er thy people meet,
> There they behold the mercy seat;
> Where'er they seek thee thou art found,
> And every place is hallowed ground.
>
> For thou, within no walls confined,
> Inhabitest the humble mind;
> Such ever bring thee where they come,
> And going take thee to their home.
>
> Here may we prove the power of prayer
> To strengthen faith and sweeten care,
> To teach our faint desires to rise,
> And bring all Heaven before our eyes.
>
> Lord, we are few, but thou art near,
> Nor short thine arm, nor deaf thine ear;
> O rend the heavens, come quickly down,
> And make a thousand hearts thine own!

It would be easy to suppose that Cowper's 'What Various Hindrances We Meet' was born out of frustration of lack of penitent-form use until one realises that he wrote it nearly 100 years before the founding of The Salvation Army:

> WHAT various hindrances we meet
> In coming to the mercy seat!
> Yet who that knows the worth of prayer
> But wishes to be often there!

Prayer makes the darkest cloud withdraw,
Prayer climbs the ladder Jacob saw,
Gives exercise to faith and love,
Brings every blessing from above.

Restraining prayer, we cease to fight;
Prayer makes the soldier's armour bright;
And Satan trembles when he sees
The weakest saint upon his knees.

O Lord, increase our faith and love,
So shall we all thy goodness prove
And gain from thine own boundless store
The fruits of prayer for evermore.

John Newton, an Anglican clergyman, took up the mercy seat theme himself when he wrote 'Approach, My Soul, The Mercy Seat', first published in 1779:

APPROACH, my soul, the mercy seat,
Where Jesus answers prayer;
There humbly fall before his feet,
For none can perish there.

Thy promise is my only plea,
With this I venture nigh;
Thou callest burdened souls to thee,
And such, O Lord, am I.

Bowed down beneath a load of sin,
By Satan sorely pressed,
By war without and fears within,
I come to thee for rest.

Be thou my shield and hiding-place,
That, sheltered near thy side,
I may my fierce accuser face
And tell him thou hast died.

O wondrous love, to bleed and die,
To bear the cross and shame,
That guilty sinners, such as I,
Might plead thy gracious name!

Fellow Anglican clergyman Hugh Stowell sees the biblical mercy
seat as a place of comfort. His hymn was first published in 1828 and
was first included in the 1930 Song Book:

FROM every stormy wind that blows,
From every swelling tide of woes,
There is a calm, a sure retreat;
'Tis found beneath the mercy seat.

There is a place where Jesus sheds
The oil of gladness on our heads,
A place than all besides more sweet;
It is the blood-stained mercy seat.

There is a scene where spirits blend,
And friend holds fellowship with friend;
Though sundered far, by faith they meet
Around one common mercy seat.

There, there on eagle wings we soar,
And time and sense seem all no more;
And Heaven comes down our souls to greet,
And glory crowns the mercy seat.

O let my hand forget her skill,
My tongue be silent, cold and still,
This throbbing heart forget to beat,
If I forget the mercy seat!

According to my 2009 survey, two mercy seats in the UK, at Exeter Temple and Winsford, bear the inscription 'Here Bring Thy Wounded Heart'. Dublin-born songwriter Thomas Moore, better-known for 'The Minstrel Boy', may well have provided the inspiration with his 1832 hymn, 'Come, Ye Disconsolate'. In it he sees the mercy seat as a place of comfort:

> COME, ye disconsolate, where'er ye languish,
> Come, at the mercy seat fervently kneel;
> Here bring your wounded hearts, here tell your anguish,
> Earth has no sorrow that Heaven cannot heal.
>
> Joy of the desolate, light of the straying,
> Hope of the penitent, advocate sure;
> Here speaks the Comforter, tenderly saying,
> Earth has no sorrow that Heaven cannot cure.
>
> Here waits the Saviour, gentle and loving,
> Ready to meet you, his grace to reveal;
> On him your burden cast, trustfully coming;
> Earth has no sorrow that Heaven cannot heal.

Baptist minister Sylvanus Dryden Phelps links the atonement of the mercy seat with the cross in 'Saviour, Thy Dying Love', first published in 1862. The first two verses read:

> SAVIOUR, thy dying love
> Thou gavest me,
> Nor should I aught withhold,
> My Lord, from thee.
> In love my soul would bow,
> My heart fulfil its vow,
> Some offering bring thee now,
> Something for thee.

At the blest mercy seat,
Pleading for me,
My feeble faith looks up,
Jesus, to thee.
Help me the cross to bear,
Thy wondrous love declare,
Some song to raise, or prayer,
Something for thee.

A year later, William Dix wrote his narrative Epiphany hymn, 'As With Gladness'. In it, following the Old Testament perspective that this is where God is, he sees the mercy seat as the destination – the fulfilment – of spiritual searching. For Dix, it is where we should offer ourselves to God. The first three verses read:

AS with gladness men of old
Did the guiding star behold,
As with joy they hailed its light,
Leading onward, beaming bright,
So, most gracious Lord, may we
Ever more be led to thee.

As with joyful steps they sped
To that lowly manger bed,
There to bend the knee before
Him whom Heaven and earth adore,
So may we with willing feet
Ever seek the mercy seat.

As they offered gifts most rare
At that manger rude and bare,
So may we with holy joy,
Pure and free from sin's alloy,
All our costliest treasures bring,
Christ, to thee, our heavenly King.

Baptist Annie Hawks's 'Who'll Be The Next To Follow Jesus?', which appeared in the 1899 song book, is the most recent of non-Salvationist mercy-seat hymns to come into Army use. It begins:

> WHO'LL be the next to follow Jesus?
> Who'll be the next his cross to bear?
> Someone is ready, someone is waiting;
> Who'll be the next a crown to wear?
>
> Who'll be the next to follow Jesus?
> Come and bow at his precious feet;
> Who'll be the next to lay every burden
> Down at the Father's mercy seat?

The poetic image of the mercy seat so far has borne a close resemblance to the Old Testament pattern – a place of communion, comfort and contrition.

The fact that these songs are still included in the Song Book and are in current use suggests that Salvationists, or at least those responsible for editing the Song Book, approve of the mercy-seat pictures painted by the songs.

In the 20th century, all new additions to Army song books on the subject of the mercy seat came from Salvationist writers. Once in Salvationist hands, it becomes less clear whether the mercy seat in a song refers to the physical bench in the Army hall, the figurative concept of communion, comfort and contrition it embraces, or both.

Only one mercy-seat song did not survive transition into the 1986 edition. The anonymously penned 'With A Sorrow For Sin' appeared in every edition since the first in 1899. It was dropped from the 1986 edition, although not, one suspects, for its reference to the mercy seat:

> WITH a sorrow for sin must repentance begin,
> Then salvation of course will draw nigh;
> But till washed in the blood of the crucified Lord,
> You will never be ready to die.

We've his word and his oath, and his blood seals them both,
And we're sure the Almighty can't lie;
If you do not delay, but repent while you may,
He will soon make you ready to die.

And that you may succeed, come along with all speed
To a Saviour who will not deny;
So kneel down at his feet, at the blest mercy seat,
And he'll soon make you ready to die.

When the fight we have done, and the victory won,
We to mansions of glory shall fly;
There eternally sing to our Saviour and King,
For his love made us ready to die.

What the song does tell us is that the writer saw the wooden bench as a place for making peace with God – a place of conversion.

Captain Strong, whose song was also first published in the 1899 Song Book, similarly sees the mercy seat as a place of salvation:

A NEEDY sinner at thy feet,
With broken heart I bow
For pardon at thy mercy seat;
O Jesus, save me now.

Strong Friend of sinners, hear my cry,
And set my sad heart free;
My sins demand that I should die,
But I believe in thee.

To thee, the sinner's changeless friend,
My all I fully give;
The living water, Jesus, send,
O let me drink and live.

In 1921, Arthur Gibby won a *War Cry* song competition with 'There Is A Mercy Seat Revealed'. In it he sees the mercy seat as a place of atonement:

> THERE is a mercy seat revealed,
> A glorious throne of sovereign grace,
> Where broken hearts may all be healed
> And truly feel love's warm embrace.
> O trembling soul, dispel thy fear,
> By faith through Christ to God draw near.
>
> The smoking flax God will not quench,
> Nor will he break the bruisèd reed;
> His justice and his love do blend
> When guilty souls for mercy plead.
> Come, sinner and backslider, fall
> Before his throne, for pardon call.
>
> Tears of repentance will not save,
> Nor yet good works for sin atone;
> The sacrifice that Jesus gave
> Must be thy plea, and that alone.
> No other name, however high,
> Can bring thy soul to Heaven nigh.

Likewise, Edward Joy sees the mercy seat as a place of comfort and forgiveness:

> IS there a heart o'erbound by sorrow?
> Is there a life weighed down by care?
> Come to the cross, each burden bearing,
> All your anxiety, leave it there.
>
> *All your anxiety, all your care,*
> *Bring to the mercy seat, leave it there,*
> *Never a burden he cannot bear,*
> *Never a friend like Jesus.*

No other friend so keen to help you;
No other friend so quick to hear;
No other place to leave your burden;
No other one to hear your prayer.

Come, then, at once; delay no longer;
Heed his entreaty, kind and sweet;
You need not fear a disappointment;
You shall find peace at the mercy seat.

There were three new additions to the 1986 song book. In G. Kaleb Johnson's 'Songs of Salvation', first published in *The Musical Salvationist*, 1934, it is the physical bench as a place of forgiveness that is in the writer's mind – as the last verse shows:

Hearts that were broken and bleeding,
Torn by remorse and grief,
Came to the mercy seat pleading,
Finding complete relief.
Love in its fulness is flowing
Here, where all sins depart,
Pardon and mercy bestowing
Freely on every heart.

Albert Orsborn wrote 'Where Lowly Spirits Meet' in July 1939 at the request of General Evangeline Booth. The General wanted to include it in special prayer meetings held around the world for the forthcoming High Council, when a new General would be elected. In his song, Orsborn portrays the mercy seat as not only a place of communion but also a common factor of worship, uniting Salvationists throughout the world:

WHERE lowly spirits meet
Instant in prayer,
All at one mercy seat,
One plea to share,

With thee we intercede,
Leader of those who lead,
Heart of our Army's need,
Make us thy care.

Let not thy people boast,
Empty are we,
Martial and mighty host
Though we may be.
Naught of our own we claim,
Forth from thy heart we came,
Thou art our altar-flame;
We live by thee.

Where secret rivers rise,
Lead us to grace;
Even through clouded skies
Show us thy face.
Own us thy people still,
Seal us within thy will,
And in thy holy hill
Stablish our place.

The most recent song, which first appeared in *The War Cry* in October 1952, was written by Doris Rendell. In it she traces the scriptural origins of the mercy seat as an encouragement to finding deliverance, healing and peace at today's penitent forms:

IN days long past the mercy seat
Was made of purest gold;
'Twas placed upon the sacred ark,
Love's meaning to unfold.
Within the holiest place God planned
Redemption's grace to show;
More sacred now is Calvary's hill
Where healing waters flow.

Thy blood, O Jesus, spotless Lamb,
Once lifted up to die,
Was shed to cleanse our fallen race
And lead to realms on high.
No one too sinful, or too low,
Too desolate, too blind,
But here before thy mercy seat
Can full deliverance find.

O hallow now our mercy seat,
Thou Son of God most high!
Here may the lame man leap for joy,
The dumb sound joyful cry,
The sin-sick soul, though wearied sore,
By evil power possessed,
The halt, the blind, the great, the small,
Find peace from sins confessed.

We seek the healing of thy cross,
The mercy of thy grace;
Here at this sacred mercy seat
May we behold thy face;
Here may we glimpse thy holiness,
Here on our souls descend,
Here may we meet, and talk with thee,
Our Master and our friend.

More than 50 years on, the hope that 'at this sacred mercy seat may we behold thy face' is still the desire of those who kneel there.

Chapter 11

The Mercy Seat In Verse

THE mercy seat is not only sung about it is also the subject of poetry.
Here is a selection of poetic insights and perceptions.

Soldier of Christ

CALLED out to follow him, by love set free.
Could higher honour be vouchsafed to me
Than this, freely bestowed on Calvary –
Soldier of Christ?

I have not chosen; he hath chosen me
That I a warrior of the Cross may be,
Girded my trembling arm for victory –
Soldier of Christ.

The word of high command sounds in my ear,
Bidding me seek the lost, to Christ so dear;
I kneel and plead His love to cast out fear –
Soldier of Christ.

When to high Heav'n my cry mounts falteringly,
When to battle I go haltingly,
Still, by his grace, I will fight valiantly –
Soldier of Christ.

One crowning day of days, low at his feet
I'll lay my armour down, then rise to meet

My King, who called me at His Mercy Seat –
Soldier of Christ.

Doris N. Rendell
(The Merchant of Heaven and Other Salvationist Verse, 1944)

Angels Guard the Mercy-Seat

'And the cherubims shall stretch forth their wings on high, covering
the mercy-seat with their wings' (Exodus 25:20 *KJV*)

WHEN Moses built a temple with the ark of God therein,
God bade him build a mercy-seat for offering of sin:
By sprinkling with atoning blood this mercy-seat of gold,
The death of Christ on Calvary was to the world foretold.

The cherubims stretched forth their wings above the mercy-seat,
And guarded well the place where souls with God were wont to meet:
Thus God gave them protection from the enemy around,
And met them in the holy place where perfect peace was found.

And thus he meets with you and me around the mercy-seat,
Providing peace and pardon which in Christ we find complete,
His guarding angels spread their wings to keep us in his care,
While we in close communion kneel and talk with Jesus there.

Irena Arnold
(More Poems of a Salvationist, 1945)

The Ark of Care

'Uzzah put forth his hand... and took hold of it' (2 Samuel 6:6 *KJV*)

UPON thine own dear shoulders' sway
Are borne the weightiest burdens of each day;
The teeming, lurking fears of anxious thought,
The doubt that laughs at what my work has wrought;
Just help me, Lord, to leave them there –
The ark that carries all my care.

Sometimes – impatient, quick – I leap
To steady, and a firmer hold to keep.
'Nay – nay, my child! Touch not this sacred load,
'Tis mine!' a Voice rebukes. 'You watch the road.'
May I obey, walk straight and free,
And leave the ark of care with Thee.

So, balanced, poised in Love's own arms,
The burden rests: of failures, needs, alarms;
Thou dost not need resourceful powers of mine
To steady and control that which is thine!
O, Bearer of the ark of care,
My life I leave, and trust it there.

Heather J. Kirkpatrick
(*The Jubilant and Other Salvationist Verse*, 1947)

The Mercy Seat

NOT just a form placed here by kindly hands,
Inscribed with words of welcome, light and love;
A meeting-place of Heav'n and earth, it stands
As emblem of the Mercy Seat above:
Where burdened souls may kneel and, keeping tryst,
Shall find awaiting them the living Christ.

I knew the pain of trespass unforgiv'n
And bore the anguish of unpardoned sin;
Too long in vain my better self had striv'n
Some joy to find, some peace of heart to win.
Bereft of all resource, and half-afraid,
I heard Love's invitation, and obeyed.

Kneeling I prayed, with penitential tears
Falling as tributes of a contrite heart;
Pardon, and cleansing from the sins of years,

Courage and pow'r to choose the better part –
These things I asked of him whose word is true,
And rose believing, saved and born anew.

Then to this form a second time I came,
But deeper now my purpose and my plea;
I sought a further blessing thus to claim,
And here in glad surrender bowed the knee.
Mine it should be by selfless love to live;
My Lord's to use all that such love can give.

O form! The lowly instrument of God:
I bear your image in my heart this day;
E'en while I live to spread his love abroad
I shall have need of you whene'er I pray:
Daily I shall in heart return to you,
My full, glad consecration to renew.

Will J. Brand
(*The War Cry* 16 July 1960)

On the Mercy Seat
(The Assembly Hall, Denmark Hill, with echoes of Exodus 25)

NO cherub pair or plate of solid gold
Adorns the place we call our Place of Prayer,
But silent splendour draped in colours bold
Stands guard each end, relaxed in gentle air.
The seat, rough wood now elegantly trimmed
And varnished to resist those briny stains
Of penitential tears forgiveness-rimmed,
Which flow to those of joy as guilt soon wanes.
Then where's God's word? Not underneath it all,
Removed from sight for none to view again,
Not in an ark preserved for mere recall,

110

But opened, read, proclaiming truth so plain.
Is this our boast, this seat of humbled pride?
'Tis but one place communion-sanctified.

Paul du Plessis
(The Evangelists sessional magazine, 1967)

The Mercy Seat
(An echo of Denmark Hill)

THE doors stand wide invitingly
A spring day's joy to greet,
And sunlight falls like patterned gold
Athwart the Mercy Seat.

So Unadorned that Mercy Seat
And yet magnificent;
So silent, yet its eloquence
Refining thoughts present.

The flag stands proudly sentinel
Above the place of prayer;
Its graceful folds protecting
Keep tireless vigil there.

That sanctuary holds holy day
When to the Mercy Seat,
While music merges into prayer,
Come young and reverent feet.

As priests drew near their altars high
With covenant of blood,
So come these dedicated ones
To covenant with God.

Their vow once made, forthwith they go
Their solemn charge to meet;

This memory living in their hearts –
A sunlit Mercy Seat.

Albert Mingay
(*My Day for Living* 1970)

Utterance

WHEN at the Mercy Seat in prayer I kneel,
Having no words and making no advance,
Lacking the skill to give me utterance
For my unshapen thought, my mute appeal;
May I recall that always there is One
Who waits upon my need and will present
My very silences, with their intent
Made crystal clear, to Him upon the throne.
Giants in prayer have long since testified:
The Spirit helpeth our infirmities;
This affirmation my assurance is;
Seeking His help, I shall not be denied.
In prayer not unaccompanied, alone,
The Spirit comes to make my cause His own.

Will J. Brand
(*With Sword and Song* Will J. Brand 1975)

The Way of Prayer

HERE in this quiet hour, this still retreat,
I bend the knee before Thy Mercy Seat;
For here I fain would pray,
Attentive only to Thy voice,
None else to hear, none other to obey:
Spirit alone with spirit,
Deep unto deep communing,
As in Thy 'circling presence
A little while I stay.

Hear me, O God, in heaven, Thy dwelling-place;
Bow down Thine ear, who art not far from me;
As pants the hart when heated in the chase
So pants my soul for Thee.

Not as passing shade come Thou to me,
O Life and Breath of all reality;
I may not now behold
Nor touch Thee, than my self more real:
Yet faith will clutch Thee with unyielding hold:
Speed not, O Time, our meeting,
Cast not thy veil about Him,
For God Himself is present
His purpose to unfold.

Too soon the busy hours with large demands
And urgent tasks will seek to lade my hands,
Yet, casting all my care
On Thee, O God, the spacious life
That springs eternal I with Thee may share:
Thy holy hill ascending,
Seeking Thy habitation,
Tranquil in heart, pursuing
The royal way of prayer.

Will J. Brand
(*With Sword and Song* Will J. Brand 1975)

Beside the Mercy Seat

HE had a troubled face
And sometimes bitter words would slip
Too easily from tongue and lip,
Darting like sudden sparks from ugly fires
Of deep resentment and of proud desires.

I thought – judging his words –
His goal was just as high as earth
And that his measuring of worth
Was taken always by a badge of rank,
Of treasure weighed and counted in the bank.

But once I saw him new,
Silent, as though an angel hand
Had touched his lips. I saw him stand
As one communing in the courts above,
His meek eyes quiet, purified by love.

Which man is he? I ask.
The discontented one of yesterday?
Or this, with striving washed away,
Surveying now, with happiness complete,
A sinner kneeling at the Mercy Seat?

Are there two men? Or one
Who made a covenant with God
Long since, and faltered where he trod?
And has he loosed his hold on worldly dross,
Moved by this sinner praying at the Cross?

The servant named by God
For holy skills and loving art
May not from his true name depart;
To be another he cannot afford
For near the sinner he is near his Lord.

Catherine Baird
(*Reflections* 1975)

If the Mercy Seat Could Talk

I'VE heard ten thousand whispered prayers,
Confessions to the Lord,

As heavy hearts find peace of mind restored.
Mistakes and wrongs of all the years
Come tripping to my ears;
The comfort of a Father's voice is heard.
This is the sign that God's at work,
I am his hallowed ground:
Assurance once again he's answered prayer.
There's always something special about knee-prints in my hand,
The knowledge of a God who understands.

I've seen the hardest ruffian cry
And wash me in his tears,
The wand'ring son with Father reconciled,
The faces of the children as they've knelt to make their prayers
And promises. And I have seen God smile.
Where now this sign that God's at work
On me his hallowed ground?
Yesterday they queued just to get near.
I'm sat upon and spat upon. The worst misuse of all
Is acting though I'm never even here.

I'm painted on, I am left bare
I'm honoured and revered,
Carpetted, roped-off and polished well.
I'm all dressed up at harvest time
With carrots in my ears,
Museum piece admired throughout the year.
I'm not worn thin by elbow marks.
I don't erode with tears.
Suspicion screams at those who visit me.
Statistical reports record my sad and slow demise.
Is this the sign that God's at work? I cry.

Nigel Bovey 1985

Mercy Seat?

IS this the mercy seat,
This manger place
Which seems so full of love,
Of good, of grace?

And will God talk to me,
Tell me his will,
Here, wrapped in silences,
So soft, so still?

I touch this tiny hand,
I see this face;
The God I'm looking for
Is in this place.

My heart prepared itself
Its Lord to greet,
And kneels with joy before
This mercy seat.

And must I bring a gift,
Some worth, some wealth?
Is it enough for me
To give myself?

Give him your yesterdays,
Tomorrows too.
He asks for nothing else
But you!
Just you!

John Gowans
(*O Lord, Not More Verse!* 1999)

Within This Place
(Reflecting on the significance of kneeling at the mercy seat)

Here is the God who keeps my heart,
My life, my all, within his grace;
My soul protected by his love
This very hour, within this place.
And so secure that soul must be,
Since Jesus bled and died for me.

Within the spheres of life's routines
Shines grace to lighten every hour;
The trivial round, the common task,
All held by gracious, gentle power.
And what a wealth of grace I see
In Christ who bled and died for me!

My joys and triumphs find him here,
My doubts and loves, my hopes and needs.
Here, all is shared, and all confessed
To him who loves and intercedes.
Such endless charm, immense and free,
That he should want to die for me!

The kindest judgments he can find
Are bathed in grace, in mercy clad;
My sins forgiv'n; a Saviour's blood
Is shed to make poor sinners glad.
My chains fell off! And I am free!
Since that same Saviour died for me!

Stephen Poxon 2009

Chapter 12

Personal Reflections

FOR most Salvationists the true value of the mercy seat is not found in prose or poetry but in personal use. The mercy seat is a special, sacred place where they make life-changing decisions and meet with their Lord. Years later we may not recall the exact wording of our prayer but we do remember the occasion.

The following is a collection of personal reflections from correspondents. They graciously provide us with the most important perspective of mercy-seat use – that of the user.

Katie Harlum

I WAS introduced to the Army through the pub ministry. I have been attending the Army for around six years, two of which were in the training college. I am in my first year of officership.

Being new to the Army I have had to adjust to the language and the use of symbols in ceremony. (In some respects I am still adjusting.) When I first came to the Army, I could see the meaning of the uniform, as it was an active sign of an inward commitment. However, I struggled with many 'Army Barmy' ideas, especially the reason for – and the use of – the mercy seat.

I picked up that the mercy seat was a place of prayer and would occasionally see somebody kneeling there. It seemed very public and the unspoken indication was that is was the 'naughty seat' and a place for somebody to be redeemed.

In time I went to the mercy seat myself but felt no attachment or change after my visit. It wasn't just once but several times after pouring my heart out on the sacred wood in a public display I would walk away feeling even more vulnerable than before.

For me, the mercy seat was not a blessing as nothing changed in my circumstances but the fact my cries could be heard from the back of the hall. I continued to seek comfort in going forward after powerful appeals but still came away feeling the same.

I continued to pursue but sensed that only more experienced Salvationists were able to hear God through this act and that I had somehow missed the boat. I then rested in the fact that I could only lead others to the mercy seat and although I had knelt with them, before them and after them I was not to find any peace in the act for myself.

Having read some of the history of the mercy seat, I began to wonder whether it was outdated or maybe not relevant to today's times and people.

The International Spiritual Life Commission's call to the mercy seat says:

'We call Salvationists worldwide to recognise the wide understanding of the mercy seat that God has given to the Army; to rejoice that Christ uses this means of grace to confirm his presence; and to ensure that its spiritual benefits are fully explored in every corps and Army centre.'

There was a bold claim that the seat was used to meet with God. This was too much for me to swallow as it felt too neat and tidy for the likes of God and his spontaneity. This clean-cut idea of the mercy seat was not my experience at all.

I was to be broken many times in my willingness in faith for change but walked away with faith but no change. Again I thought that it didn't apply to me.

It was only last week in a meeting at the training college that I felt God's nudge after a sermon on faith. I felt the call to go forward to the mercy seat in obedience to a faith issue I'd been having since my first attempts to find God's restoration there.

I was almost sick as the preacher's words pierced my heart. She spoke about faith as though it was easy but I knew God was challenging me not to have more faith in him but to believe that finally he was going to answer my prayers for change.

As I sat there, uncomfortable, I knew that every tear that I'd shed and every prayer I'd previously made at the mercy seat was heard and now was the time to act in faith and go forward to where God had required me, at the mercy seat.

I felt nervous and justified myself by telling myself that the preacher wouldn't ask for willing participants.

I was wrong. There was a call to go forward. I withheld for a moment but I knew that this had nothing to do with Army symbolism but God calling me to trust him in the process of the impossibilities of my life. I could not even begin to imagine how God was going to answer my lifelong prayer but I had to believe and trust and my first step was to go forward.

When I got to the mercy seat I was at peace, anything could have been going on behind me and I wouldn't have taken any notice at all. It wasn't vulnerability that I felt but empowerment by the Holy Spirit. God was going to act but it would require a step of faith on my part.

This was the beginning of a journey and I knew it was going to be tough, but God was intervening by his grace. It was by God's grace that now was the time to receive the blessings and my willingness to place my doubts before God showed me I was living right in the centre of his will.

By this experience, God firmly rebuked me about my scepticism of his work in and through the symbols and ceremonies that in the past had felt empty and lifeless. I was humbled by God by the very thing of which I was critical.

A week later my faith was tested and I was brought back to the commitment I had made at the mercy seat. I praise God for the opportunity this experience gave me.

Eric Himes

AS a child growing up at my corps I thought it was quite natural to kneel at the mercy seat and talk with God. I can remember the excitement I felt when I prayed at the altar (another name for the mercy seat). My heart raced. I could hardly catch my breath as I walked back to my seat after praying at that sacred place. I can't remember what I prayed in those early memories but I know that afterwards I felt good. I felt better.

As I grew older I began to realise that people prayed at the mercy seat because they wanted something to happen. They were compelled to apologise, to sacrifice, to grow, to commit. I remember seeing one retired officer kneel there each Sunday, as he knelt on one knee and put his hand on the holiness table. He seemed desperate for something. I thought he was crazy.

When I was a child I was comfortable at the mercy seat but when I grew older – and came to a realisation of my sins – I began to pity others who went forward to pray. And so I sat in my pew with my other adolescent friends, hands folded and head bowed, peeking at the sinners who knelt at the penitent form. I judged them and, in doing so, avoided judging myself.

However, as a teenager there were many times when I was so moved by the Holy Spirit that I was compelled to bring my convictions to the mercy seat.

I often cried and prayed with friends and hoped that I would be free from whatever was ruling me at the time. I was earnest in my faith and knew that God was giving me a space and opportunity to be honest and vulnerable. And that space was often found between the platform and the first pew – at the mercy seat.

I want to be a part of a Salvation Army that believes in the mercy seat. I want to fight in an Army that aches with urgency to win the world for Jesus; an Army whose soldiers know the beauty of humbling themselves before God, who get their knees dirty and have clean souls. I want to be the kind of soldier who is desperate for sanctification and who pursues holiness.

Carl Eliasen

I ONCE read that one great tragedy in the Church today is 'the drought of contrite tears at the Altar'. May God save our beloved Army from that drought!

How encouraging to see, in some Hispanic corps in the USA, the healthy practice of Salvationists kneeling at the altar with their Bibles open when they first arrive at the hall, preparing in mind, heart and soul for the meeting.

In the 1970s, when my late wife and I pioneered the work in Portugal, to get to the office we had to pass through the hall. One morning, I was moved to find a woman kneeling all by herself at the penitent form. It was the janitor, before she started her daily work.

Another emotional moment happened in Finland where I was invited to lead the 1990 Congress. An officer from Estonia was present, wearing uniform for the first time after many years of privation enforced by the Communist regime.

When the altar call was made, she went forward. The mercy seat was full with seekers, so the counsellor suggested that she knelt at a chair instead. 'No,' insisted the officer, 'I want the real thing!'

Christine Mayes

SINCE 1980, when I first stepped into a Salvation Army citadel, I have seen a few mercy seats, although not all my appointments have included one. Nevertheless, even in aged care and other social appointments I've found God can use anything, anywhere, as his mercy seat.

I remember, early in my officership, coming home from visiting my family interstate and trying to decide if I should attend the night meeting, seeing as I was in civvies. I decided to bite the bullet, intending to just slip into the meeting unnoticed and quietly sit, and be refreshed by the Holy Spirit.

I managed to find a seat in the back row, thinking no one would notice me and I could just relax in the company of God and my fellow worshippers.

Well, you can be off duty from your appointment but not off duty from God.

When the appeal was made, a fellow worshipper asked me if I would pray with her, there in our seats. After recovering from the initial shock that someone 10 years or so my junior would want me to pray with them, I knelt with her in the quietness while everyone else was standing facing the platform – her talking quietly to God and me listening and silently asking God for direction as to the words to say to my sister in Christ.

There was no age barrier, no differences between soldier and officer, and no thought of time. After a brief hug, the mountain-top experience was over and as I again took my seat I was reminded once again of how God works in a mysterious way.

God had seen fit to use me as his instrument of peace. I had done nothing, but that place had become holy ground – because God was present.

It's a long time ago now but the memory reminds me that God's grace can transform anything into a mercy seat if he chooses. I have seen a pew, a chair, a wheelchair, a dining table, a picnic table, even a lift, a stairwell and a drum transformed into a place where God came near.

If, as Scripture tells us, God can transform water into wine, and clay into a vessel, then there are no boundaries to what else he can transform into his mercy seat.

Jennifer Heaton

I USED to be very reluctant to kneel at the front and it took some time for me to make an initial commitment. However, when I was feeling at my lowest time, when our son, Jonathan, took his own life in 2002, nothing could have kept me from kneeling at the mercy seat. My husband and I did this on the Sunday after Jonathan died and the prayerful support from those present was of unbelievable value.

I think it is one of the strengths of the Salvation Army service that anyone can publicly ask for and receive prayer at the mercy seat.

David Hammond

THERE is a wide proliferation of interpretations of what the mercy seat means and what Salvationists use it for. I am not sure this is a good idea. I fear that the Founder's love for the mercy seat was because it is there that the miracle of conversion takes place, and where the Army's first purpose is established.

I see the mercy seat as a disappearing metaphor in our ministry, although there will be some glorious exceptions. Certainly, it has lost it effectiveness so that one seldom sees the transformation of yesteryear in our meetings.

I feel deeply about the need for our mercy seat as a line of demarcation between the old life and the new, which was once so characteristic of a good Army meeting. The new broom of praise and worship style has contributed in no small way to including everyone in our meetings, whether or not they know anything about conversion.

I find this very sad. What little I know about other evangelical denominations confirms that the clear difference between being saved and being unsaved is a major weakness in their salvation ministry.

I have found that the interest level in the mercy seat is very low. Not many people are willing or ready to have a discussion about their conviction around the mercy seat, unless it happens to be a once-in-five-year congress, when people go forward by the hundreds.

I wish it were not so. I doubt very much if the present trend can be altered or changed. I wish it could. The Founder built the Army around the mercy seat. General Albert Orsborn was right when he said, 'When it goes out, we go out.'

Lalkiamlova

I KNELT at the mercy seat in our village corps as a young boy and accepted Jesus as my Saviour; I signed the Junior Soldier's pledge there.

When, in my teens, my friends and I committed some very youthful and not very nice misdemeanours and got caught – my mother sent me to the mercy seat instead of physically punishing me. This action had a significant effect on me and at that mercy seat I confessed my sin and received forgiveness.

Still in my teens, I felt God calling me to the ministry. I knelt at the same mercy seat at midnight and said 'yes' to the Lord.

Some time later the prayer hall was moved to another location in our village but the villagers, knowing the significance the mercy seat at the old prayer hall had for me, erected a cement mercy seat which has become my Bethel. Whenever I visit the village, I kneel there and rededicate myself to the Lord.

Keith Hampton

LAST year in Caboolture, Australia, we outgrew our corps buildings. So, after six months of not having any outreach Sunday children's programme, I was challenged by Commissioner Joe Noland's DVD *Altars in the Street*. I sat and wept as I watched it and the echo of some of our people suggesting we that we 'don't do' children's work, and concentrate on other things, was going around my head and my heart.

I called together a group of people interested in commencing a new Sunday school on Sundays and looking for a place to have this new emphasis in our corps, as we only had one citadel, and no place to have Sunday school, or so I thought.

I used to drive regularly past the Seventh Day Adventist Church and on Sundays it was empty, so I rang and made an appointment to see the pastor, with a view to renting their building on Sundays. Eventually, our church moved in on Sundays. We ran Sunday school at nine, followed by the Sunday service at 10.30 am. Each Sunday we would take the stackable seats and make a mercy seat and a long table and cover it with the holiness cloth from the old citadel and make a holiness table.

Our divisional leaders came to the first meeting in our new set of rented buildings and my wife and I led the meetings. After my wife, Ruth, preached a sermon on faith, I led the appeal and invited the congregation to come forward in faith and to accept what God had for them.

Many came forward to the mercy seat and holiness table – all of two weeks old and made from different bits of plastic each week, but still signifying a place of prayer and commitment. One woman, not used to Army protocols, sat on the mercy seat. One of our female soldiers went and sat on the mercy seat with her and lovingly guided her to the Lord and to a new life in Christ.

In the past few months I have felt led to preach a series on holiness. I tried to keep it pretty simple. That first Sunday the mercy seat was lined with seekers and a number of Salvationists purposely moved to the holiness table.

During one meeting an elderly soldier made her way to the holiness table as the band was playing the tune to the words 'Come home! Come home! Ye who are weary, come home.' What a focal point of decision-making and commitment! We thank God for the bits of plastic that form a place of special significance in our Salvation Army corps.

But our plastic chairs are not the only mercy seat. I was talking with one of our employees in my office. We started talking about his home life and life in general and he started to talk to me about what was a very stressful time in his life. This man is an adherent member in the corps and was coming to meetings spasmodically. As we shared, I asked him if he ever shared all his stressful situations with God, as God was into sharing our life stories with us. He said he didn't.

On my desk was my laptop with last week's sermon still on it. I opened the sermon my friend had missed and showed him Holman Hunt's wonderful painting of 'Light of the World', which depicts Jesus standing at the door of our hearts with all the weeds crawling up the door.

I told my friend that the door doesn't have a handle on the outside, only on the inside and that it is up to us to invite Jesus in to our lives or not.

'Would you like to open the door of your heart to Christ?' I asked him.

'Let's do it,' he answered. And the laptop became a mercy seat.

Gordon Swansbury

ON my first Sunday in Kenya in 1957 I attended the meeting in Thika conducted by the Divisional Commander. During the prayer meeting I noticed a comrade, later discovering that he was the corps visiting sergeant (of whom there were several), walking up and down the aisle and pointing to certain members of the congregation who, at his signal, went forward to kneel at the mercy seat.

This was an unusual procedure, to my thinking, but I also noticed that none of the seekers was being counselled.

The Divisional Commander, on my enquiry, enlightened me. He said that a strong point in corps activity was area visitation, with the aim of getting the unconverted saved in their homes. Where this was achieved, the sergeant would say, 'On Sunday I want you to attend the meeting, and when I give the signal during the prayer meeting I want you to go forward and kneel at the mercy seat. You will do this as a witness to your decision to accept Christ as your Saviour, and the congregation will welcome you in their fellowship as a seeker.' It was rare indeed throughout the territory that the mercy seat was unvisited.

In Nairobi Central Corps, where the attendance every Sunday was 1,000-plus, when the appeal was given, invariably the long mercy seat would be lined again and again; with far too many seekers to allow for individual counselling.

As the seekers rose from their kneeling, the recruiting sergeant and his team of helpers would sort them out, directing the soldiers or known Christians to return to their seats. If asked why they had come forward, the common reply would be, 'Because I want to be blessed'. In some cases they would describe a problem with which they needed help.

New cases would be directed to the rear hall where their particulars would be written down and counselling given. They would be asked if it was their wish to become Salvationists, and if so they were directed to attend a class on Saturday mornings for a course of instruction.

This would continue for 13 months. On the first stage they were called 'watafuta', or 'seekers', which lasted for a month. This was to ensure that they were intent on continuing. The second stage lasted six months, and they were called, 'wanafunzi' or 'learners'. On the third stage they were called 'waongofu', roughly meaning those who were seen to be going straight; to ensure that they measured up to the standards of Salvationism.

During those 13 months they were given theoretical and practical instruction about Christian living, some Bible teaching, and education about the Army. In addition, on Saturday afternoons they had their own open-air meetings conducted by the recruiting sergeant.

At the end of their period as *wanafunzi* they would parade before the platform and receive acknowledgment of their status. At the end of the 13-month period they would be in uniform, stand on the platform with their Bible and Song Book in hand, recite certain points of their learning, and be sworn in as soldiers. This was usually done twice a year, including the Easter Sunday meeting. It was not unusual for around 150 new soldiers to be sworn in during the course of the year.

Paul du Plessis

MY own spiritual pilgrimage has been to a large extent a deepening awareness of God, and receiving his grace. The mercy seat has played an important, though by no means exclusive, part in that pilgrimage.

I've seen the mercy seat in numerous settings and used (or not used) in a variety of ways. One memorable experience was in rural Zambia in the 1970s where the mercy seat was often fashioned out of a few logs of rough timber simply lashed together with the bark of a tree.

When travelling through the town of Kafue we stopped to see the site where Salvationists gathered each Sunday under a tree. They'd gathered a few storm water drainpipes lying around and set them up in rows as benches would have been in the usual corps hall. But there it was again – the mercy seat, another storm water drainpipe. They showed me the place where they planted the flag each week just alongside their drainpipe mercy seat.

In many settings in South Asia we found there was no mercy seat in the prayer halls, as they tend to be called. We worked hard to get them to be an established part of Army worship. Altar calls were seldom made except in special and sometimes massed meetings. They were a feature of the annual revival meetings. People often queued up for prayer rather than kneel at a mercy seat.

One of the memorable moments of our years in leadership of the Southern Africa Territory was the public handing over to General Paul Rader of a book of a few thousand Salvationist signatures that endorsed our commitment to reconciliation.

During the morning meeting of the territorial congress we gave a last-minute opportunity for anyone present to sign the book at a central mercy seat in the auditorium. Placing the book on the mercy seat seemed to me symbolic of the process of cleansing we wanted to be experienced by God's grace operating in the process in which we'd been engaged.

Executive officers then processed to the platform with the book. They were moments of significance and, for many of us, charged with emotion. But behind the moment was an immense amount of hard work, teaching, discussion, heart-searching, debate and even disagreement. But for me it all came together at that mercy seat.

Sandra Dalziel

AT our corps the mercy seat is definitely used for the purpose for which it was intended and used often. One particular way is that when anyone is leaving the district – and we are a very mobile community – people who wish to pray go to the mercy seat where the person who is leaving is kneeling. They rest a hand on them and pray for them.

We can have a mass of people gathered around one person praying for them. This shows that we are a church family and very often those who go and pray are people who don't otherwise partake in the meetings, but feel they can join a group in silent prayer.

But the mercy seat is also used like a climbing frame before, during and after the meeting apart from when somebody is kneeling there. We have half a dozen under-fours, who like to use it to play games, to colour or to slide throughout the meeting.

Daryl Lach

I WAS a corps cadet in the 1960s. Our brigade was asked to perform 'General William Booth Enters Heaven' at several corps in the Metro area. One night we were at the Joliet, Illinois, corps. One of the retired officers there was Brigadier Margaret Norris, who was the unofficial mercy-seat sergeant. One of her trademarks was to walk along by the altar giving out paper tissues to those who needed them.

This night in Joliet during the revival service people were at the altar and the brigadier was doing her thing with the tissues. Our brigade was sitting at the back of the hall watching all the activity, when a very rotund woman made her way forward to the altar with tears in her eyes. Brigadier Norris met her and handed her a tissue.

It was obvious that the woman would have great difficulty kneeling. Brigadier Norris seemed to sense that this woman needed something more than simply standing to pray near the altar, so without flinching she helped the woman turn around and sat her down on the altar and began to pray with her.

To us teenagers at the back of the hall it was one of the funniest sights we'd ever seen and on the way home there were the obvious jokes like, 'My all is on the altar'.

As a young Salvationist I attended many mass meetings and congresses with people streaming to the mercy seat but they are a blur in my memory. Forty years on, I now see what the brigadier did as one of the pivotal moments in my development as a Christian.

The sight of Brigadier Norris handing out tissues and gently helping that woman to the mercy seat left the deepest of impressions for all time. Of such is the Kingdom of God.

Joanna Spice

I have been attending the Army since February 2007. For me the mercy seat is an incredible place of prayer. I find it sad that many people see it as only a place to go when someone has done wrong.

The first time I went to the mercy seat all I remember is knowing I should have done it the week before. I felt disappointed in myself for being a coward – thinking everyone would be watching, would they be wondering what I was doing? Hating myself for those thoughts.

I'd not known what I'd say to God when I got there, and if I'm honest that worried me – I hate not being organised, not having a plan – but God understood far better than I could have anticipated.

He picked me up from my seat in the back row (where I liked to hide). He guided me, led me, surrounded me with love and somehow I ended up on my knees at the mercy seat.

131

I just started praying, asking him if there was any way he could forgive me – there was a lot of baggage beside me at that special place. But I found it didn't matter. I could have come with any amount – a truck load – and it would not have mattered.

I then asked God if there was any space for me in his family. Would he care enough to come into my life and save me from myself, from my past, from whatever the future would throw at me? I knew it was a lot of asks – I'd come to a point of wondering who I was having the nerve to ask for anything, when I had nothing to offer.

At that point two others joined me to pray with me. They held me as I shook from head to toe. I knew without a shadow of a doubt that something very special was happening for me. I'd gone to the Lord asking if there was a chance of forgiveness, and he met me and let me know gently that it was OK.

Over time I've been to the mercy seat for many reasons and I've learnt that that's OK too. I've been to the mercy seat with tears of thanksgiving in my eyes. I've been there just to pray for understanding.

One Sunday I woke up knowing that this was the day that I could no longer put off, no longer run from. I knew I had to go to the mercy seat. I'd been arguing with God, but when God wants us to do something he does not give up until we see things his way.

I felt so apprehensive about going to the meeting I almost wanted to stay home. God knew this and guided a few other people to help me. When I got to the hall my friend Christine said she was going to sit next to me. Later she saw me trembling from head to foot and asked me if we should go to the mercy seat. I could hardly move. If Christine hadn't taken me by the hand I would not have gone forward. But I knew in my heart it was where I had to be, I knew in my heart there was no other way, and I thank God for providing once more for my needs.

This time at the mercy seat I knew what to say. Scared and feeling totally inadequate I did what the Lord had brought me here to do. I prayed, oh how I prayed!

My prayer was one of submission. I guess I opened my hands, my heart and my mind. I said, 'Lord, you have led me to this point. I surrender myself heart, mind, body and soul to you – for whatever you want from me, I will follow in obedience whereever you lead me.'

For six weeks I'd run around in circles, tried to argue with God that his plans for me were wrong. I tried to walk away, but he held me firm, showing me, guiding me, teaching me, laughing at me.

The sense of peace that flooded me that day at the mercy seat was the most incredible feeling I have ever known.

Chapter 13

Around a Common Mercy Seat – the Mercy Seat and Other Denominations

THE Army is not alone in benefiting from Brengle's holiness teaching. Nor are we alone in appreciating the value of mercy-seat response. For while the widespread use of the mourner's bench has long since dropped out of Methodist practice, a number of other denominations recognise the benefits not only of calling people in response to the preached word but also of providing a place for that response.

The Free Methodist Church does not have a formal mercy seat, but it does use the altar call to elicit responses for salvation and sanctification. The respondents are required either to kneel at the Communion rail or step up onto the platform. The appeals are spontaneous rather than frequent and patterned.

(In my book *The Mercy Seat*, I referred to The Emmanuel Holiness Church. Founded in 1917, it used to use the mercy seat for salvation, holiness, healing and general spiritual stocktaking. In recent years, member churches have become independent. None of them uses the mercy seat any more.)

Part of the mission of The Jesus Army, which developed from the Bugbrooke Baptist Church in 1985, is to reach the unchurched with the gospel by evangelising on the streets and in community halls. To help in eliciting spiritual decisions, Jesus Army preachers use portable backless benches at the foot of a stage or at outdoor services. These are known to Army members and described to an unchurched congregation as jargon-free 'kneeling benches'.

One of the main proponents of the mercy seat is the Church of the Nazarene. Formerly the Pentecostal Church of Scotland, it changed its name in 1915. In 1952 it amalgamated with the International Holiness Mission and was joined by the Calvary Holiness Church in 1955.

In *We Have an Altar,* Norman Oke traces the Nazarene use of the mercy seat, or altar, to the American revival of the early 1800s. The Methodist mourner's bench became the Nazarene altar every bit as much as the Salvationist mercy seat.

Oke sees the main value of the altar as a means to create atmosphere. 'The invitation has been given,' he writes, 'the seekers are kneeling by the altar. Now comes the crux of the entire evangelistic battle... This altar-atmosphere is one essential we cannot do without.'

To maintain the primacy of the altar, Oke suggests, architects employed to design Nazarene churches should 'be clearly alerted to the fact that we build our sanctuary from the altar as a central focus: the altar is not an after-thought'.

Being the focal point of the building is just one way in which Nazarenes and Salvationists share the same view of the mercy seat. It is used by adults and children for salvation, holiness and personal prayer. Sometimes its use is preceded by an altar call. At other times people come forward during times of worship.

The altars vary in design. Some have a ledge 20-24 inches above the ground. Others have no ledge. Some are adapted Communion rails.

Nazarene archivist Stan Ingersol outlines the denomination's approach in America:

'In Nazarene churches, the altar has always meant more than simply a Communion rail but a place of prayer, usually in response to an altar call summoning sinners to repentance and believers to sanctifying grace. However, it has also been a place to gather round for general prayer during Wednesday night prayer meetings or at other times when the pastor might call the congregation down for prayer.

'In recent years, many churches in the United States have begun inviting people to pray at the altar about general concerns during the Sunday morning worship service. Churches that have adopted this practice generally devote about 10 minutes of the worship service to this aspect. Usually the altar will be lined with people praying, while the rest of the congregation remains seated. Pastors who do this on Sunday morning also will occasionally specify the invitation to the altar, for instance, inviting those who want prayer for a troubled marriage, or those who want to pray for healing for themselves or others. Such invitations are often keyed to the theme of the morning's sermon.'

The following extract from a report of a 2009 preaching tour in the Solomon Islands by Dr Jesse Middendorf, published on the Nazarene website, bears many similarities of early-day *War Cry* reports.

'People crowded into the sanctuary, while others stood outside doors and windows. At the end of the message, the altar was lined with seekers who poured out their hearts in prayer. "It was more like an old camp meeting service than anything I have seen in years," Dr Middendorf witnessed.'

The camp meeting is still a feature of the Nazarene calendar, particularly in the States. At these meetings people respond to God – for salvation, sanctification and healing – at the altar.

Like Salvationists with the mercy seat, Nazarenes trace a common source of their altar to the camp meetings of American revivalism in the 1800s.

To conclude, it seems that apart from the absence of inscriptions, the Nazarene altar and Army mercy seat are synonymous in function, style and purpose. There are many who worship like the Salvationist. We share a very common mercy seat.

Chapter 14

Pitfalls of Free Fall

FROM being a 'penitent form' where the big two crises, salvation and sanctification, were resolved, for many people the mercy seat has become a 'place of prayer'. More than a quarter of respondents to my 2009 survey say they refer to the mercy seat as 'the place of prayer' (see Appendix A for details). The specialist corner shop has become a general-purpose supermarket. Some might see the change in usage not as a selling up but as a selling out. Their concern is that a broadening of the range has led to a cheapening of the goods. While for others any use is good use.

David Hammond from Canada is concerned that the original purpose of the mercy seat is getting lost in the transition:

'In recent years the mercy seat has been used for almost everything under the sun. A former territorial commander was fond of saying, "There is no reason why you should not come to the mercy seat." People now come for anything: like looking for a job, or the healing of arthritis. It seems to me that the original purpose of the mercy seat has been lost in the change. I do not deny that a place of public prayer has blessing and significance for some people, but one wonders if much of what people find could not be found as easily where they are sitting – after all, our places of worship are houses of prayer, are they not?'

As well as being an experienced corps officer, Arthur Brown has spent many years as an itinerant preacher. He observes what he sees to be a number of shortcomings in a free-fall approach to the mercy seat:

'There are Salvationists who see the mercy seat as a place to resolve any emotional upset, including that of being moved by a songster piece. This leaves the meeting vulnerable to disruption in the first ten minutes. As I understand it, Wesley made use of the Communion rail for seekers registering decisions only at the conclusion of a meeting. Having heard the gospel, the opening was made to come and publicly accept Christ through repentance and faith.'

Problems are not new. Not all use is good use. The Army did not inherit a flawless form. In the early days, there was little room to kneel at crowded mercy seats but there was room for improvement, as William Booth outlined in *Addresses to Staff Officers*:

'I suppose no officer in his senses would advocate the abandonment of this method, or undertake to deny its usefulness, either in the past or in the present, as – (i) A help to decision. (ii) A confession to Christ. (iii) An encouragement to officers and soldiers in their efforts to save the people where it is judiciously used. (iv) A preachment to the ungodly. (v) An inducement to others to decide.

'It is the abuse that is objectionable, and the sooner the abuse, not only of that, but of every other useful method, is abandoned the better... What is wanted in the use of the mercy seat is not abandonment, but correction and improvement.'

He then suggests some correctives:

'To begin with – (a) It should be taken more seriously. Made an altar. (b) A more exact explanation of its meaning should be made when the invitation is given. (c) It might be used less frequently. (d) You might take people directly into the ante-room who have been to the penitent form several times before. Although I do not know: "Seventy-and-seven" times. (e) You might make more exact and descriptive announcements of numbers. (f) There should be more thorough work done with the penitents when they are there. Getting to the roots. It is the holding back of the sword from blood that is the secret of most of our penitent-form failures. (g) You would not like me to abandon the penitent form. I would not, if I could; and could not, if I would.'

Although Booth acknowledged the faults (including that of overuse) he concluded that the mercy seat was here to stay. It is the responsibility of today's users to identify its current misuses and set about correcting them.

One of the dangers to avoid is to attribute to the mercy seat a power that it does not possess. We cannot allow fanciful theories to grow around the mercy seat as they have the long-lost Ark of the Covenant. The mercy seat is a place for spiritual reality not for superstition.

Perhaps Vera Williamson's experience best highlights the need for vigilance:

'In a meeting in a Third World country so many people came forward in response to the invitation that most could not kneel at the mercy seat. A high-ranking officer urged those kneeling at a distance to at least walk forward and touch the mercy seat. I was saddened by the dangerous misconception being conveyed. If we use the mercy seat, people should be taught not only its uses but its limitations and dangers.'

In *Salvationist,* 16 February 1991, Dale Bishop, commenting about the use of the mercy seat in soul-saving, writes:

'We have such a strong attachment to the mercy seat that we behave as if it is necessary to salvation. Might that kind of attitude prove a hindrance to God's work in men's hearts?… We would be wise to keep this in mind whenever we are tempted to think that a convert who knelt at the mercy seat is somehow more "saved", or saved in a better way, than one who knelt elsewhere. In reality, all that matters is that the sinner comes in penitence to the Father and puts his faith in the efficacy of Christ's sacrifice.'

We must avoid investing the act of coming to the mercy seat with power it does not possess, as though all life's conflicts will be resolved simply by making our way to the front.

In my 1994 survey Bram Baird highlights another kind of power – putting pressure on people to kneel.

'There is a danger,' he writes, 'that by stressing the penitent form or mercy seat we will continue to excuse ourselves for inadequate preparation of converts and put unnecessary barriers in the way of seekers…

'I have seen visiting preachers, including some who should have known better, prolong a prayer meeting with an insistence that someone present was under conviction and that the meeting must not close until that one was saved. On one occasion, a senior officer conducting the meeting literally pulled a member of the congregation from her seat and led her unwillingly to the penitent form. We never saw the unfortunate lady again.'

Baird goes on to suggest a subtler pressure, that of group acceptance:

'The other side of the same coin was the attitude of the grumpy local officer who objected to receiving new soldiers, because he had never seen any of them kneeling at the penitent form. I have never regarded the act of kneeling at the mercy seat as a ritual, but if we are to insist on it before anyone can become a soldier, then a ritual it will become. In that case, we should at least expect it to be performed with dignity.'

While there are those who insist that a mercy-seat visit is a prerequisite to enrolment, uniform wearing and even necessary to salvation, there are others who want to stop uniform-wearing Salvationists from using the mercy seat.

In the 1994 survey, Geoff Blurton noted that overt pressure is sometimes put on Salvationists not to kneel. He recalls:

'I once spoke with someone who felt that it was not the appropriate thing for a uniformed songster to make a public decision at the mercy seat. This was on the grounds that people "might get the wrong impression" or feel that if a songster did such a thing the spiritual standard of the brigade would be questioned. How glad I was when an officer on furlough (and in uniform) made a decision at the mercy seat the next week!'

The pressure not to kneel is not often so clearly brought into the open. With ropes and rails long since removed in many corps, it's closed minds that often regulate today's use and non-use of the mercy seat. A general atmosphere of cynicism and hardheartedness is likewise no incentive to kneel out from the crowd.

Superstitious power and surreptitious pressure must be braved and broken if the place of prayer is to regain its rightful place in Salvationists' thinking.

In some corps there are physical as well as mental barriers to be overcome. A band cluttering up the aisles and access to the mercy seat with instruments and stands is not unheard of. The subliminal 'message from the band', to use a time-honoured phrase, is that we don't expect – maybe even want – anyone to use the mercy seat.

A cluttered mercy seat is not a modern phenomenon. Joseph Pugmire in *The Officer*, July 1924, writes:

'The workers appointed to the penitent form should be instructed to keep it sacred and not allow it to be used as a hat rack and umbrella stand, or a dumping place for band instruments.'

For General Bram Tillsley, the focus of mercy-seat misuse is how the invitation is given. In correspondence, he writes:

'The greatest weakness is the manner in which we invite people to use the mercy seat, that is the transition from proclamation to invitation. The invitation should be an extension of the sermon. Perhaps some basic reminders would be in order:

'Allow adequate time so the invitation is not rushed. Avoid an apologetic approach to this most important moment.

'If using songs or choruses, it is helpful to inform the organist/pianist of what we plan to use. The congregation should be familiar with the songs and the music should be pitched in a slightly lower key. Avoid a continual changing of songs/choruses.

'There should be real warmth in the invitation and it should not be forced. The sincerity of the leader will go a long way in bringing about a response.

'Avoid becoming agitated if there is no visible response. Our task is to proclaim the Word; it is the Spirit's work to bring about a response.

'Brengle said he carried a mercy seat in his heart. Therefore the virtue is not in a physical altar. This means that, on occasion, we simply invite people to stand or kneel just where they are.

'My own approach has always been to appeal firstly to God's people. This takes away the suggestion that the mercy seat is only for "sinners". As John Gowans puts it: "We're all seeking the same Saviour: We're all seeking the self-same Lord."'

The General hits an essential point: If people are not using the mercy seat, is it because they are not being given the appropriate invitation or opportunity? Put another way, if meeting leaders are not seeing the mercy-seat response they would like, do they need to address what goes before an appeal, and look at how an appeal is made?

Geoff Perry, who was converted at an Army mercy seat as a boy, is also concerned about the invitation or appeal.

'Too often,' he says, 'an appeal, where there is one, is given in an attitude of take it or leave it. Yet the mercy seat has always been a place where people can get saved – which, I fear, is itself a phrase that is dying out among Salvationists – and a place to claim the blessing of holiness and full salvation.'

Another area to address is that what happens once people are at the mercy seat will determine whether they will return in future. One respondent to my 2009 survey says that they are put off from going to the mercy seat because they've seen confidential seeker cards left lying around on public view.

An article entitled 'From Penitent Form to Soldiering' in *The Field Officer*, July 1906, addresses the twin concerns of inadequate counselling and insufficient follow-up:

'The importance of linking up the work done at the penitent form with that in connection with the healthy state of the soldiers' roll should be obvious to every field officer,' it begins. 'Most likely it is, but for some reason or other it is undeniably the case that a larger proportion than it is at all possible to regard as inevitable of those who "come out" are lost to the Army if not to God.

'We have spoken with soldiers who have told us that if they had been properly shepherded they would have joined the colours years before they did... we have had officers confide to us the interesting fact that when they "came out" as trembling souls to the mercy seat, no one, not even the field officer, whose burning words had prompted the surrender, took the trouble to speak to them – much less take their name and address and arrange for visitation.'

The article continues with observations from a Major Cunningham of South Africa:

'Oh! The many wry, distorted and deformed souls there are around nearly every one of our corps, who are everlastingly quibbling about soldiership, wearing of uniform, the use of tobacco, or the going to this and that place of amusement; who might have been blessings and joys to every one of us, and happy, useful soldiers of The Salvation Army, if only they had been rightly dealt with at the penitent form; but some of them were never dealt with at all, some were dealt with by people who were incapable of doing it, and some were "hurried through" in a slipshod fashion, which, to say the least of it, was discreditable to all the parties concerned. Seeing the great amount of labour it took to land them at the penitent form, we might very naturally have expected that far more anxiety and greater care would have been shown in getting the question of their conversion and their future career rightly settled.'

General Jarl Wahlström sees danger when mercy-seat counselling is too hurried and superficial. In correspondence, he writes:

'To avoid these dangers the use of a counselling room is recommended. Kneeling at the penitent form is a sign of obedience and willingness to surrender to the will of God, and thus an act of witness. But the more detailed counselling should take place in a room set aside for this purpose.'

Catherine Bramwell Booth maintained counsellors should be direct and thorough in their work. She is quoted in *With Colours Waving*:

'Make sure that they [the penitents] have been urged to confess their sin and made to pray aloud themselves. In those first moments of seeking, the soul is ready, in its sense of need, to speak of things that, later, it will be almost impossible to approach. The very circumstances give the dealer with souls the right to inquire and instruct.'

Catherine Baird suggests that a similar sympathetic-but-firm stance should be taken with children:

'When we talk with a child at the penitent form we must have a definite idea of what we want to do for him. We want to help him to feel the nearness of God; we want him, if he has done wrong, to

145

confess it and be forgiven; we want him really to make a new start; we want him to leave the penitent form knowing that, though he will be tempted to do wrong, Jesus is always beside him to help him overcome.'

If the gaining of a sense that Jesus is always beside the seeker to help them overcome is the goal of all who use the mercy seat, then there is no room for complacency. Misuses must be corrected. The booklet *How to Counsel Seekers,* based largely upon *Orders and Regulations for Local Officers*, is one attempt at correcting mercy-seat misuses. It starts with the assertion that 'all Salvationists should be qualified and trained to counsel seekers at the mercy seat at any time'.

It continues:

'Counsellors should do all in their power to guard against the dangers to which the use of the mercy seat is exposed; in particular:

Relying upon the act of coming forward, instead of upon the work of grace which God does in the soul.

Regarding the mercy seat as a kind of "confessional" for the easing of a guilty conscience, when there is no sincere determination to forsake sin.

Going to the mercy seat misguidedly, and thereby robbing the action of its true spiritual significance.

Inadequate counselling which often results in seekers going away disappointed through not reaching victory.

Failure to realise that what takes place at the mercy seat is only elementary yet vital in God's work of grace, and should be followed by continual spiritual progress.'

When Commissioner Ian Cutmore presented the discussion paper on 'Our Emphasis on the Mercy Seat' at the International Leaders' Conference in Hong Kong in 1995, he did so armed with data collated from an informal opinion poll he had conducted among delegates at the International College for Officers. He told the conference:

'Every officer who commented would like to see the penitent form used more often and more effectively. There was no dissenting voice. What is apparent from the comments of these officers is the need to give more prominence to the penitent form as a place of prayer as well as a place of penitence (although, of course, there is always a need for penitence in the life of the believer).'

What exercised Cutmore was, 'Why are we discussing using the mercy seat more, anyway?

'Do we want to preserve tradition or are we being led to use the mercy seat more widely and more often as is entirely appropriate for the Army today? In some parts of the world, there are no longer large numbers of unsaved people in our meetings. If there were we would probably not be discussing this matter now as the penitent form would be in constant use. Should we then be looking more earnestly as to how to get in touch with the unsaved again?'

Ian Cutmore feels Salvationists need to be clear why they are concerned about the non-use or under-use of the mercy seat. In correspondence, he writes:

'I suspect we sometimes feel guilty that fewer people are getting saved at the mercy seat. I think it's easier to encourage our people to use the mercy seat as a means of grace than to get to grips with attacking the devil's hold over the unconverted. I believe we need to ask ourselves honestly whether our enthusiasm to see the mercy seat used as a means of grace is a way of taking the pressure off getting the unsaved into our meetings. It's possible to have a corps where the mercy seat is frequently used and yet no one is getting saved. We need to ask ourselves whether we are happy with such a situation.'

Ian Cutmore is right to remind us that 'more' does not always mean 'better'. If we are using the mercy seat as a means of grace we must beware that it does not become a means of escape. The question he poses is inescapable, for how we view the mercy seat is how we view the Army.

As a permanent mission to the unconverted dare we settle for anything less than using the mercy seat as our main strategy for getting people saved? Or, as the following chapters investigate, is it simply a case that in some parts of the Army world the mercy seat is being sidelined in favour of other avenues of grace?

Chapter 15

The Mercy Seat and Creative Response 1

IN considering the place of the mercy seat and other elements of Salvationist worship, the International Spiritual Life Commission acknowledged that: 'We do not deny the value of the symbolic in religion.'

In my 1994 and 2009 surveys of the UK Territory, a number of respondents said that on occasions they invited people to do something other than use the mercy seat and that such responses were equally valid. Widely mentioned alternatives included: raising a hand, standing in one's place, standing at the front of the hall either at the holiness table or the mercy seat, pastoral visitation and the use of a separate room for prayer and counselling.

These, and the use of the drum in open-air meetings, accord with the general practice around the Army world. However, my 2009 international survey also reveals practices including the washing of feet or hands in Mexico, the building of a stone altar in the USA, the lighting of candles in Sweden, the placing of written prayers on the mercy seat in Malawi and the taking of a card or a stone as a commitment reminder in Southern Africa.

From the Australia Southern Territory, Mal Davies writes:

'In some meetings there might be a task to indicate a personal response to the message, such as collecting a bookmark from the mercy seat, writing a prayer and depositing it in a receptacle or praying in small groups.'

From the USA Western Territory, Ian Wild describes how on special occasions such as Good Friday and Easter Day 'a cross has been placed at the front of the chapel and people fill out prayer cards and nail them to the cross'.

Jude Gotrich has seen a wide range of what she calls 'non-permanent fixtures in the sanctuary'. She catalogues:

'Small cross on a table with pieces of mosaic individually placed or small candles lit to form a cross at a set point in the room;

'A chain-link fence set up like a wall and small strips of ribbon were placed by the petitioner;

'Flag pins on a map of the world;

'Rocks stacked as an altar such as was used by Jacob at Bethel (Genesis 35);

'Burning barrel – during times of confession where burdens were written down on paper and then consumed in a fire – much the same done at summer campfires;

'Lighting of candles (either actual wax candles, battery operated or glow sticks) and placing them on a furnishing in the room;

'The lighting of a candle and sharing it with another as an act of peace after a grievance;

'Receiving a prayer request that has been placed on an altar and participating in a prayer service by the taking of that written petition;

'Writing on a large wall covered with paper or even a portable wall (bulletin board) with various aspects of prayer (confession, thanks, requests, encouragement, etc);

'Stones placed in water;

'Sand poured out on the ground or into a central bowl;

'Bread broken from a single loaf and shared with a prayer partner;

'Water basin and water poured over the hands of the petitioner by an elder or officer;

'Prayer circles randomly formed as a response;

'Silence.'

Since the mid-1990s, similar 'non-permanent fixtures in the sanctuary' have appeared in the UK. Post-sermon, non-mercy-seat responses have become more varied in nature and more widespread in use. Activities such as lighting a candle, writing a prayer, hammering a nail into a cross, washing of hands or receiving a bookmark have become associated with what is called 'creative response'. Typically the responses involve members of the congregation leaving their seats and moving towards the front of the hall, or to another part of the hall. Sometimes the mercy seat is involved; sometimes it is not. Often a creative response is designed to fit the specific theme of the meeting. For example, a meeting and sermon about journeys might involve the use of paper footprints.

In one sense 'creative response' is an inadequate term. Can, for example, meaningful response be anything other than creative? Is the receiving of spiritual resources at the biblically provenanced mercy seat somehow less than creative? For the sake of shorthand, however – as inadequate as that may be – when discussing a non-mercy seat, post-sermon response I will use that term here.

Anyone hoping to identify the first appearance of creative response within the United Kingdom Territory in a precise time-place-date format is likely to be disappointed. Just as the introduction of the mercy seat within Salvationist worship was more tortuous than instantaneous, so creative response is the result of evolution rather than overnight revolution.

Today's Salvationists are arguably more open to influences from other denominations than ever before. (Other denominations might well say the same of their members.) Salvationists, Baptists, Anglicans and others sing from the same PowerPoint slide. They browse the same Christian websites, play the same worship CDs, read the same books, listen to the same speakers, pray at the same 24/7 events and attend the same teaching holidays at Spring Harvest and the like. They mix and match. They give and take. They adopt and adapt. They cross international borders. They cross-pollinate.

What works in one church is tried in a corps or conference. What works in one corps is adapted by other corps. The process is loose, sporadic, informal and pragmatic. The philosophy of 'If it works, let's use it' is symbolic (maybe even symptomatic) of the present, postmodern age. Unlike the mercy seat, these things are not carved in *Orders and Regulations*.

151

There is, therefore, no one person responsible for the emergence of creative response within Salvationist worship.

In response to the emergence of creative response in the UK, since the mid-1990s the exploration of creative worship, creative response and the mercy seat has formed part of the training of the next generation of Army officers at the William Booth College, Denmark Hill. As cadets are already exposed to new ideas before they commence training, it should be recognised that not all that is learned at college comes from the official curriculum.

In 1998 the college received validation for its officer training course from the University of Gloucestershire. Since then, graduating cadets attain a diploma in higher education. In that year the teaching of preaching and meeting leadership (formerly known as Platform Ministry) was incorporated into two new modules: Communicating with People and Biblical Interpretation and Preaching.

Training Programme Director Sheila Dunkinson explains:

'The Communicating with People and Biblical Interpretation and Preaching modules incorporate exploration of creative worship, while still maintaining the balance of expectations about what worship can be. Level One sets in place the basics of planning and leading worship in formal and informal settings. It includes sessions on all-age and group-specific worship, which include a number of creative methods.

'Level Two looks at ways the Bible can be interpreted other than through a formal sermon. One of the texts used in the module is Dan Kimbell's *Emerging Church, Emerging Worship*, which gives an idea of the range of experiences the cadets are encouraged to explore.

'At both levels, the assessment of a cadet's worship leadership and preaching includes comments on the use of creative and participatory elements in their meetings. Over the past few years, module leaders have widened the definition of a Sunday meeting to enable cadets on placement to suit their style to that of the corps they are visiting, while still being formally assessed.'

As at corps, the exploration of creative worship and creative response within the college context appears (similarly to some people's experience of holiness) to have been more of a process than a crisis. It seems creative worship and creative response ideas were being explored at the college by the mid-1990s.

In 1994 one of the aims of Year 2 Platform Ministry course was to 'offer a creative approach to worship and meeting leadership demonstrating the use of creative ideas in worship'.

The 1999 module descriptor for Hermeneutics (which replaced Platform Ministry in that year) reads:

'Prepare and present ways of worshipping and preaching that reflect the multi-dimensionality of human nature and move beyond the word-based mentality of the past.'

The teaching of creative response was not included in the curriculum as a requirement of validation by the University of Gloucestershire. It has happened because of perceived spiritual needs of UK Salvationists. The college is responding to what is happening in the territory, particularly in corps in which it places cadets for training. It is a recognition of what educationalists call 'learning styles' and what the rest of us might call 'getting through'.

College tutor Sue Pegram explains:

'The rationale behind the teaching of creative worship is to respond to the changing context in which officers minister and the increased awareness of the variety of ways in which different people find it helpful to engage with, and respond to, God.'

Fellow college tutor Kathryn Stirling adds:

'The teaching of creative worship has developed from a deeper understanding of the ways in which people respond – not in terms of mercy-seat response, but rather how in general people respond to things that are presented to them. We discuss with cadets the need to be sensitive and appropriate in their choice of response invitation.'

Sheila Dunkinson points out:

'Cadets explore the discomfort some people feel at being asked to participate in something unfamiliar, and to reflect upon their responsibilities as worship leaders to take account of these responses.'

One area of response where some Salvationists are comfortable is the mercy seat. The mercy seat as a distinctive of Salvationist worship is a central and vital component of the preparation of cadets for meeting leadership.

As part of the Communicating with People module, cadets study 'The Mercy Seat in Salvation Army Worship and Leading a Time of Response'. Aspects covered include the biblical background and theology of the mercy seat, its place within Salvationist history and the spiritual principles and everyday practicalities and sensitivities of mercy-seat use.

Cadets receive instruction – and are assessed – on the conducting of a mercy-seat appeal, including how to make the transition between sermon and appeal, what kinds of things to say in an appeal and how to say them. In another part of the course, cadets receive guidance on mercy-seat counselling and pastoral aftercare.

Kathryn Stirling explains:

'We fully recognise that the mercy seat is a distinctive of Salvationist worship and that *Orders and Regulations* requires a mercy seat to be available for use in every meeting, therefore we prepare cadets in appropriate use of the mercy seat.

'Because there is more than one way to respond to God, we also discuss with cadets the value of encouraging other responses. It might, for example, be appropriate to give a congregation the opportunity to sit and reflect – in silence or with music, with or without a series of images to look at – which, in turn, might lead to response at the mercy seat. It might also be the case that a congregation would find value in putting something on – or collecting something from – the mercy seat, and maybe kneel at the mercy seat as they do so.'

This view is shared by Training Principal Norman Ord:

'We're finding that as people become more accustomed to making a response through creative worship, so they are rediscovering and re-using the mercy seat.'

The picture emerges that, as far as preparing cadets for ministry is concerned, creative response and mercy-seat use are regarded as complementary rather than conflicting approaches.

On a territorial level, to use a medical analogy, the general practice appears to be to use the mercy seat. But in some situations some practitioners offer creative response as a complementary remedy for a spiritual need.

There are a number of questions regarding creative response that I suggest those interested in the mercy seat (and, if I may be so bold, those not interested in the mercy seat) would do well to address. Why is creative response popular in the UK? What effect is creative response having on mercy-seat usage? Is creative response, like the Army's experience of the Toronto Blessing in the 1990s, a passing phase? Is it more than a fashionable thing to do? Is it the next stage in the ever-changing history of the mercy seat? To what extent will creative response make the mercy seat redundant? Can they happily co-exist?

In answering such questions we need to hold two seemingly conflicting principles in equilibrium. The first is that Salvationists believe in a God who can do miracles without the help of magnificent sermons, musical sections or mercy seats. We believe that spiritual transactions do not depend on anything – including the mercy seat – other than God's grace and our co-operation.

The second is that, as we have seen in earlier chapters, from its earliest days God has blessed the Army at the mercy seat, a construction and a concept (as later chapters will unfold) with biblical connections and sacramental connotations.

The International Spiritual Life Commission spoke about not denying the significance of the symbolic in religion. To say that William Booth was not afraid of symbols is an understatement. His idea of a crimson-based banner for the Christian Mission predates the founding of The Salvation Army. The entire Salvation Army is a militaristic metaphor. Uniform, ranks, officers, soldiers, corps, crest, flags, commissionings, marching orders, cartridges, Articles of War – everything that makes The Salvation Army (and Salvationists) distinctive is symbolic.

Salvationist worship, from the very beginning, has been wrapped – and continues to be wrapped – in symbolism. This does not mean, of course, that Salvationist worship is fake. On the contrary, characteristically Salvationist worship focuses on the essential biblical realities of personal salvation and personal holiness.

Could it be, then, that creative response is simply a fresh way of appealing to our love of the symbolic?

Responses to my 2009 territorial survey indicate that creative response has its attractions. A creative response to God's word in a corps where nobody has used the mercy seat for years is seen by some as a viable alternative. After all, the mercy seat has no spiritual power of its own and we believe in an any-time-any-place-any-where God.

Just as different styles of teaching get through to different kinds of pupils (adult or children) so it is possible that some types of people (adult and children) feel more connected through creative response.

Kathryn Stirling says:

'I don't see that inviting people to respond to God in a variety of ways implies that the mercy seat doesn't matter. People may respond in silent prayer where they are sitting. Some people are helped by responding in other ways, for example by receiving a paper footprint as a reminder to follow the Lord closely during the coming week. These ways of responding do not detract from the significance of the mercy seat. The emphasis should be on genuine response to God, and people can be helped by having the opportunity to respond in a variety of ways. This can help to keep worship fresh as well as challenging.

'Going to the mercy seat tends to be seen as a significant turning point in someone's life. However, not every response to God is a crisis. We can encourage people to use the mercy seat for other reasons too – for instance to pray for others or to say thank you to God. Equally, writing a prayer for ourselves or for someone else and leaving it at a cross or prayer station, for example, is as valid a response to God in worship as kneeling at the mercy seat. They can co-exist happily. What is important is that there is encouragement to respond to God.

'It is important for the worship leader and the congregation to understand why the opportunity to respond is being framed in the way it is. Sensitive and appropriate use of any means of response is vital or the result is loss of impact and reality.'

A mutual understanding between preacher and congregation is a vital ingredient of meaningful worship. For good communication to happen it not only has to be well presented it also has to be received as the presenter intended.

Church consultant Keith Morley explains:

'In terms of dynamics, there are two big questions: On the one hand, what does the preacher think they are presenting and what response are they looking for? On the other hand, does the congregation share the preacher's understanding of what's being presented and are they responding as requested?

'There are a number of issues for the preacher to consider in their meeting preparation. Do they have in mind for the response to be thematically linked to the sermon? For example, would holding a nail in a Good Friday service be appropriate? If so, the link should be clearly made and understandable to the congregation. Such added symbolism might prove useful and accessible for those people who wouldn't use the mercy seat because they can't picture in their minds the link between the sermon content and the wooden bench at the front of the hall.

'The preacher might also think about whether a creative response is to be used to prepare a path to the mercy seat or whether it will be used by itself. If it does, then the invitation to do so should be clear. The holding of a nail on Good Friday, for example, might allow worshippers then – nail in hand – to pray at the mercy seat with greater purpose, direction and clarity. For those who have difficulty overcoming the first steps, the physical action involved in going forward to receive a nail might ease the path to the mercy seat.

'Is the preacher seeking to elicit a specific response for a specific stand-alone purpose and hence wishes to make these responses separate from the normal mercy-seat activity (for example, sign a bookmark on Commitment Sunday to indicate a joining in common response as a whole body-of-Christ activity)?

'I suggest a preacher then needs to consider a number of questions in respect of the congregation. Will the congregation understand the thematic links the leader is making between the subject of the sermon and the called-for response?

157

'Is the congregation used to a creative response being a path towards using the mercy seat, or does experience suggest creative responses in that corps are replacing mercy seat activity?

'Where creative responses are presented on their own merit, does the congregation respond more readily to them than to a simple call to the mercy seat?

'While perhaps only the congregation can answer these questions with certainty, they are still the essential corollaries a preacher must seek to answer if creative response is be a regular feature of worship.'

One regular preacher and leader of worship who has used creative response as a stand-alone and as a path to the mercy seat is Matt Clifton. Comparing the fors and againsts of creative response, he writes:

'I have seen some very powerful instances of creative response: Young people writing confessed sin onto paper and then taking it out into the night to cast into a fire; elderly people coming forward to light a candle in memory of loved ones on Remembrance Sunday; people coming forward to take a nail and keep it, pressing its sharp end into their palm, thinking about what crucifixion meant for Jesus.

'The question of why have creative forms of response to augment the mercy seat seems to be like asking why have music. Why ask the songsters to sing "Share My Yoke" when you could just read out Matthew 11:28-30? The answer, of course, is that music and poetry speak deeply to the imagination and make profound, formative and lasting impressions. Likewise, creative response can resonate with the spoken message.

'In an effort to focus on "heart religion", there has been a tendency within the Army to devalue the visual. (Not that Salvationists would want to be genuflecting to icons or using rosary beads.) God created us with the capacity and need to encounter him through the imagination by means of visual beauty, symbols, metaphors, stories and myths (in the best sense of that word) – in short, by our physical senses. The Bible is writ large with symbolism, metaphor and allusion; therefore worship or ecclesiastical culture which deliberately marginalises these is impoverished.

'Leaders using creative responses are seeking to engage the imagination in the same way Jesus did when he said things such as "I am the light of the world" and "I am the bread of life". Why would he put it like that, if it didn't carry some imaginative power?

'My impression is that many corps officers intuitively understand that a fully rounded discipleship cannot be built from responses confined to salvation by faith and sanctification by faith. These are the central emphases, but the Bible calls for a much wider range of responses to its message. To use the mercy seat only as a place of repentance has made many long-term Salvationists reluctant to use it. We have had to find pastoral methods for reshaping its meaning in worship.

'In this respect, creative responses can serve as a way to nurture renewed use of the mercy seat. Sometimes, when stationed at Forestdale Outreach Centre, I invited people to come forward to a table to take something or write something, adding the invitation, "Why not move on to kneel at the mercy seat?" If they are already coming forward with other people for one thing, some people then find it easier to take a few more steps and pray at the mercy seat.

'There is, though, a vital difference for me in locating the mercy seat indispensably in the heart of our worshipping life and other creative responses, which I see as augmenting a particular meeting theme.

'Like anything else, if handled badly creative response can be tacky or gimmicky. There is also a matter of personal taste. What to me might be a gaudy, laminated, badly guillotined, clip-art disaster of a bookmark might be someone else's treasured memory of a powerful meeting. As with all elements of Salvationist worship – including the use of the mercy seat – poor quality is not an argument for rejection but for development and improvement.'

From the States, Jude Gotrich writes:

'It is important to recognise that God continually uses tactile symbols so that we have a picture of what his relationship to us looks like. The furnishings in the Tabernacle and the Temple, which included the Ark of the Covenant, had specific functions to give us information about the various aspects of our worship and our response to his speaking to our hearts.

'God never intended for us to be devoid of these symbols as they help us understand who he is and they remind us of our spiritual formation.

'The Cross is the primary example. It not only reminds us of Christ but also of the sacrificial life required of those who follow him. Everything is a metaphor, something "like" what God is relaying to us. The metaphor of the mercy seat needs to be continually explained to our congregations so that they are aware of its significance and purpose. When they serve to point us in the direction of the triune God, we are made rich.'

Let us continue, then, to consider the attractions of creative response.

Creative response is do-able. There seems to be no inner conflict about whether a person should go forward to, say, collect a stone or light a candle in the way there often is when a person feels under conviction to go to the mercy seat. Typically, there is no prolonged invitation – complete with prayer choruses – to respond in creative response. People who feel they cannot use a mercy seat because they are not physically able to kneel find many aspects of creative response do-able and feel glad to be involved.

One of the problems sometimes associated with the mercy seat is a judgmental attitude towards the seeker. In my 2009 survey, I asked: 'Why is there sometimes a reluctance to use the mercy seat?' Top of the most common answers were that the mercy seat is perceived as a place for wrongdoers and that the seeker is assumed by the congregation to have done something wrong. (See Appendix A for more details.)

Creative response does not generally come with such hurtful attitudes (real or imagined) directed at those who respond.

Some people are reluctant to use the mercy seat because of negative connotations. They fear personal embarrassment. They do not feel comfortable with being the centre of attention. They fear that by showing emotion at the mercy seat they will embarrass themselves.

Some see the mercy seat as a 'place of disgrace'. Some see it, or fear that it is seen, only as a place for penitence and that they will be talked about and/or judged if they use it. Some people are afraid that if they go to the mercy seat God will challenge them. There is the fear of the unknown and of appearing vulnerable.

Creative response offers an element of safety in numbers. When other people are responding in a matter-of-fact way, it makes participation easier. Responding in numbers also adds to the sense of corporate worship – of 'being involved' – rather than the majority of the congregation being onlookers (albeit prayerful ones) to an individual act of movement to the mercy seat.

Then there is the human factor. A preacher who faithfully invites their congregation to the mercy seat Sunday after Sunday, week after week, time after time, yet sees no response can be forgiven if they start to take it personally.

In such circumstances it would be understandable if a preacher introduced creative response not only to energise their congregation but also to gain some feedback that their message had got through. The sight of the majority of the congregation writing a prayer or collecting a bookmark from the holiness table or making some other creative response can uplift a preacher as well as the congregation itself. It can be a sign that the hard-worked-for message is being heard – that a corps is sensitive to the word and voice of God – and there is no feedback more positive for a preacher than that.

Chapter 16

The Mercy Seat and Creative Response 2

THE use of creative response provides answers for some people. For others it also raises questions. (It must be stated here that whether we're discussing mercy-seat use or creative response we are often drawing conclusions from appearances. And, as we know, appearances can sometimes be deceptive.)

Let's consider the other side of those positive aspects of creative response.

Creative response is do-able. Judging by the number of people who make a creative response compared with those who would likely have used the mercy seat in that meeting, there seems to be no inner conflict about whether a person should respond in this way. Does the lack of inner struggle – the argument with God that comes before surrender and making that step towards the mercy seat – affect the sincerity and depth of a creative response? Is there the same sense of Holy Spirit conviction with creative worship as there is with mercy seat use? Does it take more courage to go forward to the mercy seat and is it this courage that God acknowledges? Does God require more from us than easy responses?

In correspondence, Commissioner Betty Matear writes:

'My heart's reflex is that alternatives to the mercy seat are a very diluted concept. Candles and the like are aids not responses. The mercy seat is a place of community and mutual strengthening as well as private and personal response. The mercy seat is a relational place, a space for grace. We should repossess our possessions.'

Margaret Bovey shares her insight:

'I see the value for many people, especially children, in creative worship. I like many aspects of creative worship and use such ideas myself. But while I recognise that God does use such approaches, I can honestly say that I've never felt that inner churning that comes when the Spirit challenges me to go to the mercy seat by the likes of writing a prayer on a paper flower. Creative response has never touched me to the same depths.

'One aspect of creative response is the investment of creativity in meeting preparation. The related response normally requires the congregation doing hands-on activities. Such busy-ness makes me wonder whether, in an already-hectic world, we are not missing out on the vital, intimate aspect of just being – being still and knowing that he is God.'

Creative response lacks the judgmentalism sometimes directed at – or perceived by – mercy-seat users. But what about those people for whom creative response doesn't connect? What about those who stay in their seats while others move forward to light candles or post prayers? Are they subject to a participant's 'I wonder why they're not taking part'?

Creative response avoids embarrassment. But does it have the necessary challenge to personal pride that going to the mercy seat does? Does it offer self-denial? Does it require us to humble ourselves under God's mighty hand?

Some years ago I qualified as a cricket coach. During the course our instructor hammered home the importance of body language. It is difficult to get people excited in what you are saying if you speak with your arms folded or with hand in pockets, you don't make eye contact with your audience and you loll with your body weight on one hip. Body language, which is reckoned to account for 55 per cent of one person's communication to another, is an important part of sports psychology and is known to affect an athlete's (and opponent's) performance. What about the body language of Salvationist worship?

Salvationists are well known for one particular aspect of body language – clapping. There are others. There is the Army salute, which also sometimes accompanies the singing of the chorus 'Praise God,

I'm Saved!' There are action choruses, ranging from 'Wide, Wide as the Ocean' to 'If You're Happy And You Know It'. There is dance – with or without timbrel in hand. There is the raising of hands in singing or prayer. Then, there is kneeling – body language for humility and penitence.

In the film *Indiana Jones and the Last Crusade*, the eponymous hero is searching for the Holy Grail. To reach his goal he must gain entry to an inner chamber of a cave, which is defended by a number of deadly booby traps. To gain safe passage he must interpret a set of ancient riddles. To add to the pressure, his father lies dying and only the Holy Grail can save him.

The clue for safely negotiating the first booby trap is: 'Only the penitent man will pass.'. As Indy climbs the stairs towards the prize, he repeats the words again and again, trying to fathom precisely what they mean. There is no margin for error. No second chance. One false step and he's dead. So is his dad. Suddenly it dawns on him. 'Only the penitent man will pass,' he mumbles. 'The penitent man is humbled before God. He kneels.' As he drops to his kneels, a revolving blade – in true Hollywood style – springs from the rock at head height. The penitential Jones is safe.

Kneeling before God is a profound message – to God, to others and to ourselves. By kneeling we make ourselves small. When kneeling it is difficult to run away. Through kneeling we make ourselves vulnerable. Kneeling is the posture of penitence; the language of humility.

Does the body language of hands-on creative response say as much as the act of kneeling at the mercy seat?

Creative response offers safety in numbers but safety in numbers can also mean being lost in a crowd. When responding as part of a larger group, how easy is it to ask for, or receive, personal prayer? Does a collective creative response mean as much to an individual as kneeling at the mercy seat might? To what extent does creative response offer a literal as well as metaphorical step of faith towards personal commitment to Christ? To what extent do people regard those occasions when they have made a creative response as milestone events in their personal journey with God? Does seeing a collective creative response have the same effect on a congregation as the sight and sounds of someone praying at the mercy seat?

Creative response can help the preacher feel effective and valued. Preachers work at their best, much like the rest of us, when they feel effective and valued. But preaching has its pitfalls. 'The care of what men think or say', as one of Herbert Booth's songs puts it, is a big one. So are popularity, compromise and settling for second best. So is believing that a response to the sermon depends on the performance and creativity of the preacher. It doesn't. The mysteriously moving God often acts in spite of – and not because of – a preacher.

Here is one occasion I've witnessed when I've learned that lesson. During one Sunday morning meeting a new soldier was to be sworn in. The officer called for the soldier to make her way to the platform and for the colour-sergeant to join them. In the process of positioning himself behind the officer and soldier, the colour-sergeant hit the suspended fluorescent light fitting with the top of the flag, with much giggling from the younger members of the congregation. The light continued to sway through the entire ceremony.

At the conclusion of the ceremony, promises made, the officer, seemingly too keen to greet the new soldier with a kiss, omitted to commit the Army's newest soldier to God in prayer and dismissed her back to her seat. Later, the officer falteringly preached one of those hard-to-remember sermons before inviting people to respond to God at the mercy seat during the singing of the next song. As the congregation turned to the announced song, the pianist started to play the wrong tune. The officer stopped and corrected the pianist. Once the singing eventually started, four people made their way to the mercy seat.

Sometimes, all God is waiting for is for a preacher to give an invitation.

God requires preachers to be faithful. Their responsibility is to preach the word God has given them. It is then God's responsibility by his Holy Spirit to quicken hearers into response. There is a time for a preacher to stop and to let God do the talking.

166

If, though, a preacher sees a healthy creative response week after week, will there be a temptation to be satisfied, to continue getting as many people involved as possible? Will it be about numbers? Will there be a temptation not to challenge the congregation at a deeper level of commitment to God? Will the response be the focus rather than the message?

Ian Woodgate writes:

'The mercy seat is a living reality. It is the fact that the presence of God is among us. Just as in a Communion service worshippers are invited forward to respond to God, so we invite people to come forward to feed on him. For some people, the mercy seat as a space to be, reflect, pray and reach out to God is essential. For others, it is not so easy.

'In our creativity it may well be that, following the teaching from God's word, we give people an opportunity to seal what they have heard, and to take from their response something which remains firmly a part of them – not just the beauty of praying before God – but something they can see, hold, keep close: a physical reminder that they are accountable to God for what he revealed to them that day.

'If we are seeking simply to "get the people there" and offer them free goodies, then we have lost the focus on what the opportunity to invite people to respond to God is all about. That is the danger.

'Our prayer and focus needs continually to be that God's Spirit will stir his people and prompt them to make those important decisions and responses that will mark and transform their lives.'

The biggest question, as I see it, is: What is the purpose of non-mercy- seat responses? Is it a case of any response being better than no response? And is response the same as commitment?

In 2009 I carried out a poll of UKT divisional commanders. Unanimously, they said that when they visit corps for the annual inspection they ask to see the seekers register, the book which not only records mercy-seat usage, but also subsequent follow-up visits.

Mercy-seat use speaks of commitment: a biblical commitment by God to meet with his people, a commitment to God by the person who prays there and commitment by the corps officer to provide or arrange appropriate aftercare for that person.

From my personal observations of creative response, while the element of participation is high the element of commitment is less obvious. Creative response does not require records of responders to be kept. There is no formal accountability and that, I suggest, is a weakness.

If corps and meeting leaders want to move away from using the mercy seat in preference for what some people might consider less-threatening or more-inclusive responses, that may be just another step in the evolutionary story from the shriving pew (of which more in the next chapter) to the anxious seat to the mourner's bench to the mercy seat. But before we do away with the mercy seat, I suggest we need to work out exactly what creative responses signify. It is an unavoidable question. Asking people to move to the front, or any other part, of the hall in response to God must mean something, otherwise it is an empty gesture – a meaningless ritual – the antipathy and antithesis of Salvationist worship. Is it enough to be able to say that 'everybody went forward this morning', if nobody knows exactly what the 'going forward' signifies?

Such meaning must not only be clear to regulars. It must be crystalline to first-time visitors.

Allow me to illustrate. I was in a holiness meeting one Sunday morning when, after a sermon based on an Old Testament passage, the officer invited the congregation forward to receive a piece of bread. Two queues duly formed as, from in front of the mercy seat, the officer passed out the bread.

A few weeks later, early for an appointment elsewhere, I slipped into Westminster's Roman Catholic Cathedral, for a few minutes early-morning reflection. The 7 am Mass was reaching its climax. Two queues formed as people went forward to receive bread from the priest in front of the altar.

My question is: While the use of bread in an Army meeting is untypical, would a last-minute, first-time observer have been able to tell the difference between what was happening in the two services.

In 1996 Shaw Clifton presented a paper to the International Spiritual Life Commission on the subject of the sacraments. If the

Army were to re-introduce the sacraments, he argued, careful advance consideration would need to be given to a number of practical and theological questions. He writes:

'For any ritual we embrace or devise, what theology shall we attach to it? What will we tell the Salvationists of the world is the spiritual meaning and significance of it? What will we tell them is happening in the ritual that did not happen and was not available to us before we embraced the ritual?'

According to the *Oxford English Dictionary*, a ritual is 'a prescribed order of performing rites' or 'a procedure regularly followed'. In everyday use, however, the word 'ritual' sometimes has connotations of meaningless or empty repetition.

At the International Spiritual Life Commission the specific ritual under discussion was the observance of Holy Communion and baptism. While Salvationists are more likely to regard mercy-seat use as a spiritual exercise than a ritual, the general point still applies – whatever Salvationists do in worship must have 'spiritual meaning and significance'.

If the 'whatever' is the use of the mercy seat, then we must have a clear theology for it. Likewise if the 'whatever' is the receiving of a piece of bread, lighting a candle or posting a prayer on a prayer wall – or any one of a number of physical responses to God within worship – the now General Clifton's questions are inescapable.

The use of creative response can be helpful but we also need to work out the theology, spiritual meaning and significance of such responses. We must identify what did not happen and what was not available to us before we embraced that response.

By extension, I suggest we will also need to understand what it is that a creative response provides in terms of theology, spiritual meaning and significance that the mercy seat does not.

For UK Territorial Commander Commissioner John Matear, the mercy seat is the focal point of Salvationist worship – the place where people can meet with God. He writes:

'I like John Drane's definition of worship: All that I am, responding to all that God is. I thank God that The Salvation Army has within its worship tradition the opportunity for people to make public response to the Lord at the mercy seat.

'As an officer with the privilege and responsibility of regularly leading worship I always give an invitation and challenge. I believe we should preach for a decision/response and in this context the mercy seat should be focal. A practical aspect of this is that, as Territorial Commander, I am careful to ensure that in all new corps buildings there is a mercy seat that is focal and of adequate proportions within the layout of the worship hall.

'It is an inspiring and challenging truth that, as Dietrich Bonhoeffer says, "God is constantly lapping on the shores of peoples lives." In this context, the invitation and opportunity given in worship to respond at the mercy seat can be the right word at the right time and meeting leaders have the opportunity to be used by God to accomplish his purposes.

'I see no need to come up with alternatives to the mercy seat. Personal response to the Lord's will is at the heart of the mercy seat and when someone meets with the Lord in this way during worship, it has a powerful effect on all concerned.

'There is no doubt in my mind that opportunity to use the mercy seat should be encouraged and taught about. Where it is featured, focal and regularly responded to, then the spiritual climate of the fellowship is healthy. Young people need to see the older generation using the mercy seat as they seek to respond to God in worship with all their heart, soul, mind and spirit.

'I strongly advocate that we promote the use of the mercy seat in our worship. We are the inheritors of a worthy tradition in this regard and if we ignore it – or relegate its use to the personal preference of the meeting leader – I believe we are being unwise and poor stewards of that which is a precious key element in Salvation Army worship and evangelism.'

This raises a vital question: Is a lack of mercy-seat use due – in part or in whole – to a lack of verdict/decision preaching? Is the modern sermon, in an attempt to be all-inclusive and in some corps the one-size-fits-all solitary preachment of the week, failing to focus on the need to make a here-and-now personal commitment to Christ, either for salvation or for holiness? Will there come a time when people will consider themselves saved because they lit a candle or posted a prayer card?

On the subject of commitment, we come to a final consideration. If meeting leaders want to adopt creative response instead of – or even as well as – the mercy seat I suggest they need to work out the all-important questions of decision-making and pastoral follow-up.

How, in the mêlée of many people moving forward to post their written prayer, can someone who wants personal spiritual counsel and corporately focused prayer make that happen? Crucially – there and then – how can someone get saved?

Chapter 17

Refreshed and Fed?

TODAY'S Salvationists use the mercy seat for reasons other than salvation and sanctification. The burning question for some today is whether the mercy seat, generally regarded as a place of grace, has become a means of grace – a sacrament – in the minds of those who use it. Put simply, is the mercy seat the Salvationist's sacrament?

The first problem in trying to get a clear picture on this is that the signals given out are sometimes confusing. Namely, when Salvationists refer to the mercy seat as a sacrament it's not always clear whether they are speaking theologically or metaphorically. And is the same person always speaking theologically or always metaphorically?

The second trouble area is in the reception the signals get. For some people, the mere mention of the word 'sacrament' so stirs the heart that the head can't think straight. At one extreme, there's an overemotional slushiness about sacred things that are too special to allow base reason to approach. At the other, there's the over-defensive 'we're Salvationists, we don't need sacraments thank you very much' stance of the threatened, for whom even metaphorical reference is a betrayal of principles.

Most Protestant denominations observe two sacraments: baptism and Holy Communion. Some include other ceremonies in addition to the sacraments. Baptists, for example, who observe believer's baptism and the Lord's Supper, dedicate their children to God in a way similar to Salvationists. As well as infant baptism, or Christening, and Holy Communion, Anglicans practise confirmation and anointing the sick, although they do not regard them as sacraments.

The official Anglican position is stated in the thirty-nine Articles of Religion of the Church of England, which appear in *The Book of*

Common Prayer. In correspondence, the Rev Professor Richard Burridge, Dean of King's College London, writes:

'The official position distinguishes between the two Dominical sacraments (those "ordained by Christ", ie baptism and the "Supper of the Lord") and the other five (confirmation, confession, ordination, matrimony and extreme unction).'

The Catholic Church (Roman and Anglo) observes seven sacraments: baptism, confirmation, Holy Communion, reconciliation (formerly known as 'confession'), marriage, holy orders and anointing the sick (formerly known as 'extreme unction'). They are regarded as the means – the channels – by which God delivers his grace to a believer.

The Salvation Army's view that all of life is a sacrament and that it is the inner experience which sacraments represent that is essential to salvation and sanctification is well documented elsewhere. In 1998, for example, the International Spiritual Life Commission detailed the relationship between water baptism and enrolment as a Salvation Army soldier.

It is not the intention to re-examine the Salvationist viewpoint on sacraments here. However, there are occasions when someone using an Army 'place of prayer' connects with some of the truths sacraments represent.

Let's look at the seven sacraments:

Baptism

While practice and theology differ throughout the Church, baptism is universally regarded as an initiation rite. In the New Testament, the act of baptism is an outward, public sign that an inner, spiritual change has taken place. Baptism represents a putting aside of the old sinful life and a putting on of a new Spirit-filled character. Baptism symbolises being buried and raised with Christ. It is a mark that a new life – a life as a follower of Christ – has begun.

For Charles Finney the use of the anxious seat has a direct connection with baptism. In *Lectures on Revivals of Religion* he outlines the advantages of the anxious seat as a means through which people can respond to the gospel, then writes:

'The Church has always felt it necessary to have something of this kind to answer this very purpose. In the days of the apostles, baptism answered this purpose. The gospel was preached to the people, and then all those who were willing to be on the side of Christ were called out to be baptised. It held the place that the anxious seat does now as a public manifestation of their determination to be Christians.'

Salvation Army history is full of accounts of people kneeling at a mercy seat roaring drunk, finding the Saviour and then standing up stone-cold sober, reborn by the Spirit of God, and going on to be pillars of the corps. They were known as 'trophies of grace'. For them, and for millions more whose experience has been less dramatic, finding salvation at the mercy seat is the marking of a new beginning – the start of a new life in Christ.

In the Australian *War Cry*, 22 September 1934, Evangeline Booth writes:

'The penitent form is our baptismal font, where the fire of God's Spirit falls upon our soldiers. There the live coal from off his altar consumes their selfishness and sin; their love of ease and of the world; there the sanctifying wave of his blood has drenched from their garments the last remains of sin, separating them from the world, the flesh and the devil.'

It should be noted, however, that – in contrast to some baptismal theology – Salvationists do not believe that the act of kneeling at a mercy seat makes someone a Christian; nor that a person has to kneel at a mercy seat to be saved. Furthermore, baptism is a once-for-all-time experience. While a person's spiritual life might start at the mercy seat, that initial visit is not to be seen as a one-off occasion.

Confirmation

At confirmation, a candidate takes on – or confirms – for themselves the promises made on their behalf by their godparents at baptism. A bishop then prays for the candidate with the laying-on of hands for the confirmation – or infilling – of the Holy Spirit.

The mercy seat is often used as a place to make, confirm or renew promises to God. Cadets sign their Officer's Covenant at the mercy seat before they are commissioned (of which, more later). In many corps,

Junior Soldier Day of Renewal and Commitment Sunday are marked by people confirming promises through signing a form at the mercy seat. At enrolment ceremonies, new junior and senior soldiers sometimes sign their promise card or Soldier's Covenant at the mercy seat.

As the ministry of Brengle demonstrates, the mercy seat is used time and again as a place where people pray to receive God's confirmation – the infilling of the Holy Spirit.

Holy Communion

Again, while there is widespread difference between denominations in the practice and theology of Holy Communion, in essence Communion is a commemoration of the atoning death of Jesus. Anglican and Catholic Eucharist liturgies both contain variations on: 'Lamb of God, you take away the sins of the world, have mercy on us.'

Both liturgies also include a profession of faith (the saying of a creed), a prayer of confession (of which more later) and an opportunity for reconciliation between members of the congregation, through the giving of a 'sign of peace'. All of which is preparation for the going forward to receive the elements of bread (in the Roman Catholic tradition) or bread and wine (in Anglicanism). There then follows a time of solemn reflection and prayer.

The Army love feast, where biscuits and water are shared in a prayerful attitude between those gathered as a symbol that they are of one spirit, is no longer in common use. Any differences or grudges were to be sorted between the parties before they shared a common biscuit and drank water together.

In *The Officer*, September 1895, officers were reminded of the value of love feasts:

'Where sermons, preachments and exhortations have failed to bring that blessed love spirit as it should exist, the simple applications of the Love Feast have, under the blessing of God, brought peace, happiness and healing to many wounded souls and corps.'

Evangeline Booth writes:

'The penitent form is our Communion rail, where the broken links of fellowship are united: where grudge-bearing has been lost, the enemy forgiven, the estranged ones reconciled.

'The penitent form at the foot of the cross of Jesus is the gate at which the sinner, the oppressed, the wicked, have laid down their burdens; the pool where the most base, the most filthy, the most unloved, the most unwanted on earth, the most hungered for in Heaven, have been washed and made clean in the blood flowing from the heart of the Lamb of God.'

The mercy seat is a place of reconciliation. It is a place where people can get right with each other, right with themselves and right with God. Such at-one-ment is possible only through the atonement of Christ, which is the very focus of Holy Communion.

Holy orders

Within Catholicism, the taking of holy orders is regarded as a sacrament. There are three levels of holy orders: bishop, priest and deacon. According to the *Catechism of the Catholic Church*:

'The essential rite of the sacrament of Holy Orders for all three degrees consists in the bishop's imposition of hands on the head of the ordinand and in the bishop's specific consecratory prayer asking God for the outpouring of the Holy Spirit and his gifts proper to the ministry to which the candidate is being ordained.'

Rather than requiring a priestly class, Salvationist doctrine holds to the priesthood of all believers. Nevertheless, it is worth noting how central the mercy seat is on Covenant Day, the day when about-to-be commissioned officers sign their Officer's Covenant.

Correspondence with the present and a number of former training principals of the William Booth College, London, confirms the use of the mercy seat on such occasions.

Training Principal Norman Ord writes:

'The current approach is that there is an expectation for cadets to sign their covenant cards at the mercy seat, insofar as they are invited to come forward to the mercy seat and do so. In the time I have been the training principal, I have not had a situation when someone has not done so. It appears cadets are keen to sign their covenant cards at the mercy seat.'

Mel Jones concurs:

'Everyone signed at the mercy seat. We never had an expectation as such that they would do so, rather it was an assumption.

'One cadet had a baby the day before Covenant Day. As a result, we held a Covenant Day for her in my office on the Saturday with a few cadets and she signed her covenant in my office. It was a lovely occasion.'

Commissioner Robert Street writes:

'There was definitely an expectation that this would be signed at the mercy seat. In the fellowship of the session, it was seen as being at least as sacred an occasion as the public commissioning ceremony itself.

'No one declined to sign. In days leading up to the signing, I had one or two talks with cadets (at their request) about the covenant, as they asked for clarification and wanted to discuss its implications and meaning.

'The undertakings were also seen as a legal requirement in regard to each officer's relationship with the Army.'

The undertakings being seen as a legal requirement raises the question: Is it a legal requirement for an officer to sign an Officer's Covenant?

IHQ Legal and Parliamentary Secretary, Peter Smith, explains:

'The signing of the covenant is not a legal requirement if you mean by that "the law of the land". In the United Kingdom it is not necessary for an individual to sign the covenant in order to be classed as a Minister of Religion. This may be different in other legal jurisdictions.

'However, so far as The Salvation Army "law" in *Orders and Regulations* is concerned, an individual must firstly sign the Soldier's Covenant and then, before they can be commissioned as an officer, they must sign the Officer's Covenant.

'I can find no direct reference in *Orders and Regulations for Officers* to say that the covenant "must" be signed, but it is there by implication because in the undertakings it states "therefore, in addition to the promises made on becoming a soldier and those in the Officer's Covenant, a Salvationist is commissioned and ordained as an officer on condition that the following promises and declarations are made..."'

Although used in at least one division in 1985, since the establishment of the United Kingdom Territory with the Republic of Ireland in 1990 it has become common practice to welcome an incoming corps officer through an installation service. During the ceremony, the meeting leader reminds the new incumbent of their spiritual responsibilities.

There is no definitive set of words for this ceremony, but in general reference is made and promises given regarding the Bible, the flag, pastoral care, the salvation of souls and the mercy seat.

One divisional variation of the ceremony makes no reference to the mercy seat, but the following extracts from different orders of service will give a sense of the centrality of the mercy seat:

Example 1

Leader: Here is the mercy seat, to which sinners are called in repentance, and where believers find a closer communion with God. Here the lost will be saved. Here the disciple will be filled with the Holy Spirit. To this end will you make the mercy seat the focus of your ministry?'

Officers: 'We will.'

Example 2

Officiating Officer: Here is the mercy seat. It has no virtue of its own, but has a prominent place in every place of worship. A mercy seat – a place of meeting with God – may be raised anywhere and at any time – by the kitchen table, at the bedside, in the public house, in the hospital. For the Salvationist all roads lead to the mercy seat, for our service is offered with the hope that all people may meet with God in whose name it is given.

Congregation: The mercy seat is a place where pardon may be claimed, power received, peace may be restored and commitment to service registered. In our citadels this visible way to God is always kept open and may be used at any time as the Holy Spirit leads.

Officiating Officer: Do you promise to ensure that the purpose of the mercy seat to bring men, women and children to meet God, to know him, love him, serve him and seek peace will be the first purpose of your ministry?

Officer: I do.

Example 3

Officiating Officer: I charge you to make the mercy seat the focal point of your ministry. Every task, however menial, should have as its motive, the ultimate salvation of the souls of men. You are appointed to the whole district with a charge to 'Go for souls'. Do you promise to direct your efforts to the saving of souls?

Corps Officer: I do.

Divisional and territorial leaders are similarly installed. In some versions of the ceremony the newly installed officers are invited to kneel at the mercy seat while the meeting leader prays for them. The installation ceremony is also used in other territories around the world.

From being the place where a response to the call to officership is often made, through the place of covenant to the place of renewed ministry focus, the mercy seat is intertwined with the holy calling and sacred outpouring of Salvation Army officership.

Marriage

In the Roman Catholic Church a married couple are, through their love, devotion and faithfulness, ministers to each other of God's grace. They are to help each other advance in holiness and co-operate in God's redemptive plan by raising their children in the faith. They also recognise the presence of God in their union.

Although Salvationist couples would not readily describe themselves as 'ministers of a sacrament', their aspirations for their life together differ little from that of Catholic spouses.

Although not a general practice, at their wedding some Salvationists mark the start of their new relationship by praying at the mercy seat – their first act together as a married couple (after the groom has kissed the bride, of course).

Similarly, for those who in later years renew their wedding vows, the mercy seat is a place for receiving God's blessing and grace.

Anointing the sick

When a Catholic is seriously ill or infirm through old age, they may call on a priest to anoint them with oil and pray for them.

According to the *Catechism of the Catholic Church*:

'The sacrament of Anointing of the Sick has as its purpose the conferral of a special grace on the Christian experiencing the difficulties inherent in the condition of grave illness or old age.'

Practising the scriptural teaching of James 5:14: 'Is any of you sick? He should call the elders of the church to pray over him and anoint him with oil in the name of the Lord' is not the sole preserve of Catholicism. Other denominations – including Orthodox, Anglican, Lutheran, Pentecostal, Charismatic – and some Salvationists anoint the sick and pray for their healing.

Anointing a person with oil at an Army mercy seat in the course of a public meeting is a rare occurrence. The mercy seat, though, is used as a place for prayer for healing – physical, emotional, mental and spiritual – either for the seeker themselves or on behalf of others.

Reconciliation

The sacrament of reconciliation includes a number of elements: repentance, conversion, confession, forgiveness, reconciliation and penance. The aim is to reconcile the penitent sinner with their Maker and with their community – the Church.

In pre-Reformation Catholicism the sacrament was known as penance. The Anglo-Saxon *Ecclesiastical Institutes*, translated from Theodulphus by Abbot Aelfric around AD 1000, explains the procedure:

'In the week immediately before Lent everyone shall go to his confessor and confess his deeds and the confessor shall so shrive him as he then may hear by his deeds what he is to do [by way of penance].'

The idea of 'shriving' is found in 'shrovetide' and 'Shrove Tuesday'. It was a pre-Lenten time of confession in preparation for forty days of prayer and fasting. The *Oxford English Dictionary* defines the verb 'to shrive' as: '(of a priest) hear the confession of, assign penance to, and absolve' and '(of a penitent) submit oneself to a priest for confession etc.'

In what may be the earliest forerunner of the Army mercy seat, this confessing took place at a special pew, known as the shriving pew. In

Princes, Pastors, and People, Susan Doran and Christopher Durston explain:

'Everyone was required to confess at least once a year, and most did so during Lent, immediately behind or in front of the rood screen in the church. There were no closed confessional boxes but some churches had a special faldstool or "shriving pew", where the penitent knelt before the priest in private.'

Confession is not solely the preserve of Catholicism. Anglican priest Richard Burridge writes:

'Private, individual confession has been part of Anglicanism since the Reformation. The Exhortation to Communion in *The Book of Common Prayer* (which was written in 1662, well before the Anglo-Catholic movement came into being) contains the following:

"Dearly beloved, on ——- day next I purpose, through God's assistance, to administer to all such as shall be religiously and devoutly disposed the most comfortable Sacrament of the Body and Blood of Christ; to be by them received in remembrance of his meritorious Cross and Passion; whereby alone we obtain remission of our sins, and are make partakers of the Kingdom of heaven... my duty is to exhort you... to search and examine your own consciences, (and that nor lightly, and after the manner of dissemblers with God; but so) that ye may come holy and clean to such a heavenly Feast, in the marriage-garment required by God in holy Scripture, and be received as worthy partakers of that holy Table.

"The way and means thereto is; First, to examine your lives and conversations by the rule of God's commandments; and whereinsoever ye shall perceive yourselves to have offended, either by will, word, or deed, there to bewail your own sinfulness, and to confess yourselves to Almighty God, with full purpose of amendment of life. And if ye shall perceive your offences to be such as are not only against God, but also against your neighbours; then ye shall reconcile yourselves unto them; being ready to make restitution and satisfaction, according to the uttermost of your powers, for all injuries and wrongs done by you to any other; and being likewise ready to forgive others that have offended you, as ye would have forgiveness of your offences at God's hand: for otherwise the receiving of the holy Communion doth nothing else but increase your damnation...

"And because it is requisite, that no man should come to the holy Communion, but with a full trust in God's mercy, and with a quiet conscience; therefore if there be any of you, who by this means cannot quiet his own conscience herein, but requireth further comfort or counsel, let him come to me, or to some other discreet and learned Minister of God's Word, and open his grief; that by the ministry of God's holy Word he may receive the benefit of absolution, together with ghostly counsel and advice, to the quieting of his conscience, and avoiding of all scruple and doubtfulness."'

'Note,' writes Burridge, 'that this is an invitation to prepare in advance of receiving Communion. It is not a compulsion. An old adage, which I was taught in training for the ministry, is that "All may, none must, some should".

(That Anglican adage will also prove useful as we continue to consider helpful attitudes towards the mercy seat and those who use it. In due course we will return to it.)

In an address to staff officers in 1906, William Booth likened the mercy seat to a confessional when he pointed out:

'Do not millions go to the penitent form when they go (i) To the confessional, with the Catholic priest; (ii) To the confessional in their own pews at the churches; (iii) To the confessionals in their own chambers? They kneel by their beds and confess their sins, and ask God to blot them out.

'The confessional for many Salvationists is the mercy seat. If men sin, they must confess somewhere, or perish; so some confess in one place, and some in another.'

Today's Salvationists need little convincing that the mercy seat is still used as a penitent form. It is a place to confess our sins to God. It is a place to receive the assurance of his forgiveness. It is a place of reconciliation with our Maker. It is a place to make peace with our neighbour. It is a place of conversion.

At the mercy seat, the old Army chorus still rings true:

Here is the place for the lifting of burdens,
Here is the place of freedom from care;
Here is the place where the sinner finds pardon,
Here is the place where God answers prayer.

Chapter 18

A Place of Grace or a Means of Grace?

WE are considering the question: Is the mercy seat the Salvationist's sacrament? In the last chapter I suggested connections between some uses of the mercy seat and the sacraments observed by the majority of Christendom.

In *Mere Theology* Alister McGrath talks about the importance of shared symbols. He writes:

'For a society to have any degree of cohesion, there must be some act in which all can share, which both demonstrates and enhances that unity. The point was developed by Augustine of Hippo in the early fifth century: "In no religion, whether true or false, can people be held together in association, unless they are gathered together with some common share in some visible signs or sacraments."'

One of the 'visible signs' to provide Salvationists with a shared identity is the mercy seat. If, therefore, as the *War Cry* reporter of November 1898 who covered the Founder's farewell before going to the States put it 'the penitent form is the beautiful centre of gravitation round which all the Army's efforts arrange themselves', we need to explore further the nature of our corporate centre of gravity.

From the States, Gary Haupt, in correspondence, writes:

'The mercy seat is used as a physical destination for an invitation. In this the mercy seat offers a tangible target by which a seeking soul can measure progress toward answering a call. It is a physical signal by which a soul settles in to wrestle with God.

'The mercy seat is a physical medium of grace. It becomes an understandable channel through which the seeker perceives that God

185

is working. Although not possessing power itself, it nevertheless represents a contact with God that is known to be a venue at which God's action occurs. It may be similar to the effect created by the use of the rosary. Its power does not lie in its innate characteristics, but in its symbolism.

'The mercy seat is a rallying point for congregational action. It is often used as a place around which corps members may gather for prayer, testimony, mutual support, or even a call to action. In this sense, it is a bit like an ensign, clearly defined, endued with meaning and physically understandable.

'The mercy seat is a representation for the presence of God. To this place the invitation might be given to "meet Jesus", "meet God", "kneel at the feet of Christ" or similar phrases. Whereas we do not use very concrete representations such as statues or icons, we do invoke internal images of Christ by coupling those images to a physical place.'

In the Australian *War Cry*, 22 September 1934, Evangeline Booth describes the centrality of the mercy seat to Salvationist worship and mission:

'Many times I have given thought to the importance and work of the Salvation Army penitent form. I have wondered whether our Salvationists recognise its real value in its relationship to the work, and whether we have come to regard it more lightly than we did a few years back. Realising its inestimable service from the hour of the Army's first stroke against sin, I feel the need to enforce its claims.

'The penitent form is a foundation method of The Salvation Army's work. It is the starting post of the Salvationist. It always has been and always will be. The work done at the penitent form is not an auxiliary – it is the cornerstone. It is not an afterthought. The first breath of the Movement was breathed at the penitent form when the first penitent met his Saviour there.

'It is our first, chief, and most powerful method for fulfilling the God-created purpose of the Organisation. We did not start with a band; we did not start with the uniform, or with poor men's hotels, or slum corps, but we did start with the penitent form in the dark on

Mile End Waste, London, where the Army was born. It is not merely one of the many institutions of the Army; it is one of the vitals that can never, never change, and from which it can never be separated and live.

'Here are some of the uses of the penitent form:

'The penitent form is in one way our altar. No altar is more sacred. It is the altar upon which have been laid the offerings of the soul and service of our people for God and his Kingdom. It is the altar upon which have been laid the sacrifices of widows who have given their daughters; of fathers who have given their sons; upon which have been left the consecrations of men's souls – more precious to God than all the world's gifts.

'The penitent form is our baptismal font, where the fire of God's Spirit falls upon our soldiers. There the live coal from off his altar consumes their selfishness and sin; their love of ease and of the world; there the sanctifying wave of his blood has drenched from their garments the last remains of sin, separating them from the world, the flesh and the devil.

'The penitent form is our Communion rail, where the broken links of fellowship are united: where grudge-bearing has been lost, the enemy forgiven, the estranged ones reconciled.

'The penitent form at the foot of the cross of Jesus is the gate at which the sinner, the oppressed, the wicked, have laid down their burdens; the pool where the most base, the most filthy, the most unloved, the most unwanted on earth, the most hungered for in Heaven, have been washed and made clean in the blood flowing from the heart of the Lamb of God.

'The penitent form is our factory for ammunition. It is here the soldiers have found their zeal; it is here their sword has been re-sharpened; it is here the candidate has found courage to offer for the work; it is here where differences in the home circle have been settled; it is here where the wearing of the uniform is decided.

'The Salvation Army penitent form is the spiritual Waterloo of tens of thousands of souls. It covers all differences. It has made the saved heathen our brother. It has brought to the same level the rich and the poor, for The Salvation Army penitent form is like the love of God. "Whosoever will may come."

'The penitent-form has made us what we are.'

Evangeline paints a broad canvas yet the detail is sharp. The mercy seat is the foundation on which the Army is built and it is the cornerstone upon which all activity is aligned. It is an ammunition factory – a place where weapons are made – and a battleground – a place where weapons are used. Salvationists need not feel ecclesiastically challenged for, according to Evangeline, the mercy seat is the Army's altar, baptismal font and Communion rail.

Some fifty years later, Phil Needham, in *Community in Mission* writes:

'The mercy seat itself is symbolic of any place where a seeker after God comes in prayer. The true mercy seat is of the heart, and the outward act of kneeling at a prayer bench, or any other place, is nothing if not the outward sign of the kneeling soul.'

With talk of symbols and signs, is the question of sacraments in his mind? After all, Evangeline Booth spoke of the mercy seat as 'our baptismal font' and 'our Communion rail'. In personal correspondence, Needham clarifies:

'The phrase "symbolic of any place where a seeker after God comes in prayer" means for me that almost any place can become a mercy seat because where God chooses to speak to us and we are open to respond to him is in fact a mercy-seat setting. The actual mercy seat in a corps hall is therefore only symbolic in the sense that it represents all such places.

'When a Salvationist insists that a person confessing conversion must come to the mercy seat in the hall, then he is treating that mercy seat or ritual as an end in itself and is not understanding that the only aspect of the experience that is decisive is the kneeling of the souls before God in penitence.

'The actual kneeling of the person at our corps mercy seat is therefore only an outward act which points to a deeper experience with wide-ranging implications. As such, it is therefore a truly sacramental act.'

With which of the sacraments, though, does he equate the act of kneeling at a mercy seat?

'I would say,' he writes, 'both adult [believer's] baptism and the Lord's Supper, depending upon the experience that is taking place. When a person kneels at the mercy seat seeking forgiveness of sins and new life in Christ, the act of coming forward, kneeling at the mercy seat, confessing one's sins and then renouncing them, and then rising a new person is equivalent to adult baptism. If, on the other hand, the person comes forward for a subsequent or continuing nurturing/growth experience, the equivalence is the Lord's Supper, which symbolises the faithful's continual "feeding on Christ". And if Salvationists join together in prayer for one another as well as for the world for whom Christ died, then another strong similarity with the Lord's Supper is demonstrated – namely, the celebration of the Body's unity in Christ and their commitment to the world for whom Christ offered up his body.'

Needham is not alone. In my 1994 and 2009 surveys a number of respondents identified the mercy seat as a place of communion (See Appendices A and D for details.)

For Paul du Plessis, kneeling at the mercy seat has close associations with baptism. Addressing the Army's non-sacramental position in *The Officer* in 1983, he argues for a discovery of the truth which the sacramental symbols represent – truths beyond the sacraments. He writes:

'If baptism is particularly the symbol of submission and of death to self and then the rising to new life in Christ, we Salvationists can speak with confidence of that which is beyond the sacrament. The mercy seat (with its perhaps coincidental kneeling and rising) can environ that experience.'

General Wilfred Kitching describes the mercy seat as 'a means of grace exactly suited to the deepest human needs, and in a straight line with instinct and custom throughout our human story'.

We do well to remember, however, that it is flesh-and-blood people rather than theological propositions that are at stake here, people with emotional hungers as well as intellectual needs. People who want to be the best they can be for God. People who want to get the best God has for them.

Starting from the premise by Anglican cleric, Michael Green, that the non-sacramental churches 'are missing something', Lindsay Anderson, in *The Officer* 1981, asks:

'What means of grace have we in the Army to make up the means of grace that others find in Communion? I have come to the conclusion,' he continues, 'that the answer... is to be found in the way we use the mercy seat and in the meaning we give to it... *The Book of Common Prayer* defines a sacrament as "an outward sign of an inward grace, given to us by Christ"... It seems to me that using this definition of sacrament we can indeed look upon the mercy seat as sacramental. What is kneeling at the mercy seat but an outward expression of an inner seeking, a visible sign of a deep spiritual desire?... At the mercy seat we both give to God and receive from his hands. A sacrament indeed!'

Anderson recognises that some will find this view unacceptable. He continues:

'What means have we to facilitate spiritual Communion? The ready answer is the mercy seat, for while some may not find it easy to look upon it as sacramental, many will find it possible to use the place as a means of grace if encouraged to do so... I don't advocate a mechanical trooping out to the front, but no Salvationist should become a stranger to the mercy seat. Certainly if our people would learn to use the mercy seat as a means of grace, as they have need, then much of the hardness found in our corps towards coming forward would disappear.'

He concludes:

'I would hate to give a significance to the mercy seat that it does not hold, nor would I want to say anything that would lead folk to trust in the place instead of in God, so my final remark is this. Whether the mercy seat be the official one in any Army hall or a chair placed in front of it, or a bench put out when an "outside" hall is used for the meeting, it is not so much the place but the *coming* that is important. Let us keep the people coming to God's mercy seat.'

190

If coming to the mercy seat is a particular sacrament, rather than a general sacrament-like thing to do, we all need to be clear exactly what it signifies. As Needham indicates in the use of his phrase, 'depending upon the experience that is taking place', this is not always clear-cut. In trying to tie it down to one or two specific sacraments, the danger is we'll restrict the use of the mercy seat to a few specific categories. Of course, some Salvationists already think there's only one reason why anyone goes to the mercy seat. It's because 'they (the person kneeling) have done something wrong'.

As we have seen in the previous chapter, mercy-seat use contains elements of all seven sacraments. But these do not exhaust the reasons why people kneel at the Army mercy seat.

The mercy seat is certainly sacred. Many have found it helpful, meaningful and even life-changing. The mercy seat is certainly symbolic. The mercy seat is certainly sacramental – an outer sign of an inward reality. (Although, as with baptism and Communion, what you see is not necessarily what you get.) But is the mercy seat a sacrament in the ecclesiastical sense?

One of the attractions of Salvationist worship is that there is no formal liturgy. This isn't to say there's no formal or formulated worship. However, even in the 'low' and the informal sacramental churches the sacraments of baptism and Communion are presented within a liturgical framework. The worship leads up to that point in the service where people take Communion, move towards the font, step into the baptistery or whatever.

Unlike in a Communion service, there is no set time for someone to receive God's grace by kneeling at the mercy seat. In Salvationist worship, while people often kneel in direct response to an invitation during a prayer time towards the end of a meeting, there are other events which may trigger response at other times; the words of a congregational song, the playing of the band or the singing of the songsters. It has even been known for people to kneel at the mercy seat without invitation or emotional encouragement. Sometimes, people use the mercy seat after the benediction has been pronounced.

The writer of *The Sacraments: The Salvationist's Viewpoint* sees this any-time availability as one of the mercy seat's strengths:

'Two of the main values of the Penitent-form are that it is open to all and it is open all the time. There are no embargoes on this man or that, and there are no set times when it can be used. It is provided for all and the provision is ever available.'

In his 1951 book *The Mercy Seat,* William Burrows picks up the right time theme.

'The mercy seat is not a confessional,' he writes. 'A person is not expected to kneel there at certain stated times, though he may kneel there whenever he feels so led of the Spirit.'

Furthermore, sacramental worship generally requires a third party to administer the bread and wine, hear confession, anoint with oil, lay on hands, pour the water, immerse the baptismal candidate and so on. When a person uses the mercy seat, for whatever reason, they do not necessarily need the ministrations of another person. Indeed, sometimes that's the very last thing they need.

Another element in sacramental worship is that some churches restrict access to the sacraments. In some congregations, Communion is offered only to those who have been confirmed. Some go further and insist that only those who have been confirmed in that denomination may receive Communion. Likewise, the Roman Catholic Church does not regard the issuing of Last Rites to a dying Catholic soldier on a battlefield by a non-Catholic padre as of equal worth. In contrast, a Salvation Army mercy seat is open to all, the saved and the unsaved; the first-time worshipper and the stalwart of the corps.

Some denominations see baptism as not only essential to, but also the means of, salvation. They believe that the act of baptism regenerates the candidate (adult or child) and makes them a Christian there and then. In contrast, there is no inherent regenerative power either in the mercy seat or in the act of going forward to a mercy seat. Salvationists want neither to restrict access to the mercy seat, nor invest the wooden bench with the power of access to the Kingdom of God. As William Booth proclaimed at an Exeter Hall meeting on 13 March 1889:

'Neither water, sacraments, church services nor Salvation Army methods will save you without a living, inward change of heart and a living, active faith and communion with God.'

In sacramental worship there is a right time, a right place and a right way. Consider the theatre of the Mass. There is the script – the finely honed liturgy, constructed through centuries of use, with its priestly invocations and corporate responses, sung, chanted or said. There is the climactic sounding of the bell at the precise moment of transubstantiation, when (according to Catholic doctrine) the host is changed into the actual body of Christ. Then there's an all-pervading aroma of incense which focuses the senses on another world. There is the action – making the sign of the cross, bowing of head, genuflecting, clasping hands in prayer, lifting of the host, journeying to the altar, the giving and receiving of the host. Everything has to be just right: right person (only a priest may conduct Mass and only a confirmed Catholic may receive Mass), right time, right place, right way. Salvationist worship, however, even though it has its symbols and cymbals, is built around the principles of anyone, any time, any place, any way.

To the Salvationist, just as any meal can be a commemoration of the Lord's Supper, so any chair, bar stool or park bench can become a mercy seat. Thus using a mercy seat is 'a truly sacramental act', to use Needham's expression, without becoming an ecclesiastical sacrament. But then, Salvationists have long viewed life itself as 'a truly sacramental act'. They recognise, in the words of General Albert Orsborn, that:

> My life must be Christ's broken bread,
> My love his outpoured wine,
> A cup o'erfilled, a table spread
> Beneath his name and sign,
> That other souls, refreshed and fed,
> May share his life through mine.

General Jarl Wahlström confirms the any time, any place aspect of our worship:

'The penitent form is the central point of the hall,' he writes. 'But we believe and teach that God is not confined to any particular locality. The mercy seat may also be a kitchen chair, a hospital bed, a log or a rock at a youth camp, a drum in an open-air meeting.'

General Erik Wickberg agrees:

'I am the first to admit that any chair, any bedside can meet the need for decision. Indeed, the penitent form in itself is not essential. But the practice it has had all round the world for many years now has served as a meeting place with God.'

By way of illustration the General gives his own testimony:

'Though a son of Salvationists, I had at the age of nearly 20 no experience of salvation. I was not a Salvationist and seldom or never attended Salvation Army meetings or any other religious services. For reasons I did not at the time understand, it happened that I opened my old Swedish school Bible at random and there, in the Gospel of St Luke, I read about Jesus saying, "He who is not with me is against me, and he who does not gather with me, scatters." I did not feel this as a word for me and closed my Bible, only to open it again in the same casual way. And, believe it or not, there was the same word.

'I cannot explain it but I found myself praying and suddenly being convinced that Christ was calling me to officership in the Army. This, I can truly say, was the very last thing that could have entered my mind and I tried to put the whole thing out of my mind. But it was so real that I prayed to God, "Anything but this." Finally I got up from my knees and went to tell my parents. My father asked, "Are you saved?" "Yes," I said. "When were you saved?" he asked. My answer was, "A few minutes ago, when Christ met me."

'And this is how it all began. Without penitent form – alone with the living word.'

In sacramental circles, Communion without the elements of bread and wine (or their substitutes) is unthinkable, baptism without water impossible. The Salvationist, however, believes that the truth the mercy seat represents can be experienced, in General Wickberg's words, 'without penitent form – alone with the living word' or, in Brengle's terms, by having a mercy seat in our hearts.

For Robert Sandall, the virtue is not found in the form itself but in the act of the seeker going public:

'The Salvation Army has no altar but that which is spiritual. The custom which has grown up of enclosing a seat at the foot of the platform for use as a penitent form does not imply that it is more sacred than any other seat... The significance of a penitent form is that to kneel at it is a public confession of Christ, which could be made anywhere and in any way with equal efficacy if it were equally public.'

It was the public confession of Christ that headed William Booth's meeting agenda. Nothing should be allowed to get in the way of people finding Christ at the mercy seat. Writing at a time when Salvationist worship did include baptism and Communion, he issued the following statement in 1881:

'There must be no baptismal service that can delude anyone into a vain hope of getting to Heaven without being "born again". There must be no Lord's Supper "administered" by anybody in such a way as to show anything like a priestly superiority of one over another – every saved person being a "priest unto God"... There must never be a sacramental service at the end of a meeting so as to prevent the possibility of inviting sinners to the mercy seat.'

In the words of Robert Lowry's song, Salvationists often ask: 'What can wash away my sin?' then answer: 'Nothing but the blood of Jesus.' Salvationists will want to be clear that neither the mercy seat, nor the act of going to the mercy seat, nor praying at the mercy seat have of themselves any power to change their spiritual condition. There is only one medium that can save and sanctify: there is nothing but the blood of Jesus.

The evangelist Billy Graham was once accused of equating the act of responding to an altar call – or appeal – with salvation. In response, he issued a public statement, quoted by R. Alan Streett in *The Effective Invitation*:

'There's nothing about the mechanics of coming forward that saves anybody's soul. Coming forward is an open acknowledgment and a testimony of an inward experience that you have had with Christ. But this inward experience with Christ, this encounter, is the most important thing.'

Amen to that!

At the 1995 International Leaders' Conference, Ian Cutmore presented separate discussion papers on 'Our Emphasis on the Mercy Seat' and 'The Army's Stance on the Sacraments'. Aware of the relationship between the two aspects of worship, he does not see them in competition. In correspondence, he writes:

'The mercy seat is a sacramental means of grace for many people who use it. I feel the mercy seat as a means of grace stands alone. We must, at the same time, work through our stance on Holy Communion and baptism. We should not offer the mercy seat to our people as an alternative to any other means of grace. Let both the mercy seat and the sacraments stand alone as valid and useful in the spiritual nurture of God's people.'

In its Call to the Mercy Seat, the International Spiritual Life Commission of 1998 describes the mercy seat as a 'means of grace' – a term commonly used to mean 'sacrament':

'We call Salvationists worldwide to recognise the wide understanding of the mercy seat that God has given to the Army; to rejoice that Christ uses this means of grace to confirm his presence; and to ensure that its spiritual benefits are fully explored in every corps and Army centre.'

Called to be God's People, Commissioner Robert Street's collection of, and commentary on, the findings of the International Spiritual Life Commission, includes perhaps the clearest official statement to date regarding the relationship between sacrament and the mercy seat:

'St Augustine offered two famous definitions of "sacrament": "a sign of something sacred" and "a visible sign of an invisible grace". Salvationists do indeed have their own "signs of something sacred" and some of our symbols, such as the flag and the mercy seat, could be described as "visible signs of an invisible grace". More recently Joseph Martos has explained that "any ritual or object, person or place can be considered sacramental if it is taken to be a symbol of something that is sacred or mysterious". By these definitions, ancient and modern, the Army is a sacramental Movement. We do not deny the value of the symbolic in religion.'

In correspondence in 2009, commission member Commissioner Paul du Plessis writes:

'Those of us intimately involved in the setting up of the International Spiritual Life Commission did so recognising a deep longing among Salvationists for a deeper spiritual experience. Some felt that embracing the sacraments might help. My own conviction has remained that when we gather we need to help Salvationists seek after and experience the presence of Christ. It is then that he mediates his grace. While it is one means of grace, the mercy seat should remain a focal point in that quest.'

In a sense the Salvationist can have the best of both worlds. For many people, using the mercy seat is a holy occasion, a time when they sense the presence of God 'in a real way'. In Needham's terms, their use of the mercy seat is a 'sacramental act'. But equally the Salvationist is not robbed of blessing by not routinely kneeling at a particular place at a particular time. (Note, though, that a person robs themself of blessing when, knowing that God is calling them to meet him at the mercy seat, they do not respond.)

As seen in an earlier chapter, Phil Needham says 'the coming forward is only a sign that a search is in progress and conversion is contemplated'. We need that physical sign for ourselves. A sign not only that a search is in progress but that a destination has been reached, a decision made, a corner turned. We can take only so much head knowledge. If we are to be fulfilled in our worship we need to make room for heart experience. Giving intellectual assent is one thing but showing ourselves we mean business with God by going to the mercy seat is something our whole being needs from time to time.

If our use of the mercy seat is to mean anything at all we must be sincere. It cannot be regarded as a ritualistic routine. It dare not become an empty gesture. If, for example, we seek real mercy, we must really mean it. It's right that pride will sometimes get in the way, for a struggle with pride is indicative of our sincerity. The easier we find the journey to the mercy seat, the more lightly we will treat God's mercy. Above all, it is not the act of seeking that counts so much as the attitude of the seeker.

In his discussion with a Samaritan woman about worship, Jesus cuts through age-old, divisive arguments and traditions about acceptable worship depending on externals. Jesus points her beyond the ideas of right time, right place and right people. What counts, he says, is right attitude. 'True worshippers,' he says, 'will worship the Father in spirit and truth, for they are the kind of worshippers the Father seeks. God is spirit, and his worshippers must worship in spirit and in truth' (John 4:23-24).

Because Salvationists are sensitive to spiritual realities, they will not demean those who speak of the mercy seat in sacramental terms. Because they are a pragmatic and adaptable people, they will seek all credible means to present and give opportunity to respond to the gospel. By so doing they will be faithful to the heritage of their forebears and true to those who built the original mercy seat – the Children of Israel.

Chapter 19

The Mercy Seat in The Old Testament

THE Children of Israel were a people on the move. They had been rescued from Egypt and were heading towards the Promised Land. They were also a very careful people. They kept all their most important possessions in a portable safe – the Ark of the Covenant.

Exodus 25:10-22 gives a description of the Ark. It was an acacia wood trunk approximately one metre in length, with gold rings and poles on the side so that it could be easily carried. It was covered by a lid (the Hebrew *kapporeth*) made of pure gold, which was flanked by two golden cherubim whose wings overshadowed the lid. It was here, the Bible records, that God would meet with his people and instruct them (verse 22).

Deuteronomy 10:1-9 also describes Moses making an ark out of acacia wood and depositing the stones of God's commandment within it. This account, however, makes no mention of the construction of the mercy seat.

The word *kapporeth* appears in the Old Testament 27 times, and mainly in those books dealing with the 'orders and regulations' for worship. The other instance is in 1 Chronicles 28:11, where David, having set his heart on having a Temple in Jerusalem, commits the plans to his son Solomon. They include a room to hold the Ark and its golden lid.

William Tyndale, the first to translate much of the Old Testament directly from Hebrew into English, used the term 'mercy seat' whenever the Hebrew *kapporeth* appeared. It was an inspired term because it expressed the connotations and context of the word rather than simply its basic meaning.

More recent translations and paraphrases use a variety of words: 'mercy seat' (*Authorised Version, Revised Standard Version, Revised Authorised Version, New American Standard Bible, New Revised Standard Version*); 'lid' (*Good News Bible*); 'cover' (*Revised English Bible*); 'throne of mercy' (*Jerusalem Bible*); 'place of mercy' (*The Living Bible*) and 'atonement cover' (*New International Version*).

Before looking at the significance of the mercy seat, it is helpful to discover the contents of the Ark as outlined in Hebrews 9:4, as the mercy seat was the place where the spiritual benefits of the contents were received.

Contents

1) The stone tablets of the covenant

In Genesis 17:7, God enters into a contract or covenant with Abraham: 'I will establish my covenant as an everlasting covenant between me and you and your descendants after you for the generations to come, to be your God and the God of your descendants after you.'

Years later God invites Moses to share in a similar agreement: 'I will take you as my own people, and I will be your God' (Exodus 6:7).

God had promised Moses the same as he had promised Abraham – a two-way relationship: 'You will be my people, I shall be your God.' This was a binding agreement on both parties, but it was still only a verbal agreement. It was on Mount Sinai that Moses received the full details of the Covenant. One can imagine his delight, 'We've got it in writing... God really means it... He really will look after us... He really will love us... we've got it in writing!'

Then keep it in a safe place, said God (Exodus 25:21). So the first items in the Ark were the stones of **God's promise** – the full benefits of which were conditional on the Israelites' obedience.

2) The gold jar of manna

As the Children of Israel journeyed towards the Promised Land they had to be refuelled. Dinner, in the form of quails, would fly in. Breakfast was hand-picked honey-flavoured muesli – manna. For 40 years, six days a week, leaving double on Friday mornings (in advance of the

Sabbath), God never failed to feed his people. Moses told Aaron to keep a jar of manna as a sign that God had kept his word (Exodus 16:33). So into the Ark went a jar of manna as a sign of **God's provision**.

3) Aaron's staff that had budded

In Numbers 16, Korah leads a rebellion with 250 leaders against Moses and Aaron: 'You have gone too far!... Why then do you set yourselves above the Lord's assembly?' (verse 3). The outcome of this attempted coup was that God opened up the ground to swallow Korah and the rebels. The next day Moses was told to show the people who is in charge.

In Chapter 17, Moses takes 12 staffs, writes the name of the tribes in turn – for the tribe of Levi he writes Aaron – and puts them in front of the Ark. God said (verse 5), 'The staff belonging to the man I choose will sprout, and I will rid myself of this constant grumbling against you by the Israelites.'

The next day (verse 8) Aaron's staff 'had not only sprouted but had budded, blossomed and produced almonds'. Moses was told to keep it in front of the Ark as a reminder to the rebellious. So the staff which blossomed almonds was kept in the Ark as a reminder of **God's protection** over his chosen representatives.

The Ark of the Covenant contained:

> stones as a sign of God's promise,
> a storage jar as a sign of God's provision,
> and a staff as a sign of God's protection.

However, the contents are but foundational to the cover – the mercy seat. It is at the mercy seat that the benefits of God's promise, provision and protection are received.

Cover

Regarding this pure gold cover the Lord promised three things:

Appearance. In Exodus 25:22 God promises to meet his people at the mercy seat. When God gives the design details of the mercy seat in Exodus 25:17-20, he tells Moses to make the cover of one piece of pure gold. A cherub is to be integrated into either end, their wings forming the back and arms of a chair.

In *The Pentateuch Translated and Explained*, Hirsch points out that they are an integral part of the golden cover, rather than an appendage. They were worked from one piece of gold, not joined together from several pieces. 'The cover itself at its two extremities became the cherubim,' he writes, and goes on to explain that they represent the bearers and protectors of the Law, which is also the task of the Children of Israel. To help them in their mission, God promised that he would reveal himself to them. In Leviticus 16:2 (*AV, RSV*) God says, 'I will appear in the cloud upon the mercy seat.'

To the Psalmist, as to the Children of Israel, the mercy seat was where God sat. In Psalm 99:1 he writes, 'The Lord reigns, let the nations tremble; he sits enthroned between the cherubim, let the earth shake.' In verse 5, the seat of God becomes a stool for God: 'Exalt the Lord our God and worship at his footstool.' In Psalm 132:8 David speaks of finding a suitable resting place for the 'ark of your might'. He records hearing people encouraging each other: 'Let us go to his dwelling-place; let us worship at his footstool' (verse 7).

By the time Solomon built the Temple in Jerusalem as God's appointed resting place for the Ark, it still contained the two stone tablets, but neither the manna nor Aaron's rod (1 Kings 8:9). When the priests had finished installing the Ark into the Holy of Holies, God announced his presence in a cloud. The priests 'could not perform their service because of the cloud, for the glory of the Lord filled his temple' (1 Kings 8:11). Whether in a windswept desert tent with Moses or a gold-encrusted Temple with Solomon, the mercy seat became the sign of God's attendance and appearance. This is where God was.

Atonement. On the Day of Atonement (see Leviticus chapter 16), the High Priest made the annual sin offering for the people. Among other ceremonies, he killed a goat and sprinkled its blood on the mercy seat as a sign that atonement had been made (v 15, 16). As a result of this ceremony, the Israelites were told, 'before the Lord, you will be clean from all your sins' (16:30).

The Hebrew word used here for atonement is *kaphar*. It shares the same root – *kpr* – as *kapporeth*, the word denoting the golden lid of the

Ark. This root carries the idea of covering, as can be seen in the name for the Jewish male skullcap – 'kippah'.

'Kpr' is also found in Yom Kippur – the Day of Atonement. Gentiles today may recall this phrase if they think back to the 1973 war between Egypt and Israel, which started on Yom Kippur.

Judaism later developed and animal sacrifices were replaced by prayer. Today the Jewish perspective is that atonement is based not on sacrifice but on God's grace and human repentance. For the Children of Israel the mercy seat was the place where God forgave the sinner.

Advice. Exodus 25:22 (RSV) says, 'There I will meet with you, and from above the mercy seat... I will speak with you of all that I will give you in commandment for the people of Israel.'

On the day when Moses dedicated the completed tabernacle to God, he entered the tent to speak with God and 'heard the voice speaking to him from above the mercy seat that was upon the ark of the testimony, from between the two cherubim' (Numbers 7:89 RSV). Here was the place where God gave his undivided attention. Here was the place for divine communion. The mercy seat was the place to seek God's advice.

While Moses himself knew that God was not restricted in confining his messages to only one specific place – he had, after all, previously got through to Moses at the burning bush – the mercy seat became a special place of communication.

God's word through Jeremiah is that there will come a time when the Ark of the Covenant (and the mercy seat) will become irrelevant. A bigger truth will dawn. Looking forward to a time when the rebellious, idolatrous Israel has returned to the Lord, he records: '"In those days, when your numbers have increased greatly in the land," declares the Lord, "men will no longer say, 'The ark of the covenant of the Lord.' It will never enter their minds or be remembered; it will not be missed, nor will another one be made. At that time they will call Jerusalem The Throne of the Lord, and all nations will gather in Jerusalem to honour the name of the Lord. No longer will they follow the stubbornness of their evil hearts"' (Jeremiah 3:16, 17).

Maybe part of the reason for the Ark, including the mercy seat, not being built again is the prophetic insistence that God will do a deeper work for his people by writing his will not on stone but in their hearts. Jeremiah writes: '"This is the covenant that I will make with the house of Israel after that time," declares the Lord. "I will put my law in their minds and write it on their hearts. I will be their God, and they will be my people"' (Jeremiah 31:33).

Ezekiel speaks of a restored Israel having a heart of flesh rather than a heart of stone. Passing on God's word he writes: 'I will give you a new heart and put a new spirit in you; I will remove from you your heart of stone and give you a heart of flesh. And I will put my Spirit in you and move you to follow my decrees and be careful to keep my laws' (Ezekiel 36:26, 27). In his vision of a new Temple to replace Solomon's, which had been destroyed when Jerusalem was captured by the Babylonians, Ezekiel lists the dimensions and details of its construction and consecration. But it contains no Ark – no mercy seat.

Ezra's account of the rebuilding and dedication of the new Temple records the reinstatement of vessels looted by King Nebuchadnezzar (Ezra 5:14, 15) but no Ark – no mercy seat. His account of the dedication service includes sacrifices and the observance of Passover and the feast of Unleavened Bread, but no Ark – no mercy seat.

The Old Testament ends with the physical mercy seat no more. The reason being, God wanted to do a new thing. As he did with the Children of Israel and their Ark of the Covenant, he wanted to lead successive generations of his people forward. To do that God would provide a new covenant – and a new mercy seat.

Chapter 20

The Mercy Seat in The New Testament

WHEREAS the Old Testament concludes with no Ark of the Covenant, the last book of the New Testament describes John's vision of the heavenly temple, which includes the Ark: 'Then God's temple in heaven was opened, and within his temple was seen the ark of his covenant' (Revelation 11:19).

For centuries the mystery of the Ark's whereabouts has resulted in a number of theories and investigations. The idea that it had been taken into Egypt formed the backdrop to the blockbusting film *Indiana Jones and the Raiders of the Lost Ark* and its whip-cracking archaeologist hero.

In 1973 real-life archaeologist Leen Ritmeyer became involved with excavations on Jerusalem's Temple Mount. Although he claims to have found the spot where the Ark would have stood in Solomon's Temple, he also says that, under the present circumstances, this is the nearest we will come to finding the original.

In correspondence, he writes:

'I say "under the present circumstances" because I would not rule out the possibility of finding the Ark again. The circumstances under which it could be found, however, entirely depend on God's intentions.'

In February 2008, Professor Tudor Parfitt of the University of London's School of Oriental and African Studies was featured in *Time* magazine. His claim was that a descendant of the Ark had made its way to Africa with its priestly guardians – members of the Lemba tribe of South Africa and Zimbabwe – and that a remnant of an ark – dated to AD 1350 and the oldest wooden object ever found in sub-Saharan Africa – was stored in a museum in Harare.

In correspondence, he writes:

'According to Rabbinic sources there were two Arks – a simple wooden one made by Moses (as the account in Deuteronomy 10 has it) and an ornate golden one made by Bezalel [mentioned in Exodus 31]. The former was the Ark of War, the latter the ceremonial Ark which resided in the Temple in the Holy of Holies. It is a descendant of the Ark of War which I believe I discovered and my book – *The Lost Ark of the Covenant* – traces the history of this ark from Palestine, through Arabia and the Yemen to Africa.'

The only direct New Testament reference to the mercy seat is found in Hebrews 9:5. It is, in Parfitt's terms, the 'ceremonial Ark'. Having described the contents of the Ark of the Covenant, the writer to the Hebrews completes the picture with, 'Above it were the cherubim of glory overshadowing the mercy seat. Of these things we cannot now speak in detail' (*RSV*). This is a shame, for New Testament teaching goes considerably further than this solitary verse.

The New Testament Greek word for mercy seat is '*hilasterion*'. (It is also so used in the Septuagint – a Greek translation of the Old Testament, written between 300-200 BC – in instances such as Exodus 25:18.) It is related to '*hilaskomai*' – 'to propitiate' – and '*hileos*' – 'merciful'. Propitiation signifies the removal of wrath through the offering of a gift. It is related to the idea of appeasement and is the basis of the sacrifices ancient Greeks, Romans and others made to their gods. The idea of propitiating their gods was in the thinking and theology of Jonah's travelling companions as they shared tempest-tossed, Tarshish-bound berths (see Jonah 1). We will consider the New Testament sense of propitiation later.

A glance through various translations of Hebrews 9:5 reveals a similar word-picture gallery to that on view in the Old Testament. *Hilasterion* is translated as 'atonement cover' (*New International Version*); 'throne of mercy' (*Jerusalem Bible*); 'the place where sins were forgiven' (*Good News Bible*); 'place of expiation' (*New English Bible, Revised English Bible*); 'place of mercy' (*Contemporary English Version*) and 'mercy seat' (*Authorised Version, Revised Standard Version, Revised Authorised Version, New American Standard Bible, New Revised Standard Version, The Living Bible, The Message*).

In the Old Testament the mercy seat is where God is, where God forgives and where God meets humankind. In the New Testament these concepts of appearance, atonement and advice are fulfilled in Jesus.

Appearance

The Ark represented God's saving presence. That same presence became incarnate in Jesus. The word 'incarnate' literally means 'into flesh'. In the first chapter of his Gospel, John describes Jesus as the Word: 'In the beginning was the Word, and the Word was with God, and the Word was God' (John 1:1). While Bible scholars tell us there are philosophical concepts involved with the idea of the 'Word' (Greek *logos*), we will confine ourselves to the notion that a word – any word – is the expression of a thought. True, we may not always think before we speak, but the words we speak start off as unexpressed thoughts. We know what it is to 'speak one's mind'. This is precisely what God did. Jesus – the Word – is God speaking his mind. Jesus – the Word – is God letting us know what he thinks, what he feels and what he wants. Jesus – the Word – is God letting us know what he is like.

In order for us to understand fully what was on his mind, God expressed himself in our terms – in human form. As John recognised: 'The Word became flesh and made his dwelling among us' (John 1:14).

In the Old Testament, God promised to appear at the mercy seat (Leviticus 16:2). Jesus is God's promised appearance in the flesh. Paul writes that: 'When the time had fully come, God sent his Son, born of a woman, born under law, to redeem those under law' (Galatians 4:4). In Luke we read how Gabriel appeared to the woman in question – Mary – to tell her the intention of God and the identity of the child: 'The Holy Spirit will come upon you, and the power of the Most High will overshadow you. So the holy one to be born will be called the Son of God' (Luke 1:35). Jesus is the ultimate fulfilment of the virgin-born 'God-with-us' Immanuel of the Old Testament (Isaiah 7:14).

At his baptism, Jesus received confirmation of his identity in the voice from heaven saying: 'You are my Son, whom I love; with you I am well pleased' (Luke 3:22). In his boyhood town of Nazareth, Jesus revealed his true identity as the Messiah when he read from Isaiah 61 in the synagogue one Sabbath (Luke 4:18, 19, 21). During his ensuing ministry he went on to fulfil those words. He demonstrated that he was God appearing in flesh through word and deed. He told his disciples: 'Anyone who has seen me has seen the Father' (John 14:9) and 'I and the Father are one' (John 10:30). The working of miracles (eg, the stilling of the storm, Luke 8:22-25), the healing of the sick (eg, the paralytic, Luke 5:17-26), the casting out of demons (eg, the dumb man, Luke 11:14-26) and the raising of the dead (eg, the widow's son, Luke 7:11-17) as well as being powerful acts in themselves were demonstrations of his authority over the natural world, his authority to forgive sin, his authority over Satan and his authority over death. Authority found only in divinity.

As if to emphasise John's notion of 'flesh' that 'made his dwelling among us', in Philippians 2:5-12, Paul says that Jesus was 'in very nature God' (v 6), 'taking the very nature of a servant' (v 7), 'being made in human likeness' (v 7) and 'found in appearance as a man' (v 8).

Using a different approach to explain the person of Jesus, Paul describes him as 'the image of the invisible God' (Colossians 1:15). The Greek word for image is *eikon*, from which the English 'icon'. Again, while there are philosophical connotations, in the everyday sense an icon is a lifelike picture of a person. A subject expressed in oils, gold leaf or whatever. Secular or religious, icons are looked up to, if not worshipped. An icon is the result of the artist expressing themselves without words. Whereas for John, Jesus the Word is the mind of God, for Paul, Jesus the image is the face of God. For John, Jesus is God expressing himself verbally. For Paul, Jesus is God expressing himself visually. For both of them, Jesus is the appearance of God in a way we can understand.

Atonement

In the Old Testament the mercy seat was the place of atonement. Through his death and resurrection Jesus gave himself as an atonement for the whole world (John 3:16; Acts 4:12). In the New Testament Jesus is portrayed as the priest and the sacrifice – the offerer and the offering.

Jesus as priest

Under the old covenant, God restricted membership of the priesthood to the line of Aaron (Hebrews 5:1, 4). Priesthood was by divine rather than human appointment. The writer to the Hebrews states that Jesus' credentials were similarly established:

'So Christ also did not take upon himself the glory of becoming a high priest. But God said to him, "You are my Son; today I have become your Father." And he says in another place, "You are a priest for ever, in the order of Melchizedek"' (Hebrews 5:5, 6).

The primary role of the priest was to speak to God on the people's behalf – especially about their sin. Priests were required to be holy without being pious. They had to be able to approach God and be approachable to their people. Jesus fulfils both requirements perfectly: 'For we do not have a high priest who is unable to sympathise with our weaknesses, but we have one who has been tempted in every way, just as we are – yet was without sin' (Hebrews 4:15).

People depended on the high priest as a mediator to offer sacrifices on their behalf so their sin would be forgiven by God. When Jesus died he made the ultimate sacrifice, of which the old covenant sacrifices were but shadows: 'For this reason Christ is the mediator of a new covenant, that those who are called may receive the promised eternal inheritance – now that he has died as a ransom to set them free from the sins committed under the first covenant' (Hebrews 9:15).

While Jesus is the high priest of the new covenant as Aaron was of the old, there is one essential difference. Under the old covenant access to the mercy seat was restricted. Even though the high priest enjoyed sole access, he could not go to the mercy seat whenever he liked (Leviticus 16:2). He could enter the Holy of Holies only on one day of the year – the Day of Atonement. Under the new covenant, however, Jesus offers forgiveness to the whoever, whenever.

Jesus as sacrifice

Just as under the old covenant the high priest had to measure up to certain standards, so there were stringent standards as to what was a suitable sacrifice. To cut a very long Law short, the key requirement was that an animal should be 'without blemish'. On the Day of Atonement unblemished animals were sacrificed (Leviticus 16:3, 5).

At Calvary it was, in the words of John the Baptist, 'the Lamb of God, who takes away the sin of the world' (John 1:29). At Calvary the death of a 'without blemish' Jesus secured our eternal redemption, once for all (Hebrews 9:11-14); not by offering the blood of another but by dying in our place for our sins.

In his first letter, John describes Jesus as 'the propitiation for our sins' (1 John 2:2) and says that God 'sent his Son to be the propitiation for our sins (1 John 4:10). In both instances the Greek word is *hilasmos*. In Romans 3:25 Paul describes Jesus 'whom God hath set forth to be a propitiation through faith in his blood' (all *Authorised Version*). Paul uses *hilasterion* for 'propitiation'. Its only other occurrence in the New Testament is in Hebrews 9:5 where it is translated 'mercy seat'. *The Amplified Bible* reads, 'Whom God put forward [before the eyes of all] as a mercy seat and propitiation by His blood'. In effect, Paul is saying 'God gave Jesus as a mercy seat. Here is the place to find peace with God.'

These New Testament writers had no qualms about seeing the offering of Jesus' life as a way of removing divine wrath – the heart of the meaning of propitiation. Today, we are less likely to hear – or preach – a sermon on the wrath of God. Propitiation is a topic that, in general, has fallen out of favour with preachers, their listeners and with Bible translators.

A chronological glance through some of the better-known translations of the past 50 years shows a general linguistic and cultural trend away from the notion of God's wrath being appeased. This is how the *hilasterion* of Romans 3:35 is translated: 'an expiation' (*RSV* 1952), 'the means of expiating sins' (*NEB* 1970), 'the means by which people's sins are forgiven' (*GNB* 1976), 'a sacrifice of atonement' (*NIV* 1978), 'the means of expiating sins' (*REB* 1987), 'a way to forgive sin' (*New Century Version* 1991) and 'God sacrificed Jesus on the altar of the world' (*The Message* 2002). Exceptions include 'propitiation' (*New American Standard Bible* 1971) and 'satisfy God's anger against us' (*New Living Translation* 1998).

Theologians also are disturbed by the idea of a wrath-filled God who needs appeasing through the offering of a gift. But however we view the theological implications of Christ's sacrifice – and the atonement has many facets – the truth remains: by his death Jesus took on himself God's wrath, which humankind deserved as a consequence of breaking the Covenant. Jesus took on himself the consequence of God's wrath – the penalty for our sins – death.

On the Cross, the wrath-bearing, sin-laden, suffering-Servant Jesus became the mercy seat for all humankind, for all of time. Wounded for our transgressions, bruised for our iniquities, chastised so we can know peace with God, by Christ's atoning stripes we are healed.

Advice

In the Old Testament, God promised to speak with and guide his people at the mercy seat (Exodus 25:22). It was here that God guided Moses (Numbers 7:89). Through his ascension Jesus has become our intercessor. There are two aspects to his ministry of intercession – heavenward and earthward.

Jesus speaks for us

During his earthly ministry, Jesus prayed for his disciples, present and future (John 17:6-26). Now ascended, he continues this priestly function of speaking to God on our behalf: 'He entered heaven itself, now to appear for us in God's presence' (Hebrews 9:24). His is a permanent priesthood.

In his first letter, John pictures Jesus as a defence barrister: 'If anybody does sin, we have one who speaks to the Father in our defence – Jesus Christ, the Righteous One' (1 John 2:1). The phrase 'one who speaks in our defence' translates just one Greek word, *parakletos*. The word literally means 'one called alongside to help'. It is the word for a legal adviser, representative or advocate. The general sense is that here is someone who has the qualifications and qualities to speak sympathetically on my behalf so that I will escape the 'guilty' verdict. (And we sometimes wonder how barristers can bring themselves to defend heinous criminals.)

As an offering, Jesus paid the penalty for our sin. As an advocate, Jesus defends those who have put their trust in him. He pleads for them. He points to the fact that he has paid the penalty on their behalf. Consequently, 'he is able to save completely those who come to God through him, because he always lives to intercede for them' (Hebrews 7:25).

Jesus speaks to us

Shortly before his death, Jesus assured his disciples that it was to their advantage that he left them: 'Unless I go away, the Counsellor will not come to you; but if I go, I will send him to you' (John 16:7). The Holy Spirit would not be given until Jesus was dead, buried, raised and ascended. Once again John's word for the Counsellor is *parakletos*. The coming Holy Spirit would advise and guide the disciples just as Jesus had done. He would be *another* Counsellor (John 14:16).

The Holy Spirit is the Christian's in-built guidance system. His job is to educate and equip God's people – telling us what to do and giving us power to do it. Jesus describes the Spirit's role in these terms; the Holy Spirit is a teacher: 'The Counsellor... will teach you all things' (John 14:26); the Holy Spirit is a witness to the identity of Christ: 'When the Counsellor comes... he will testify about me' (John 15:26); the Holy Spirit is a prosecutor of sin: 'He will convict the world of guilt in regard to sin and righteousness and judgment' (John 16:8); the Holy Spirit is a reliable guide as to what is right: 'He will guide you into all truth... he will tell you what is yet to come' (John 16:13); the Holy Spirit is a revealer of God's will: 'He will bring glory to me by taking from what is mine and making it known to you' (John 16:14).

Moses received guidance at the mercy seat. The Christian receives guidance through the Holy Spirit sent by Jesus.

To summarise: Jesus has fulfilled the truths represented by the Old Testament mercy seat. He is the mercy seat of the New Covenant. The cover of the Ark of the Covenant was a representation. Jesus is the reality. Through his life Jesus became the sign of God's appearance; through his death and resurrection Jesus became the means of God's atonement; through his ascension Jesus became the dispenser of God's advice. Our kneeling at a symbolic mercy seat energises this threefold truth of Jesus into reality.

At the mercy seat we see Jesus – the full expression of God; the Word become flesh; God in understandable terms. Here we see Jesus – the face of God.

At the mercy seat we meet Jesus – the sympathetic priest and the spotless Lamb of God. Here we share in the benefits of his once-for-all sacrifice. He died once for all time. He died once for all people. On both counts that includes us. It is at the mercy seat that we can be made at one with God because of Christ's at-one-ment.

At the mercy seat we hear Jesus – the advocate who pleads for us in Heaven, the adviser who guides us while on earth. Here is where Jesus speaks to us. Here is where we can receive his Spirit in greater measure. Here is where we can become more like Jesus. Here is where we become empowered to present him to the world.

Chapter 21

Next?

IN this study we have seen how the pre-Reformation shriving pew became the anxious seat, then the mourners' bench of revivalist preaching and how later it passed into Army hands as the penitent form. We have seen how over the years calling people to make a response to the gospel at the mercy seat has helped millions of people into the Kingdom of God. We have seen that the Army is not the only denomination that uses a mercy seat.

We have seen that, over time, Salvationist perceptions have changed. For the likes of Brengle the mercy seat, or 'penitent form' as he insisted on terming it, was the place to resolve the big two crises – salvation and sanctification.

Successive generations have broadened their view. The 'penitent form', with its connotations of repentance and forgiveness, is today regarded as a more inclusive 'place of prayer'.

However, the low number of seekers recorded in seekers registers suggests that many UK Salvationists do not regard the place of prayer as the place for them. For an emerging group of Salvationists, the mercy seat is seen as one in a range of equally valid responses to God that can be made in worship. For others, however, the mercy seat is so special as to be a sacrament.

Hopefully, along the way the reader has identified their personal positional statement on the mercy seat. What we need to address now is, where next? What place, if any, does the mercy seat have in the 21st-century Salvation Army?

One answer to the last question is deceptively simple: The mercy seat will have the place 21st-century Salvationists want it to have. One lesson from mercy-seat history, I suggest, is that, while the principles of the mercy seat are rooted in ancient Scripture, the practice of mercy-seat use has always been flexible and ever-changing. Each generation has interpreted the mercy seat for its own time and culture.

Terms such as 'mourners' bench', 'anxious seat' and 'penitent form' were products of a generation of preachers who stressed sin, consequence and divine wrath and judgment. Many of the great revivals have been characterised by people's awareness of their own sinfulness and the dual need for repentance and God's forgiveness. Against such a cultural backdrop (which included a shorter life span and high mortality rates), the language of mourning over one's sin, being anxious about one's eternal destiny and repenting of one's wrongdoing connected.

Today's culture is different. The spiritual truths are timeless – we are still sinners, there is still a Heaven and a Hell and God is still Judge – but the cultural mood music has changed. The talk now is more about the love of God, the welcome God will give a prodigal child and the need to live out Christian values in a multicultural society. Linguistically, then, the term 'place of prayer' is arguably a better fit than 'penitent form' or even 'mercy seat'.

(It is not, of course, only Christians who change over time. In Victorian Britain, death was an everyday topic of conversation and sex was tabooed. Today, the reverse is the case.)

In the past, the mercy seat was often roped off. Access was allowed only after the ropes had been hooked back and the meeting leader had declared the mercy seat open for prayer. Today some corps with multi-purpose halls have a mercy seat which needs to be moved into place and assembled before worship.

In the past, Salvationists inscribed their mercy seats with aspirational and inspirational statements such as 'Here bring thy wounded heart' and 'To the uttermost he saves'. Although in 2009 the corps at Bristol Bedminster re-inscribed their mercy seat with 'He can break every fetter', the inscribing of new mercy seats is not generally practised.

For years, the mercy seat (and to a much lesser degree, the holiness table) was the only focus of a post-sermon appeal. Today, as we have discussed, many people physically respond to God in Salvation Army meetings without going to the mercy seat.

These quick, historical comparisons underline the point that how the mercy seat is regarded and used in one generation is not (and should not be) set in stone for the next. In many ways, this comes as no surprise. If Salvationism has one overriding tradition it is that its members – from William Booth's use of music hall tunes and the fakir-robe-wearing Frederick Booth-Tucker to officers preaching PowerPoint sermons and musicians using computer-generated backing tracks – have always adapted their soul-saving methods to the prevailing culture.

The anxious seat was, as we have seen, a device used by revivalist preachers to help people come to and keep a life-changing spiritual decision. It was a response to the prevailing culture. Likewise, the emerging practice of writing Post-it prayers, picking up pebbles and lighting candles is connected to the interactive culture that Sunday worshippers inhabit in the everyday 24/7 world.

Worshippers who press the red button on their TV remote to cast a vote for a talent show, feedback to national newspapers via email, join in blog discussions or share their innermost feelings on social networking sites are used to being – and want to be – part of the action.

In pondering the place of the mercy seat today and in the future, we need to do more than look at current culture and practice. History tells us that they will change. The key to mercy-seat use is in the principles.

I suggest that our consideration of the mercy seat can be collated under three areas: scriptural, spiritual and practical.

Scriptural principles

Our study of the Scriptures clearly shows that the original mercy seat was God's idea. It had no power of its own, yet it was the place – the only place on earth – where God said that he would meet with his people. It was here that he would appear. It was here that they were to atone for their sins. It was from here that he would advise them.

The Old Testament charts the way life changed for the Children of Israel. When they built the first mercy seat they were an itinerant,

217

rural people and kept the Ark of the Covenant in the portable tabernacle. When they became a city-based nation, the Ark resided in the Temple. When they were banished into exile, the Ark disappeared, the whole system of offering sacrifices ceased and the focus switched to the study of God's word.

Today, the Day of Atonement is still the most solemn event in the Jewish calendar. While most Jewish remembrances are accompanied by feasting, *Yom Kippur* is characterised by fasting, repentance and confession of sin. Today, Jews still seek God's advice through prayer and Scripture and they still look for the appearance of God in the form of the Messiah. In other words, while the original mercy seat no longer exists, its principles are still fundamental to Judaism.

For the Salvationist, the mercy seat is a physical reminder of these same scriptural principles – God wants fellowship with humankind, whoever we are and whatever we've done; God has, through Jesus, provided the means for our atonement; God does not leave us to work out life by ourselves. Through his Holy Spirit, he is willing to guide us and empower us.

These scriptural principles are at the heart of the message and mission of The Salvation Army. Without them The Salvation Army has no purpose. The mercy seat is, therefore, a billboard of a mission statement, for the Movement and for each individual Salvationist.

Spiritual principles

Aligned with those scriptural principles, Salvationist worship emphasises certain spiritual principles. Salvationists believe that whosoever will may be saved. We believe that in order to be saved a person must make a personal commitment to Christ. We believe that there is more to being a Christian than being saved; that we are called to an all-embracing holy lifestyle.

The mercy seat is a service station, not a destination. People haven't spiritually arrived just because they have gone to the mercy seat. It is, rather, the place to receive resources – to be filled – for the next leg of the spiritual journey.

Salvationists believe that God can be sought and found by anyone, anywhere, any time, without special ceremony or liturgy. While helpful, it is not necessary to go to the mercy seat in order to be saved or effect any spiritual transaction. When it comes to mercy-seat use – as Richard Burridge, speaking of his Anglican training college's attitude to participants at Holy Communion, reminds us – all may, some should, none must.

Salvationists appreciate the value of special, spiritual journeys. We mark occasions such as dedications, enrolments, covenants, renewals, commissionings and installations. Experience shows that, while it is possible and valid to make a spiritual decision wherever one is seated in a meeting, there is benefit in stepping out, making one's need visible and tracing a special journey to the mercy seat. Among other things, it triggers the congregation to supportive prayer and can later strengthen a resolve to honour that decision.

In his book *God at Work*, Ken Costa, international investment banker and Chairman of Alpha International, tells of the time he had a life-changing decision to make. He writes:

'When I was 32, I found it very difficult to decide whether to ask Fi to marry me. When I prayed, it seemed that God was in the relationship and that he was asking me to take a step of faith, but whenever I reasoned, everything seemed unclear. I rang my father, who told me that a relationship was not a balance sheet, and I would therefore never be able to balance the pros and cons! There were uncertainties that I could not give proper weight to. The idea of commitment frightened me.

'One evening we went to the opera. I still have the programme with most of the print on the cover wiped out from the sweat on my palms. We then went out for dinner. I had asked the waiter to have both Perrier and champagne available. The choice would depend on whether I would pluck up the courage to ask, and of course on what Fi's reply would be.

'She said yes, the champagne arrived and the relief was overwhelming. I felt on top of the world. Almost immediately, however, and for the only time in our marriage, I doubted the decision. The thought of lifelong commitment suddenly dawned on me. It all seemed too much and I wanted to run for cover. Forty-eight hours later, Fi and her family wanted to put an engagement announcement in the newspaper. I baulked at this idea, preferring to keep things a little more flexible! But deep down I knew the decision was right and there was little point in delaying. The announcement went in! This marked a point of no return, making a step of faith into a public act. Immediately afterwards, a huge peace came over me as I realised that God was in that decision. I have never looked back and we are fortunate to have a wonderful marriage.'

Ken's experience has many similarities with making a decision for Christ. There is the weighing up of fors and againsts, the physical discomfort and the uncertainties. Even when a decision has been made – a new relationship formed – there is the possibility of doubts and 'oh, no what have I done?' There are times when we need to turn, in Ken's words, 'a step of faith into a public act'. For many people 'going public' at the mercy seat is the act that seals their private resolve. They receive peace from God. They never look back. They go on to enjoy a lifelong relationship with the Lord.

Salvationists recognise that receiving salvation at the mercy seat is not only powerful imagery that affects those who witness it, but it is also a profound spiritual reality for the person who kneels there. For them the mercy seat becomes the river of grace that divides the new life from the old.

But for that to happen there needs to be clear invitation. Just as generally people don't get married without thought, intent, invitation and acceptance, so they don't just happen into a relationship with Christ. Likewise, holiness isn't something that is automatically absorbed over time or transferred by an osmosis-like process. A relationship with Christ is an outcome of challenge; an acceptance of invitation.

The Salvation Army belongs to the preach-for-a-verdict school of preaching. Historically, our style of preaching prepares the congregation for a make-your-mind-up time. We expect God, through the preacher, to stimulate our intellect, stir our emotions and challenge our will. We also want the opportunity for our inner struggles to be resolved here and now, not merely to go away and think about it.

Salvation preaching is verdict preaching. It is 'Will you take Jesus today?' preaching. It is 'This is what's wrong. Here's how to put it right. Will you do it now?' preaching. If we expect people to kneel at the mercy seat for salvation, they will need to hear verdict preaching.

Salvationists believe that a person can accept Christ's invitation to follow him, in the words of that favourite response song, 'Just as I am'. Sometimes, all that it needs for a person to come as they are and to find peace with God is an invitation.

Practical principles

For a meaningful invitation to be given, considered and responded to three things are required – time, space and attitude.

If a meeting leader holds the scriptural and spiritual principles of the mercy seat to be sound, then in their meeting planning they would do well to allow time for people to reflect and respond without unnecessary pressure. Even if nobody responds at the mercy seat, quiet moments in today's hectic world (and Sunday-hectic corps) are spiritual oases for every worshipper.

A last-minute appeal before the usual meeting closing time is not likely to be met with response. On those occasions when someone does go to the mercy seat two minutes before the meeting 'should' end, those who are wanting to get away to the open-air meeting/catch the bus/cook the dinner/collect the kids from Sunday school are not likely to be in the most prayer-supportful mood.

If time pressure is a regular constraint, then maybe the corps as a whole needs to weigh the importance of the mercy seat in the context of the other usual ingredients of a meeting and prioritise accordingly. If the salvation of the unsaved is the number one priority of that meeting, we may need make sacrifices and do without some of the usual meeting features that make us feel good.

A meeting leader may also need to consider which type of mercy-seat appeal is appropriate to a particular meeting. Where every member of the congregation is already saved, a weekly invitation to accept Christ as Saviour is as meaningful as asking one's spouse of 35 years to 'marry me'. If the relationship is established, it is time to help it grow.

For those corps where Sunday morning is the holiness meeting and Sunday evening the salvation meeting, there may be times when, if the Sunday morning congregation includes unsaved people, it would be more appropriate to preach a salvation message and issue a salvation invitation in the morning meeting.

In their meeting preparation, a meeting leader might invest time in working out who they think might respond and what they want to say in their appeal.

As well as time there is the question of space. If a person is under conviction, the temptation is to find any barrier to prevent them going to the mercy seat. An uncluttered, empty mercy seat works best. A mercy seat laden with flowers and collection plates sends a subliminal message – 'there's no room for you here'.

Ideally, the space in front of the mercy seat is also best left clear. Having to negotiate music stands or band instruments to get to the mercy seat is a disincentive to its use. The person under conviction is feeling bad enough already without having to get close to people or speak to them en route to the mercy seat. It may be that corps may consider the style of seating layout in a move to encourage mercy-seat response.

Mark Sawyer writes about his experience:

'We have found that the mercy seat is used more when it is in the best place. In one corps where my wife and I were corps officers we decided to move the mercy seat from its traditional place (front, middle of the hall underneath the rostrum) to the left-hand side, making a prayer corner.

'This made it so much easier for people to get to. This meant that it was actually easier to get to during the meeting. It was more visible, not crowded by any groups standing in front of it, and far more private. When people knelt there they were not uncomfortably close to people on the platform, nor did they have the leader of the meeting on a microphone speaking above their heads.

'Because space to the side of the platform was more private, it was conducive to making commitments. The number of people using the mercy seat rose dramatically. In the following four years, we recorded more than 700 commitments in the seekers register. One factor was the simple moving of the mercy seat to a better place in the hall. It was still the focal point of worship and with the way the hall was designed, it still looked very central to all that took place.

'As visiting speakers, at corps where there is a portable mercy seat we sometimes ask if we can move it to where it will be most accessible and private. On every occasion we have done so, the mercy seat has been used. While this is just one factor, I think it is something meeting leaders and corps officers should think more seriously about.'

Accessibility also extends to a person's physical mobility and agility. Some people don't respond at the mercy seat, even though they want to, because they feel they should kneel but physically cannot. While, as we have seen, the Disability Discrimination Act covers the relatively few newly built or refurbished corps in the UK, doesn't every corps want to make it possible for everyone who wants to use the mercy seat to do so?

In some corps, the answer might be to make physical changes to the mercy seat. In all corps a solution could be for it to become common practice for people (even occasionally those who can kneel) to stand at, or even to sit on, the mercy seat.

For a congregation to accept someone sitting on the mercy seat might well need something of a sea change in attitude. (At one corps at which I was teaching about the mercy seat, I made as if to sit on their highly polished mercy seat. As I lowered myself, the sharp intake of breath from some of the songsters spoke volumes.)

By contrast, at another corps I have seen a corps officer sit on the mercy seat and invite the congregation to do likewise. Three people did.

If anything determines the future of the mercy seat it is attitude. We reap what we sow. A positive, focused attitude towards the mercy seat will likely result in regular meaningful use. A take-it-or-leave-it approach – from preacher or congregation – usually leads to people leaving it.

When an appeal comes across as unconvincing or as an afterthought, the preacher's attitude shows through in the way that they say it. When a person feels that they can't go to the mercy seat because they sense (from past experience or present perception) that they'll be criticised or judged by others in the congregation, then that corps will reap what it has sown.

If Salvationists are unconvinced of the mercy-seat principles that have been a hallmark of our worship and evangelism, then they will need to come up with other God-blessed methods of spiritual response. For if our investigation of the mercy seat has told us anything, it is that humans are built to respond. The human psyche reaches out to mystery. The human intellect reaches out for understanding. The human spirit reaches out for God.

It is the divinely ordained mission of The Salvation Army to tell people that God will meet them where they are, that he offers them the gift of eternal life and that he will be their constant companion in this life and the next. It is a characteristic – a distinctive – of Salvationist worship to invite people to respond to God – to meet him and be transformed by him here and now.

The practice of mercy-seat use has changed, is changing and will change. The mercy seat's future lies in the following of the scriptural, spiritual and practical principles of the mercy seat. So, too, does the future of The Salvation Army.

Appendix A

2009 Mercy Seat Survey

TO gain a current picture of how others viewed the mercy seat, I enlisted the help of fellow Salvationists. On 21 February 2009, an article and survey form appeared in *Salvationist*. An online survey form was also posted on the UK territorial website and circulated via the Corps Officers' extranet. A letter inviting mercy-seat details was also placed in *The Officer*.

As well as using the same questions as in the 1994 survey, I also added a question about a reluctance to use the mercy seat. The results of the 1994 survey appear in Appendix D for comparison.

My aims were:
To update the data compiled in the 1994 territory-wide survey.
To investigate possible changes in actions and attitudes that may have happened in the intervening 15 years.
To investigate the area of mercy-seat use reluctance, arising from the 1994 survey.

RESPONSE
1. A total of 180 responses were received.
2. Not all forms were complete in every detail.
3. Each of the 18 divisions of the UK Territory as at 21 February 2009 is represented in the responses.
4. Inscription details were received in respect of 327 (46%) of the territory's 709 corps, outreach centres and plants.

FINDINGS
All findings are based on corps in existence on 21 February 2009.

1. Mercy seat inscription by corps.

Data is now available for 327 corps. This compares with 283 corps in 1994.

117 (35%) mercy seats have inscriptions. 210 (65%) have no inscription. In 1994 the relative percentages were 32 and 68. Inscription details for individual corps are in Appendix B, which includes inscriptions recorded in the 1994 survey from corps extant in February 2009.

For comparison, 1994 inscriptions are in Appendix E.

2. Style of wording.

There are 49 styles of wording in use. This is the same number as in 1994. Thomas Burfitt-Williams (THQ Property Department) points out that for halls rebuilt or refurbished since 1994, no corps has ordered a newly inscribed mercy seat.

As a number of corps with mercy-seat inscriptions recorded in 1994 have since closed, the fact that the number reported has stayed the same is more likely to be due to the fact that additional corps were reported in 2009. It is not due to a revival of adding inscriptions to mercy seats.

In the summer of 2009 Bristol Bedminster, after some years of having no inscription, inscribed their mercy seat with the old inscription of 'He Can Break Every Fetter'. The reason given was because 'corps folk felt something was missing'. To date, there has been no discernable increase in mercy-seat use since the new inscription.

The most common inscriptions are: 'Jesus Saves', 'To The Uttermost He Saves' and variants of 'Pardon Peace Power Purity'.

The overwhelming majority of inscriptions relate to salvation. If inscription describes perception, then the mercy seat was primarily seen by those responsible for the inscriptions as a place for salvation.

Frequency of style of wording is in Appendix C. It includes wording recorded in the 1994 survey from corps which still existed in February 2009. For comparison, the frequency of 1994 inscriptions is in Appendix F.

3. Have you ever used or seen others use the holiness table as a focal point for public decision?

145 respondents answered this question.

Yes 49%. No 51%

The near 50:50 divide is in sharp contrast to the respective 1994 figures of 31% and 69%.

Reasons given for using the table include:

An alternative to the mercy seat for those who cannot kneel

An overflow of the mercy seat when it is full

The reception of special collections, such as altar services and of prayer cards

A place of focus on special occasions such as Easter, Whitsun and Commitment Sunday

A place to go when invited to seek and receive the 'blessing of holiness'

A place of prayer and commitment

A place for flowers and the collection plates

Selected responses:

'We use it all the time. We have a cross on the holiness table, so it might be the cross rather than the table that people respond to.'

'We use it regularly and sometimes put a chair next to the holiness table for anyone who needs special prayer to sit on.'

'Very often they stand at the holiness table to signify their public commitment.'

'I saw it used in around 1949 when holiness was preached on Sunday mornings.'

'Never heard of the holiness table until I read about it on the armybarmy blog.'

'We have a new holiness table but I'm still not sure what it's for. I've been a soldier for six years.'

It appears that the use of the holiness table is on the increase. The reader must decide how many of these uses constitute 'public decision'.

4. Which term do you use most often: mercy seat, penitent form, both equally, neither (in which case what do you call it?)?

171 respondents answered this question.

The terms in use are as follows: mercy seat 67%, mercy seat and place of prayer 11.7%, mercy seat and penitent form 7.6%, place of prayer 7.0%, penitent form 3.5%, altar 1.2%, nothing 1.2%, mercy seat/penitent form/place of prayer 0.6%.

The two respondents who answered 'nothing' did so because they worship at centres which do not have a physical bench.

In 1994 the percentages were: mercy seat 71%, mercy seat and penitent form 14% place of prayer 14% and penitent form 1%.

It would appear that the use of the term 'penitent form' is not dying out, as some might have supposed given that it is often regarded as an old-fashioned term. It also appears that the use of the non-specific 'place of prayer' is on the increase. More than a quarter (26.3%) of respondents refer either completely or partly to 'place of prayer'.

5. What do you see as the purpose of the mercy seat?
There were 150 responses to this open-ended question. The main perceptions were those of a place of prayer and a focal point to worship.

Keyword incidence: Prayer 63; Meeting with God 25; Commitment 17; Forgiveness 17; Public 17; Communion 14; Decision 13; Focal point 11; Respond 10; Grace 10; Repentance 8; Confession 7; Dedication 6; Thanks 6; Public declaration 4; Sanctification 4; Altar 3.

Selected responses:

'The mercy seat is a visible throne for an invisible God. A multi-sensory aid to focusing thoughts and prayers of an individual and community towards their God and each other.'

'It is the place to make your first "decision" – to ask for forgiveness and give your life to Christ. A place to receive forgiveness and grace whenever feeling called to do so. A place to find help when I cannot cope.'

'A place for communion with God and to receive the prayer support of the corps fellowship.'

'A place to express an holistic and obedient response to the Holy Spirit. Often the depth of response is accompanied by an urge for physical expression such as singing, dancing, raising one's hands, reclining or sitting at this place of spiritual significance. Each serves to express a particular response and releases the whole being to the Holy Spirit. A penitent posture can also signify self-denying, humble obedience.'

'I believe the act of moving forward is helpful to those making a decision and also encourages others to respond to the Spirit's promptings. I also believe it is important for the whole corps to be able to support seekers in prayer.'

'To go to talk with the Lord and to renew my life with him.'

'Moving to the mercy seat helps a person seal the heart decision as there's no going back.'

'A place of response to God, whether penitence, intercession or holiness.'

'It is a place of grace where we can come and meet with God whatever our need.'

'It is appropriate for all spiritual decisions: salvation, holiness, restitution, repentance, responding to the call to officership, reconciliation between corps members, recommitment. It is suitable for young and old, whether kneeling at, sitting at or near or standing before.'

'An opportunity for God to have a personal appointment with us.'

'Whatever purpose the mercy seat had in the old days of the Army, I doubt it has that purpose now.'

'The mercy seat is the meeting place with our Saviour and the lifeblood of the Army, where a person can come publically and claim Christ as their Saviour, as witnessed over the years. It is also the place for bringing all human need as the Holy Spirit leads.'

6. Meeting leaders: Why do you give the invitation to come to the mercy seat?

There were 94 responses. The most common were related to prayer and spiritual growth as Christians.

Keyword incidence: Response to God 24; Prayer 23; Commitment 18; Meet with God 15; Need 7; Salvation 7; Decision 5; Forgiveness 4; Rededication 4; Repentance 3; Strengthen decision 3; Witness 3; Guidance 2; Healing 2; Holiness 2; Submission 2; Thanksgiving 2; Worship; Intercession.

These 19 headings suggest that people are invited to use the mercy seat for many reasons. Even at this, it is not exhaustive.

It should be noted that the top answers of response to God, prayer and commitment also feature among the top of the purpose of the mercy seat question.

It appears the early-day focus of salvation and sanctification associated with the use of the term 'penitent form' is not as strong as it was. It might also be deduced that today's invitation is a more general 'come and respond to God' rather than 'come and be saved' or 'come and claim the blessing of holiness'.

It should also be noted that the mercy seat is fulfilling the need. The main reasons meeting leaders give an invitation – response to God, prayer and commitment – are also what respondents see as the main purposes of the mercy seat.

While two respondents said that they invite response at the mercy seat out of 'tradition', there is overwhelming support for the use of the invitation.

Selected responses:

'We must always preach for response.'

'I always preach for response.'

'I need to give people the opportunity to respond for salvation or holiness.'

'I believe it is important to encourage people to respond to what they have heard.'

'Sometimes you feel that it is necessary to make a public statement about how you feel and this strengthens your closeness with the Lord.'

'For some people making a public decision will help them continue. It also helps the congregation to support with prayer.'

'As a holiness movement, the invitation to kneel at the mercy seat is an important part of our worship.'

'It is a place where people meet with God in a special way, so I give the invitation regularly.'

'There is power in stepping forward in faith for God to meet with you.'

'Coming forward for prayer allows people to feel free and safe.'

'A public confirmation of an inward decision is likely to be firmer and longer lasting.'

'In every meeting people need the chance to make a public decision for God.'

'Because the mercy seat is a place where burdens can be lifted.'

'An invitation might be the thing a person was waiting for.'

While most of the responses refer to inviting people to use the mercy seat in the hall, one retired officer reminds us that God also works outdoors and that sometimes all he requires is for someone to do the inviting:

'I mainly make the invitation because with money pouring in at beach meetings I was conducting, I realised that money was the wrong harvest. In great fear, I promised the Lord that in the many beach meetings to come I would invite people to give themselves to him. There was no difficulty getting a crowd, but only God knows the cost of that first effort. That summer on the promenade 30 people claimed salvation. I have not failed the invitation since.'

7. What do you expect to happen when someone kneels at a mercy seat?

There were 153 responses. The answers divide into two areas: the mercy-seat user and the onlookers. The over-riding expectation is that when someone uses the mercy seat they will meet God there. There is also an expectation that God will in some way change the user's life as a result of that encounter.

Keyword incidence for mercy-seat user: Meet God 43; Change 17; Forgiveness 5; Make commitment 4; Need met 4; Receive a work of grace 3; Get saved 2; Receive healing 2; Repentance 2.

So far as others in that meeting are concerned there is a high expectation that someone, not necessarily the corps officer, will go to the mercy seat and offer to pray with and/or counsel the mercy-seat user. The rest of the congregation is also expected to provide prayer support for that person.

Only three respondents mentioned a follow-up pastoral visit by the corps officer. I suggest this level of response does not reflect the importance of such visits, and wonder if it is an accurate level of expectation.

Keyword incidence for onlookers: Prayer/counselling offered 55; Congregation prayer support 18; Pastoral follow-up 3.

Selected responses:

'After the meeting I will follow up anyone who goes to the mercy seat.'

'At the mercy seat I can become aware of something that might need following up.'

'Anything can happen at the mercy seat. It may be a time spent alone or with support. It may be a simple time of serious quiet prayer and commitment. Very often it is much deeper. The act of going forward is not taken lightly and is often cathartic.'

'God will meet their need. The counsellor will help with good advice. The congregation will pray in support.'

'I don't necessarily expect anything, but I have experienced a mighty moving of the Spirit when I have knelt at the mercy seat.'

'My expectation would be a supportive atmosphere followed by encouragement. Sadly, my experience is one of indifference and irritation from many Salvationists.'

'There will be a new beginning in their life.'

'Sadly, not much. The design of the mercy seat makes it difficult to counsel others, compared with, say, an altar rail.'

'They will meet with God and renew their relationship with him.'

'That they will be truly saved.'

'Long experience suggests that very little, if anything, happens.'

'My grandfather followed an Army band from an open-air meeting in a drunken state. He knelt at the mercy seat and rose sober. I have seen people's lives change in miraculous ways at the mercy seat. I have seen people lay their new-born babies at the mercy seat and others tear up their cigarettes and leave them on the mercy seat.'

8. What does kneeling at the mercy seat signify?

There were 136 responses. Some people focused on the action, some on the attitude of the mercy-seat user.

Among the actions were such phrases as 'meeting with God', 'getting closer to God', 'expressing a need of God's help' and 'making an act of dedication'.

Attitudes included 'repentance', 'humility', 'submission', 'believing', 'reverence' and 'contrite'.

The main themes were those of meeting God, humbling oneself before God, expressing a need and wanting to pray.

The similarity with the keywords for mercy-seat expectation should be noted.

Keyword incidence: Meeting with God 22; Humility 17; Expression of need 16; Commitment/recommitment 15; Prayer 11; Submission 10; Repentance 9; Clean heart/infilling of Holy Spirit 6; Closeness to God 6; Consecration/dedication 6; Obedience 5; Surrender 5; Decision 4; Faith 4; Forgiveness 4; Reverence 4; Bowing 3; Change 3; Help 3; Penitence 3; Response 2; Trust 2; Contrite; Determination; Get right with God; Grow; Intercession; Sincerity; Thanksgiving; Vulnerability.

Selected responses:

'For some, hallelujah, it is still the place where God meets to offer salvation. The significance will forever be that that particular mercy seat was the place where that person was saved. For most Salvationists and friends I believe kneeling at the mercy seat is more of an outward sign of inner renewal, repentance or commitment. For many the significance in kneeling is not only to bring their needs to God but also to seek the support of the congregation who will then pray for them.'

'How much you love the Lord.'

'You are responding to the Lord. You know it doesn't matter who else is around, you need sorting by the Lord for whatever you need.'

'It means I want to be close to God.'

233

'A sign that a person is willing to testify to others that they are trying to get right with God.'

'It means trusting in the Lord to guide me when I need help, also thanking God for something special that has happened to me, such as the birth of a grandchild.'

'It is a declaration that you want to grow in your relationship with Jesus.'

'That people want to change.'

'That there has been a movement of the Holy Spirit in someone's life and a desire to act upon God's leading.'

'The higher authority of God being recognised.'

'That you want to seek mercy or forgiveness, or you want to give yourself to the Lord.'

'That God is working within you.'

'Our willingness to be obedient to God's call on our lives.'

'Submission. Some older Salvationists see going to the mercy seat as the way that a sin is acknowledged and repented, allowing them to go back into uniform.'

'A public act of prayer and personal walk with God in a community of worshippers.'

9. Are there suitable alternatives to the mercy seat?

150 respondents answered this question. 41 people said categorically that there is no suitable alternative to the mercy seat.

Alternatives suggested by the others included using any seat, raising one's hand, standing in one's place and standing at the front of the hall for prayer (with or without the laying-on of hands). The holiness table, a prayer room or prayer stations, the drum, the lighting of candles, the writing of prayers and a cross were also mentioned as ways of responding to God.

At some corps, chairs are provided near the mercy seat for those for whom it is difficult to kneel.

There was a general recognition that any thing, anywhere, can become a mercy seat.

Selected responses:

'Of course, there are alternatives but the historical and physical presence of the mercy seat in such a prominent place in our halls lends itself to ease of invitation at significant times during worship. If, however, counselling becomes protracted, I would be happier to know that there was an appropriate place where the counsellor could take the seeker for further discussion.'

'I firmly believe that any place can be a mercy seat, even a kitchen sink. I vividly remember leading someone to Christ while peeling potatoes.'

'There isn't a suitable alternative. The mercy seat should never be removed.'

'There may be alternatives in some churches but I feel Salvationists should cherish the mercy seat as unique to the Army and Scripture.'

'There is no alternative that conveys everything the mercy seat does.'

'To say that the mercy seat is the only place to meet God is not true, so any alternative is great.'

'An alternative could be anywhere but I firmly believe that within worship the place of response must be central alongside the word of God. I was once told that every word we preach must cross the mercy seat because we are preaching for response.'

'A standard altar rail works much better. I have found that more people make a commitment, or find healing through prayer, while sitting around the tables in our community hall than at the mercy seat.'

'Yes and no. In our ministry we have used various other methods to draw people closer to God. For example, a basin and towel, prayers written by the congregation pinned to a cross and love feasts. But should these methods be used more and the mercy seat less?'

'Other forms of opportunity to respond – lighting of a candle, taking a prayer card or other symbolic item.'

'There should be other ways in which people could make a response, whether that's some other activity such as writing on prayer hands, picking up a bookmark, taking a stone with a cross on it.

However, traditional Salvationists don't always react well to this sort of thing. Newer people will have less baggage. However, somebody told me they won't come to the Army because of this requirement to kneel at the front – it can be seen as too outward.'

'The mercy seat is just one tool. We have also used prayer lines, fire tunnels – creative worship ideas that have helped in response times.'

'We use the mercy seat and other responses such as inviting people to pray with each other where they sit, offering bread, lighting candles, the list is endless. But we never do them without inviting people to kneel and pray at the mercy seat.'

'There is nothing as simple as the mercy seat. In other churches when people are asked to move to the front in response there is not the same atmosphere when people stand around seemingly aimlessly until someone might come and pray with them. The mercy seat can be used in creative ways to make it more accessible, such as a prayer station or placing something on it for people to take away to help them continue responding to God.'

'The mercy seat itself does not have actual importance. The importance is in the use of the place and the significance of that use. To this end, anything can be a mercy seat.'

'Any place, any time but the mercy seat provides a public witness as well as a secret tryst. Knowing that other people have witnessed one's decision provides a strong incentive to remain strong in the face of subsequent temptation.'

10. Why is there sometimes a reluctance to use the mercy seat?
150 respondents answered this question. Reluctance comes mainly from the embarrassment or fear of what other people in the congregation will think of a mercy-seat user. It is recognised that the mercy seat is wrongly perceived as 'the place to go when you've done something wrong'.

There are also practical reasons. These include a lack of privacy, a lack of invitation, poor counselling, the inability to kneel and time constraints.

Respondents say there is a need for better teaching about the mercy seat and its use.

Keyword incidence: Embarrassment 31; Place for wrongdoers 27; Assumption of congregation of wrongdoing 23; Fear 19; No/unclear invitation 9; Lack of teaching 8; Pride 7; Judged 6; Lack of privacy 6; Lengthen meeting 6; Draw attention to self 4; Gossip 3; Lack of use 2.

Selected responses:

'Could it be that the terms "mercy seat" or "penitent form" might give the impression that we only go there if we have committed some terrible sin? The "place of prayer" is somewhere saint and sinner can go.'

'People do not like being perceived as sinners.'

'Seen as irrelevant and outdated perhaps.'

'Because they are having a hard struggle to make a decision.'

'A general lack of wishing to commit to anything.'

'British reserve.'

'Shyness. People not feeling at ease with others looking on.'

'The devil suggests all manner of inconveniences. Insufficient time. A lack of prayerful atmosphere.'

'Embarrassment. Fear of gossip. Feeling it's an interruption to the service. Unwillingness to share with anyone else. Fear that the prayer will be seen as an attention seeker.'

'We have become too performance orientated. Our methods are focused on attractional Christianity. We are out to impress, as a result our spirituality has suffered.'

'Because it is not necessary.'

'Because of the historical baggage that this is where one goes to repent of sin.'

'Some people believe the mercy seat is a one time, one-way ticket and that once they've made an initial commitment it is not needed again.'

'Some people think it is beneath them to use the mercy seat.'

'Older people who call it the penitent form may think you have done something wrong. A need exists for re-education. We don't have this problem in our corps. People just think there's no need to use the mercy seat.'

'It takes courage to move to the mercy seat, in some ways that makes using the mercy seat even more of an important occasion.'

'Some people are put off because they don't want to be recorded in the seekers register. It is not a book I use these days.'

Additional insights

Survey respondents were invited to add general insights and comments. These range from the need to invite people to the mercy seat to not liking flowers being stood on the mercy seat. The following sample responses are an indication of a wide range of thinking about the mercy seat:

'An invitation to use the mercy seat should be made in every meeting. We had a particularly difficult meeting following a promotion to Glory of one of our soldiers. When the invitation was given to stand at the mercy seat almost all the congregation responded.'

'I am very uncomfortable when I see the mercy seat used for dumping things on, a place for children to play or a place to sit.'

'We get hung up about the mercy seat. While it's appropriate to have a focal point where people can go and pray or be saved, this can happen anywhere. I worry that we who reject the sacraments are making the mercy seat into something more than a simple piece of furniture where people can pray.'

'The mercy seat is an old, wonderful idea that should be preserved for use in the modern day.'

'There will always be a need for the mercy seat. Perhaps the name should be spoken about more often.'

'There needs to be more education about the mercy seat. Meeting leaders need to understand that not everybody is familiar with what the mercy seat signifies.'

'The mercy seat is one of the fundamentals of the Army. Don't change the fundamentals, rather help them be relevant in a newer climate.'

'The huge challenge is to work out how to integrate the mercy seat into postmodern, friendly forms of church which don't have formal Sunday services the way corps do. Those of us involved in planting need some insights from other Salvationist planters.'

'Sadly, the mercy seat has been removed from our corps. Sometimes we have a few chairs in a corner near a cross.'

'When I arrived at this corps there was no mercy seat or anything to say this was The Salvation Army. We now have a cross and a mercy seat. People now say it feels like a church and they often use the mercy seat for prayer and rededication. We must never lose sight of the mercy seat.'

'The mercy seat at my home corps is rarely used and people are reluctant to testify. In great need of the mercy seat I went to a corps where it is well used so I could find peace of mind through prayer and support at the mercy seat.'

'It would be useful for there to be regular articles in the Army press on the meaning of the mercy seat and holiness table and for readers to share their experiences.'

'There is a great need for mercy-seat counsellors, and for them to be properly trained.'

'Since forming a ministry team to be available for mercy-seat counselling, more people have used the mercy seat.'

'Used during 24/7 prayer weeks and in an empty hall at the beginning and end of day.'

'Children are much less reticent to use the mercy seat than adults.'

'The mercy seat is central to my Christian expression.'

Bottom Line

Going by mercy-seat inscriptions, in the past the mercy seat has been seen primarily as a place for sinners to receive salvation – a penitent form rather than a mercy seat.

This survey suggests that there is a move from the terms 'penitent form' and 'mercy seat' towards using the term 'place of prayer'. One of the reasons for this may be the fact that 'penitent form' in particular and 'mercy seat' less so have cultural connotations of being 'the place where you go when you've done something wrong'.

When people sense they will be judged or assumed that they've committed a particular sin, they are reluctant to use the mercy seat.

The 2009 survey responses suggest that there is a general understanding between meeting leaders and congregation about the purpose, significance and expectation of the mercy seat and its use.

The 2009 survey suggests that rather than the mercy seat being primarily a place of salvation or sanctification, where the dividing line between the old life and new life is drawn, its primary function is as a place of personal prayer for the believer.

Appendix B

Mercy Seat Inscriptions
By Corps 2009

**(according to 1994 and 2009 mercy seat survey response.
Where there is any difference, the 2009 response has been used.
Corps stated as at February 2009)**

Corps	Inscription
Abergavenny	n
Addlestone	n
Alnwick	n
Alton	n
Andover	n
Ashton-in-Makerfield	n
Attercliffe	To The Uttermost He Saves
Aylesbury	n
Ayr	Pardon Peace
Balham	n
Bargoed	n
Barking	There Is Mercy In Jesus
Barnsley	He Saves To The Uttermost
Barrow-in-Furness	To The Uttermost He Saves
Basildon	n
Basingstoke	n
Bath Temple	Jesus Christ Is Lord
Beccles	Jesus The Name Above All
Bedford Congress Hall	n
Bedworth	Jesus Saves

Belfast Citadel	n
Belfast Sydenham	Jesus Christ Is Lord
Bicester	n
Birkenhead	n
Birmingham Citadel	n
Birmingham Erdington	n
Blackburn	n
Blaydon	n
Bognor Regis	n
Bolton	n
Boscombe	n
Bourne	n
Bradford Idle	n
Branksome	n
Bridgwater	n
Brightlingsea	n
Brighton Bevendean	Jesus Saves
Bristol Bedminster	He Can Break Every Fetter
Bristol Citadel	n
Bristol Easton	n
Bristol Kingswood	n
Bristol Knowle West	God Is Love
Briston	Come Unto Me
Brixham	My Peace I Give You
Bromley	n
Bromsgrove	n
Buckingham	n
Burgess Hill	n
Burton-on-Trent	To The Uttermost He Saves
Bury St Edmunds	n
Camberwell	n
Cambridge	n
Campbeltown	n
Canterbury	n
Cardiff Canton	n

Cardiff Ely	n
Cardiff Grangetown	n
Carlisle Citadel	n
Carshalton	n
Castleford	n
Chalk Farm	n
Chatham	n
Chelmsford	n
Cheltenham	To The Uttermost He Saves
Chesham	n
Chester	n
Chester-le-Street	n
Cirencester	n
Clacton	n
Clapton	n
Clay Cross	n
Clitheroe	n
Clowne	n
Clydebank	n
Colchester	n
Connah's Quay	n
Coventry City	n
Cradley Heath	n
Cramlington	n
Crawley	n
Crewe	n
Crowland	Pardon Peace Purity
Croydon	Deliverance
Cwmbran	n
Darlington	n
Deptford	n
Derby Central	The Promises Of God Are Sure
Dereham	n
Diss	Pardon Peace Purity
Douglas	God Is Love

Downham Market	Repentance
Driffield	At The Cross There's Room
Droitwich Spa	n
Dudley	n
Dundonald	Holiness Unto the Lord
Dunstable	n
Ealing	n
Easington Colliery	n
Eastbourne	n
Eaton Bray	n
Eccles	n
Edinburgh City	n
Edinburgh Gorgie	n
Erskine	n
Exeter	Here Bring Thy Wounded Heart
Fakenham	n
Farcet	n
Feltham	n
Findochty	n
Forestdale	n
Fraserburgh	Jesus Saves
Gainsborough	Grace
Gateshead	n
Gibbonsdown	n
Gillingham	n
Glasgow City Centre	n
Gloucester	n
Gosport	n
Govan	n
Grantham	n
Grimsby	n
Guildford	n
Guisborough	n
Hadleigh (Essex)	n
Hadleigh (Suffolk)	Pardon Peace Power

Halifax	n
Harpenden	n
Hartlepool	n
Hastings Citadel	From The Uttermost To The Uttermost
Haverhill	Peace Pardon Purity
Hedge End	n
Hemel Hempstead	n
Hemsworth	n
Hendon	n
Hereford	n
Hinckley	Ye Must Be Born Again
Horden	n
Horsham	n
Hounslow	Pardon Power Peace Purity
Hove	He Saves To The Uttermost
Hucknall	n
Hull Icehouse	n
Hythe	To The Uttermost He Saves
Inverness	n
Ipswich Bramford Road	Jesus Never Fails
Ipswich Citadel	n
Isle of Wight	n
Ivybridge	n
Kidderminster	n
Kilmarnock	n
Kinlochleven	n
Kirkcaldy	To The Uttermost He Saves
Kirkwall	n
Knottingley	n
L'Islet	n
Larne	Jesus Saves
Launceston	n
Leadgate	n
Leamington Spa	n
Leeds West Hunslet	n

245

Leek	n
Leicester Central	Pardon Peace
Leigh-on-Sea	n
Leighton Buzzard	n
Leytonstone	n
Lincoln	n
Liverpool Walton	n
Lochgelly	To The Uttermost He Saves
Lockerbie	n
Londonderry	He Can Break Every Fetter
Long Eaton	n
Longton	n
Loughborough	n
Lowestoft Citadel	n
Lowestoft South	To The Uttermost He Saves
Luton	n
Maddiston	n
Maesteg	He Will Break Every Fetter
Maidstone	n
Maltby	Jesus Saves
Malvern	n
Mansfield	n
Margate	Jesus
Middlesbrough Citadel	n
Milton Keynes Central	n
Minster	n
Mirfield	n
Mold	Jesus Saves
Morecambe	n
Morriston	n
Motherwell	n
Newbiggin-by-the-Sea	n
Newcastle City Temple	n
Newcastle-under-Lyme	n
Newry	He Can Break Every Fetter

Newton Abbot	Bring Him Thy Sorrow
North Walsham	Jesus Saves
Northampton East	n
Norwich Citadel	Jesus Is Lord
Norwich Mile Cross	n
Notting Hill	n
Nottingham Arnold	n
Nottingham Aspley Green	Place Of Prayer
Nunhead	n
Oakengates	n
Oxford	n
Paignton	n
Paisley	n
Parkhead	n
Penarth	n
Penge	n
Penrith	n
Penzance	n
Peterborough Citadel	n
Peterborough Ortons	n
Pill	Jesus Is Lord
Plumstead	Salvation Full And Free
Plymouth Congress Hall	n
Plymouth Exeter Hall Whitleigh	n
Pontypool	n
Poole	n
Poplar	To The Uttermost He Saves
Portadown	Pardon Peace Purity
Portobello	Jesus Never Fails
Portsmouth Citadel	n
Potton	n
Rayleigh	He Can Break Every Fetter
Reading Central	n
Reading Lower Earley	n

Redhill	To The Uttermost He Saves
Redruth	Boundless Salvation
Regent Hall	n
Rhyl	n
Ripon	n
Rochdale	n
Rock Ferry	The Mercy Seat
Romford	n
Rothwell	n
Royston	Pardon Peace Purity
Rugby	Forgiveness
Rushden	n
Rutherglen	n
Sacriston	n
Saltcoats	Jesus Saves
Scarborough	n
Selby	Pardon Peace Power
Shaw	n
Shepton Mallet	n
Sheringham	Come With Thy Sin
Shildon	n
Shirebrook	n
Shiremoor	n
Shoeburyness	n
Shotton Colliery	n
Shotts	n
Sittingbourne	Jesus Saves And Keeps
Skegness	Pardon Peace Purity
Skewen	Power Pardon Peace
Sleaford	Pardon Peace Power
Smallthorne	n
South Woodham Ferrers	n
Southampton Shirley	Come To Jesus
Southend Citadel	n
Southend Southchurch	n

Southport	n
Southsea	Be Ye Reconciled To God
Southwark	n
Springburn	n
St Albans	Pardon Peace Power
St Mary Cray	n
St Sampson	It Matters To Him About You
Stafford	n
Staines	n
Staple Hill	n
Stapleford	Jesus Saves
Stenhousemuir	n
Stirling	Ye Must Be Born Again
Stockport Heaton Norris	n
Stockton	n
Stratford	Emmanuel
Street	n
Strood	n
Stroud	He Is Able To Save
Sunderland Millfield	n
Sunderland Monkwearmouth	n
Sutton	n
Swadlincote	n
Swanage	n
Swansea	He Will Abundantly Pardon
Swindon Citadel	n
Swindon Gorse Hill	n
Swinton	n
Taunton	n
Teddington	n
Teignmouth	Precious Saviour
Tenby	n
Tewkesbury	n
Thornaby	n

Thornton Heath	Pardon Peace Power Purity
Tiverton	n
Truro	Pardon Peace Power
Tunstall	n
Wakefield	n
Wallasey	n
Wandsworth	n
Watchet	Jesus Will Save You
Waterbeach	Jesus Saves
Wellingborough	n
Welwyn Garden City	Pardon Peace Purity
Weston-super-Mare	n
Whitby	Jesus Saves
Willenhall	n
Winsford	Here Bring Thy Wounded Heart
Woking	n
Wokingham	Jesus Never Fails
Wollaston	n
Wolverhampton	n
Wood Green	n
Woodbridge	n
Woodford	n
Woodhouse	Peace Pardon Purity
Worcester	n
Worksop	n
Worthing	n
Wrexham	n
Yeovil	n
York	n

Mercy Seat Inscriptions With Frequency 2009

At The Cross There's Room
Be Ye Reconciled To God
Boundless Salvation
Bring Him Thy Sorrow
Come To Jesus
Come Unto Jesus
Come With Thy Sin
Deliverance
Emmanuel
Forgiveness
From The Uttermost To The Uttermost
God Is Love (2)
Grace
He Can Break Every Fetter (3)
He Is Able To Save
He Saves To The Uttermost (2)
He Will Abundantly Pardon
He Will Break Every Fetter (2)
Here Bring Thy Wounded Heart (2)
Holiness Unto The Lord
I Bring Thee All
It Matters To Him About You
Jesus
Jesus Christ Is Lord (2)
Jesus Is Lord (2)

Jesus Never Fails (3)
Jesus Saves (11)
Jesus Saves And Keeps
Jesus The Name Above All
Jesus Will Save You
My Peace I Give You
Pardon Peace (2)
Pardon Peace Power (5)
Pardon Peace Power Purity
Pardon Peace Purity (6)
Pardon Power Peace Purity
Peace Pardon Purity (2)
Place Of Prayer
Power Pardon Peace
Precious Saviour
Repentance
Salvation Full And Free
Seek Ye First The Kingdom Of God
Tell It To Jesus
The Mercy Seat
The Promises Of God Are Sure
There Is Mercy In Jesus
To The Uttermost He Saves (10)
Ye Must Be Born Again (2)

Appendix D

1994 Mercy Seat Survey

TO gain a wider picture of how others viewed the mercy seat, I enlisted the help of fellow Salvationists. In February 1994, I sent a survey form to every corps officer in the British Territory via DHQs. A total of 690 forms were sent.

In March 1994 a letter inviting mercy-seat details was placed in *Salvationist* and in *The Officer*.

My aims were:

1. To compile a record of inscriptions on mercy seats from every corps in the territory. (There are no official records.) Allowing for non-responses, respondents were invited to submit mercy-seat inscriptions from corps other than their present appointment. Where a response came from that quoted corps, the response of the incumbent was taken as authoritative and the reported version deleted.

2. To determine whether inscription styles were time and/or area related. In the event it was not possible to determine when many of the corps surveyed were opened. It was not possible to determine when any mercy seat was inscribed. In some cases the inscription had been changed or deleted over the years.

3. To determine the common usage – and thereby perception – of the terms 'mercy seat' and 'penitent form' among contemporary practitioners.

4. To investigate contemporary experience of the use of the holiness table as a place of response.

5. To investigate current perceptions of the mercy seat.

6. To investigate practitioners' expectations of mercy-seat appeals.

7. To investigate alternatives.

RESPONSE

1. Altogether, 215 forms were returned and form the total sample. This represents a 31% response rate from the survey population. According to a spokesman from Gallup, professional pollsters look to the purity of the sample rather than its size to assess its validity as a true indicator of public opinion. Given that response was voluntary, I can only hope the sample is a representative cross-section of officer-opinion. It is interesting to note that street surveys typically draw national inferences from the answers of only 1,000 people.

2. Not all forms were complete in every detail.

3. Some responses were given verbally by the incumbent. The details given were restricted to corps and inscription.

4. Replies were received from each of the 24 divisions of the UK Territory as at 14 February 1994. Highest response was West London with 21, lowest was North West with two.

5. Inscription details were received in respect of 283 (41%) corps in the territory.

FINDINGS

1. Mercy seat inscription by corps.

A total of 90 (32%) mercy seats have inscriptions. 193 (68%) mercy seats have no inscriptions. This means that 2 out of every 3 mercy seats have no inscription. Individual corps inscription details are to be found in Appendix E.

2. Style of wording.

There are 49 styles of wording in use. The most common are: 'To the uttermost he saves', 'Jesus saves' and variants of 'Pardon peace power purity'. Details of inscription frequency are to be found in Appendix F. There are 31 word styles, including the catch-all 'pardon peace power' and its variants, relating directly to salvation. These 31 styles account for 80 of the corps surveyed. If inscription describes perception, then the mercy seat was seen overwhelmingly by those responsible for the inscriptions as a place for salvation.

The following are inscriptions from corps that are now closed, or mercy seats which have been replaced with a new or no inscription, or are in the present young people's hall:

At the cross there's room
Come unto Jesus
Come unto me
Come with thy sin
Faith mighty faith
He can break every fetter
He is able
He will abundantly pardon
Here bring thy wounded heart
His promises are sure
Jesus never fails
Let the children come
Make Jesus your choice
Pardon peace power
Pardon peace power purity
Salvation is full present free
Seek and ye shall find
They that are whole have no need of a physician
To the uttermost
To the uttermost he saves
Underneath are the everlasting arms
Ye must be born again

Two respondents were able to trace the style change over the years. Bolton's inscription in the 1920s was 'Underneath are the everlasting arms'. In the 1930s this became 'To the uttermost he saves'. From the 1940s to 1990 it was 'Pardon peace purity power'. The corps moved into a new hall in 1990 where the mercy seat is blank.

The mercy seat at Bristol Citadel, which is also now blank, has undergone numerous facelifts: 'Ye must be born again' to 'Come with thy sin' to 'Jesus never fails'.

David Blackwell (THQ Property Department) observes, 'In the post-1945 halls, inscriptions were discouraged but individual corps chose inscriptions which divisional commanders agreed.' This is endorsed by the survey. Reports were received from 22 corps which had opened, reopened, or been rebuilt since 1945, only four (18%) of which have inscriptions on the mercy seat.

Since 1990, 11 corps in the survey had either been opened or moved into a new hall. Three (27%) have an inscription. This move away from inscribing the mercy seat is confirmed by the observation of Roland Sewell (THQ Property Department): 'In the 20 or so new halls I have been involved with in the past six years none has a legend, and the designs differ markedly.'

A number of responses came from other parts of the world.

Joan Stevenson recalls her husband making a mercy seat out of old table tops for the training college in Johannesburg, South Africa. It was inscribed, 'Making ceaseless intercession'.

Vera Williamson from New Zealand records the mercy seat in the Catherine Booth Hospital chapel, Nagercoil, India, as 'Come unto me', written in English and Tamil. In the Booth-Tucker hall in Nagercoil the mercy seat read, 'Able to save to the uttermost'.

James Ling says that there are no inscriptions on mercy seats in Hong Kong.

Erling Maeland suggests 'Jesus receives sinners' is a common inscription in Norway.

Alice Joyce records that the inscription at Pittsburgh Temple in 1961 was, 'O come let us bow down, let us kneel before the Lord'.

William Roberts records 'From the uttermost – Jesus saves – to the uttermost' as the words above the mercy seat at the Harbour Light Centre in Detroit, USA.

Leslie Rusher remembers the inscription at his home corps of Brunswick, Melbourne, as 'Jesus is mighty to save'.

Sixty-seven word styles were received in total from all sources.

3. Which term do you use most often?

Mercy seat 71%, penitent form 1%, both equally 14%, place of prayer (respondents' suggested option) 14%.

The following selected comments typify the tangle of terminology:

'I do not like the term "mercy seat" so we always use "the place of prayer".'

'I seldom use either the term "mercy seat" or "penitent form" since it seems that both carry a one-sided connotation. I prefer to talk about our "place of prayer".'

'I wish someone would outlaw the use of the phrase "place of prayer" when referring to the mercy seat. I've even seen a hall where that is the legend emblazoned across the back of the mercy seat. Are people afraid of the traditional title?'

'Americans would prefer "altar" to either "mercy seat" or "penitent form". This is not great theology but it is user-friendly.'

4. Have you ever used or seen others use the holiness table as a focal point for public decision?

Yes 31%. No 69%.

Reasons for using the table include:

To receive holiness rather than salvation

Rededication on Commitment Sunday/New Year's meeting

Placing of commitment cards and altar service gifts

Signing Articles of War/junior soldier's promise

Signing of junior soldier renewal cards

Because the seeker was physically unable to kneel at the mercy seat

When the mercy seat was full

A place of prayer for healing

A place of reconciliation for soldiers who had become estranged from fellow Salvationists

The place around which a love feast is held

5. How do you perceive the mercy seat?

There were 56 responses to this open-ended question. The main perceptions were those of a place of prayer and a focal point to worship. The keyword incidence is as follows: Prayer 13; Focal point 11; Meeting with God 9; Decision 6; Commitment 5; Communion 4; Grace 4; Public declaration 4; Forgiveness 3; Rededication 3; Altar 2; Confession 2.

257

A number of respondents identified a link between the mercy seat and the sacraments, although in doing so did not necessarily express their own theological viewpoint.

'The mercy seat has no merit of its own. However, I feel that we often find having a focal point, a symbol, a tangible to represent the intangible (a sacrament?) to be helpful. For Salvationists the mercy seat can help in this way.'

'The mercy seat provides Salvationists with a tangible expression of response to the Spirit. In a sense it is a substitute for the Communion response.'

'The mercy seat is an integral part of Army worship as much as Communion is to other churches.'

'The mercy seat is the place of special communion with God, although I would have difficulty expanding on that idea. It's the Communion rail in the Salvation Army hall. But any place can become our Communion rail.'

'The mercy seat is a place for receiving God's grace in whatever way one needs it. Although not essential, I believe there is value in open confession of one's need... I believe this open confession can be a powerful experience, possibly compensating for our non-use of sacraments like believers baptism.'

'The mercy seat is a sacrament in Army terms, a place of Holy Communion and baptism.'

'At some corps I have called the morning meeting a "Communion meeting", implying that a specific opportunity would be given for all to kneel at the mercy seat towards the end of the meeting. The only advance notice given to the congregation was when I told them at the start of the meeting. The sermon would end 15 minutes or so before the normal time and music would be played as people came forward. There was no counselling, no audible or formal prayers, just this moving to the place of prayer. One can't do this very often, but whenever we have tried it we have seen a significant response, both in numbers and in changes of heart.'

'I believe the unresolved emotional tensions of our people can be attributed to the fact that we neglect the celebration of the Lord's

Supper. There are those who say that the mercy seat is our means of grace that replaces the Lord's Supper. Whilst I cannot accept this, I do recognise that the reason why some people disrupt a meeting in this way is because they need the outward grace offered through the sacraments. I have never been to a Communion service where someone has short-circuited the proceedings by asking for an immediate urgent Communion before everyone else. But I have been in a number of meetings where people refuse to wait until what I would consider mercy seat appeal time... Whilst I would like to see a "proper time" to come to the mercy seat, ie, when the invitation is given, I am reluctant to say that no one can come while the meeting is in progress, despite the fact the privilege is abused.'

6. What does kneeling at the mercy seat signify?

There were 51 responses. The main themes were those of an act of submission to God, an asking for his help and a request for help from fellow-Christians.

Keyword incidence: Submission 9; Need of God 8; Asking for congregation's help 6; Meeting with God 5; Public declaration 5; Penitence 3; Initial response 2.

Comments included:

'I see no significance in kneeling at the mercy seat. Decisions can be made anywhere. The mercy seat is often the starting point or a ratification point in a decision-making process.'

'Nothing. People should be allowed to use the mercy seat without feeling that they have sinned.'

'The lack of use of the mercy seat in many corps mirrors the reality that many Salvationists never "bend the knee" in prayer.'

7. Why do you give the invitation to come to the mercy seat and what do you expect will happen there?

There were 39 responses. This question had the widest range of answers. The most common was related to receiving holiness and spiritual power to grow as Christians. Rededication, penitence, forgiveness and intercession were the next most frequent.

Keyword incidence: Holiness 6; Rededication 4; Forgiveness 3; Intercession 3; Penitence 3; Guidance 2; Prayer 2; Salvation 2; Thanksgiving 2; Change of heart; Commitment; Deliverance; Healing; Reconciliation; Repentance; Strengthen decision; Worship.

These 17 headings demonstrate the wide range of functions invested in the mercy seat. Even at this, it is not exhaustive. Writes one officer: 'We should encourage people to use the mercy seat to say "Please" and "Thank you" and in particular to ask, "What next?"'

Another observes: 'Children use the mercy seat more than adults.'

'We have to get away from the stigma that the mercy seat is a place where only sinners go. Unfortunately it has lost its meaning as people can be quite cruel to those who use the mercy seat by saying things like, "I wonder what he has done."'

'Kneeling at the mercy seat is sometimes used to gain the ear of a sympathetic counsellor which, while important to the seeker, may not be of a spiritual nature.'

'During the earlier years of my officership the mercy seat had, to some extent, become an end in itself, and was often applied as a "success" rating for an officer. Quantity mattered rather than quality.'

'Sadly, the mercy seat is used very rarely because of embarrassment.'

'Many Salvationists... give the mercy seat a sort of ritual power as the place to go when you've done something wrong or "lost your saved".'

'I think Salvationists perceive it as a place where things can be put right, whatever the reason for them going wrong in the first place.'

'A local officer told me that someone could not attend recruits classes because he had not knelt at the mercy seat.'

'I was locking up the hall after the carol service when Bill returned and asked me what he had to do to join the Army. As it was rather late, I arranged to visit him at home the next day. While I was there, I explained to him the way of salvation and we knelt at his kitchen table, where he gave his life to Christ. The sad thing is that such a conversion was not acceptable to the corps folk. He hadn't knelt at the mercy seat and according to their thinking you couldn't be saved unless you did. Eventually I had to say to Bill, "You'll never be accepted here unless you go out to the front." He did and he was, but I always felt it was sad that custom was considered more important than experience.'

'I wish the rails had never been taken away. I know our halls are multi-purpose but I find it difficult to explain to people in the mother and toddler club that this is a special place and not to be climbed over or sat on to drink tea. I know it has no special merit, but to me it is a special place.'

'To be able to approach the mercy seat without completing an obstacle course would encourage the first-time seeker or at least be less off-putting.'

'The Ark, tablets, cover and cherubim have all vanished, raising no emotion from the people of Israel. My fear is that one day our mercy seat will disappear from our halls without Salvationists raising an eyebrow. This will be because they do not know what it stands for. They will then have to find new places for flowers, collecting plates, band music, tracts and decorations of all sorts which sometimes clutter the mercy seat.'

'I recall the horror of a distressed person telling me that she had been told at the mercy seat that it was not possible to pray for anyone other than oneself there.'

'In almost all corps the mercy seat is regarded as sacred and people are scolded for standing on it, sitting on it or putting cups of tea on it. In one appointment, the mercy seat was merely a bench which was often used as a seat during the week. This we believe is the right attitude.'

'Perhaps being older soldiers they feel they don't need the mercy seat, I don't know. It makes appeals for decisions difficult as the attitude of "I'm all right" is a hard one to break down.'

'Many people refrain from using the mercy seat for fear of someone immediately pouncing on them to give them counsel.'

An officer, describing herself as 'new to the Army', writes: 'I do not think the mercy seat is a good idea. Some of our older people have become immune to invitations to respond.'

8. Are there suitable alternatives to the mercy seat?

There was widespread acknowledgment that methods other than the use of the mercy seat were equally valid. Raising a hand, standing in one's place, standing at the front of the hall either at the holiness table or the mercy seat, pastoral visitation, and the use of a separate room for prayer and counselling, were widely suggested as alternatives.

Sitting on or standing at the mercy seat by those who found kneeling difficult was also suggested.

A few mentioned the practice of calling people forward to be ministered to through the laying on of hands or anointing with oil – for healing, or to receive the infilling of the Holy Spirit.

One respondent suggested: 'The Eucharist is the obvious alternative.'

No one admitted regularly using any of these as alternatives, although one said: 'I stress the need for the mercy seat of the heart.'

The general feeling was that, while there were valid alternatives, none was a better alternative to the mercy seat.

'Kneeling at the mercy seat', according to one respondent, 'puts the decision "on the sleeve" as well as "in the heart".'

'I do not think an alternative is necessary. But the positioning, appearance and comfort could be improved to enable people to use the mercy seat. To be able to approach the mercy seat without having to complete an obstacle course would be less off-putting to the user.'

It was also widely recognised that wherever and however a person seeks God, there needs to be supportive aftercare.

Bottom Line

Going by mercy seat inscriptions, the prayer bench has in the past been seen primarily as a place for sinners to receive salvation – a penitent form rather than a mercy seat.

Judging by the responses from today's practitioners, the prayer bench is now seen as a mercy seat rather than a penitent form. Its primary use is in strengthening the experience of the saints, rather than in facilitating the conversion of the sinner.

Appendix E

Mercy Seat Inscriptions By Corps 1994

Corps	Inscription
Aberdeen Woodside	n
Abergavenny	n
Addlestone	n
Alnwick	n
Alton	n
Andover	n
Ashton-in-Makerfield	n
Ashton-under-Lyne	n
Ayr	Pardon Peace
Balham	n
Bargoed	n
Barking	There Is Mercy In Jesus
Barnsley	He Saves To The Uttermost
Barrow-in-Furness	To The Uttermost He Saves
Basildon	n
Bath Temple	Jesus Christ Is Lord
Belfast Citadel	n
Bicester	n
Birkenhead	n
Birmingham Citadel	n
Birmingham Erdington	n
Birmingham Goodwill	n
Birmingham Sparkhill	n
Blackburn	n
Blaydon	n

Bognor Regis	n
Bolton	n
Boscombe	n
Bourne	n
Boyne	n
Bracknell	n
Bradford Idle	n
Bradford West Bowling	n
Bridgwater	n
Brightlingsea	His Blood Can Make The Vilest Clean
Brighton Bevendean	Jesus Saves
Bristol Bedminster	n
Bristol Citadel	n
Bristol Easton	n
Bristol Horfield	Seek Ye First The Kingdom Of God
Bristol South Goodwill	God Is Love
Brixham	My Peace I Give You
Bromley	n
Bromsgrove	n
Buckingham	n
Burgess Hill	n
Burnley Accrington Road	Come With Thy Sin
Burton-upon-Trent	To The Uttermost He Saves
Bury St Edmunds	n
Bush Hill Park	Pardon Peace Purity
Cambridge	He Can Break Every Fetter
Campbeltown	n
Canterbury	n
Canvey Island	n
Cardiff Ely	n
Carlisle Citadel	n
Carshalton	n
Castleford	n
Cefn Mawr	n
Chalk Farm	n

Chatham	n
Chelmsford	n
Cheltenham	To The Uttermost He Saves
Chester	n
Chester-le-Street	n
Cirencester	n
Clacton	n
Clapham	n
Clay Cross	n
Clitheroe	n
Clowne	You Must Be Born Again
Colchester	n
Connah's Quay	n
Cramlington	n
Crawley	n
Crewe	n
Crowland	Pardon Peace Purity
Croydon Citadel	Deliverance
Cullen	Christ Receiveth Sinners
Cwmbran	n
Deptford	Jesus Saves
Diss	Pardon Peace Purity
Dorking	n
Douglas	God Is Love
Downham Market	Repentance
Driffield	At The Cross There's Room
Droitwich	n
Dudley	n
Dumbarton	Down At The Saviour's Feet Burdens Roll Away, Darkness Turns To Day
Ealing	n
Easington Colliery	n
Eastbourne	n
Eaton Bray	n
Eccles	n

Edinburgh City	n
Erskine	n
Exeter	Here Bring Thy Wounded Heart
Farcet	n
Felling	n
Feltham	n
Findochty	n
Fleetwood	Jesus Saves
Fraserburgh	Jesus Saves
Gainsborough	Grace
Gateshead Citadel	n
Gillingham	n
Glasgow City Centre	n
Gosport	Peace Power Pardon
Govan	n
Grimsby Citadel	He Can Break Every Fetter
Grimsby Victoria	n
Guildford	n
Halifax	n
Hanley	n
Hanwell	n
Harpenden	n
Hartlepool Temple	n
Hastings Citadel	From The Uttermost To The Uttermost
Haverhill	n
Hemel Hempstead	n
Hemsworth	n
Hendon	n
Hinckley	Ye Must Be Born Again
Hollinwood	n
Horden	n
Horsham	n
Hove	He Saves To The Uttermost
Hucknall	n
Hull Icehouse	n

Hythe	To The Uttermost He Saves
Ipswich Bramford Road	Jesus Never Fails
Ipswich Citadel	n
Kidderminster	n
Kingston-upon-Thames	Pardon Peace Power Purity
Kirkcaldy Sinclairtown	To The Uttermost He Saves
Kirkwall	n
Knottingley	n
Launceston	n
Leadgate	n
Leamington Spa	n
Leeds West Hunslet	n
Leek	n
Leicester Central	Pardon Peace
Leigh-on-Sea	n
Leighton Buzzard	n
Leytonstone	n
Lincoln Citadel	n
L'Islet	n
Liverpool Clubmoor	I Bring Thee All
Liverpool Edge Hill	Pardon Peace Power Purity
Liverpool Kensington	n
Liverpool Walton	n
Lochgelly	To The Uttermost He Saves
Lockerbie	n
Londonderry	He Can Break Every Fetter
Long Eaton	n
Longton	n
Loughborough	n
Loughborough Junction	To The Uttermost He Saves
Lower Earley	n
Lowestoft Citadel	n
Lowestoft South	To The Uttermost He Saves
Maesteg	He Will Break Every Fetter
Malvern	n

Manchester Harpurhey	Pardon Peace Power
March	Jesus Saves
Margate	Jesus
Marlow	n
Middlesbrough Citadel	n
Middlesbrough North Ormesby	n
Milton Keynes Central	n
Morriston	n
Motherwell	n
Newbiggin	n
Newcastle Temple	n
Newport IoW	n
Newton Abbot	Bring Him Thy Sorrow
North Walsham	All The Promises Of God Are Sure
Northampton East	n
Norwich Citadel	n
Nottingham Arnold	n
Nottingham Aspley Green	Place Of Prayer
Nottingham Bulwell	n
Oakengates	n
Oldham Lees Road	n
Paisley	n
Parkhead	n
Penarth	n
Penge	Pardon Peace Power
Peterborough Ortons	n
Pollokshaws	Pardon Peace Power
Pontypool	n
Poole	n
Poplar	To The Uttermost He Saves
Portsmouth Citadel	n
Rayleigh	He Can Break Every Fetter
Reading Central	n
Redhill	To The Uttermost He Saves

Redruth	Boundless Salvation
Rhyl	n
Ripon	n
Rock Ferry	The Mercy Seat
Rothwell	n
Royston	Pardon Peace Purity
Rugby	Forgiveness
Runcorn	Salvation Full And Free
Rushden	n
Rutherglen	n
Ryde	Peace Pardon Purity
Sacriston	n
Saltcoats	Jesus Saves
Scarborough	n
Selby	Pardon Peace Power
Sevenoaks	n
Shaw	n
Shepton Mallet	n
Shirebrook	n
Shiremoor	n
Shoeburyness	n
Shotton Colliery	n
Shotts	n
Skegness	Pardon Peace Purity
Skewen	Power Pardon Peace
Smallthorne	n
Somerset Evangelical Unit	n
South Croydon	Boundlesss Salvation
South Woodham Ferrers	n
Southampton Shirley	Come To Jesus
Southend	n
Southport	n
Southsea	Be Ye Reconciled To God
Southwark	n
Springburn	n

St Albans	Pardon Peace Power
St Sampson's	It Matters To Him About You
Stafford	n
Staines	n
Stapleford	Jesus Saves
Staple Hill	n
Stenhousemuir	n
Stirling	n
Stockport Heaton Norris	n
Stockton	n
Stratford	Emmanuel
Street	n
Strood	n
Stroud	He Is Able To Save
Sunderland Millfield	n
Sunderland Monkwearmouth	n
Sutton	n
Swadlincote	n
Swanage	n
Swansea	He Will Abundantly Pardon
Swindon Citadel	n
Teignmouth	Precious Saviour
Tenby	n
Tewkesbury	n
Thornton Heath	Pardon Peace Power Purity
Tiverton	n
Truro	Pardon Peace Power
Tunstall	n
Wadhurst	n
Wakefield	n
Wandsworth	n
Warley	n
Watchet	Jesus Will Save You
Waterbeach	Jesus Saves

Wealdstone	Pardon Power Peace
Welwyn Garden City	Pardon Peace Purity
West Bromwich	n
Weston-super-Mare	n
Whitby	Jesus Saves
Winsford	Here Bring Thy Wounded Heart
Wokingham	Jesus Never Fails
Wollaston	n
Wolverhampton Goodwill	n
Wood Green	n
Woodhouse	Peace Pardon Purity
Worcester	n
Worthing	n
Wrexham	n

Appendix F

Mercy Seat Inscriptions With Frequency 1994

All The Promises Of God Are Sure
At The Cross There's Room
Be Ye Reconciled To God
Boundless Salvation (2)
Bring Him Thy Sorrow
Christ Receiveth Sinners
Come To Jesus
Come With Thy Sin
Deliverance
Down At The Saviour's Feet Burdens Roll Away, Darkness Turns To
    Day
Emmanuel
Forgiveness
From The Uttermost To The Uttermost
God Is Love (2)
Grace
He Can Break Every Fetter (4)
He Is Able To Save
He Saves To The Uttermost (2)
He Will Abundantly Pardon
He Will Break Every Fetter
Here Bring Thy Wounded Heart (2)
His Blood Can Make The Vilest Clean
I Bring Thee All
It Matters To Him About You

Jesus
Jesus Christ Is Lord
Jesus Never Fails (2)
Jesus Saves (9)
Jesus Will Save You
My Peace I Give You
Pardon Peace (2)
Pardon Peace Power (6)
Pardon Peace Power Purity (4)
Pardon Peace Purity (6)
Pardon Power Peace
Peace Pardon Purity (2)
Peace Power Pardon
Place Of Prayer
Power Pardon Peace
Precious Saviour
Repentance
Salvation Full And Free
Seek Ye First The Kingdom Of God
Tell It To Jesus
The Mercy Seat
There Is Mercy In Jesus
To The Uttermost He Saves (12)
Ye Must Be Born Again
You Must Be Born Again

Appendix G

Orders And Regulations

LIKE many aspects of Salvationism, the mercy seat has long been the subject of *Orders and Regulations*. The first set of *Orders and Regulations for Field Officers* was published in 1886. They contain no mention of the mercy seat.

The penitent form or mercy seat was first mentioned in *Orders and Regulations* in 1917, 50 years or so after it was first used.

A survey of *Orders and Regulations* through the years also highlights the change in terminology from 'penitent form' to 'mercy seat' and 'holiness altar' to 'holiness table'. The term 'penitent form' has not been used in *Orders and Regulations* since the 1974 edition.

The term 'holiness altar' is first mentioned in 1925. It was replaced by 'holiness table' in 1950.

The following are relevant extracts that relate to the mercy seat and holiness table.

O & R for Field Officers, 1917
Bk. II, Pt. III]   Indoor Sunday Meetings   [Chap. V, Sect. 7
Section 7. The Penitent-Form

1. The Commanding Officer [C.O.] is responsible for seeing that the Recruiting Sergeant has the Penitent-Form available at the moment it is required. The forms used for penitents should never be removed or used for any other purpose than that of a Mercy Seat.

a) The Penitent-Form approved by the National Headquarters is recommended, but no structural alterations may be effected without the consent of the Divisional Commander, in harmony with the Regulations relating to Property.

b) The official design is a form, fixed at the foot of the platform, enclosed, when not in use, by a heavy red cord suspended to short posts placed at suitable distances apart, the enclosed space being carpet.

c) Whilst discouraging mere formalities, the F.O. [Field Officer] should encourage his people to regard the Penitent-Form with feelings akin to reverence; he must see that it is maintained in a cleanly condition.

2. The C.O. must see that the Recruiting and Penitent-Form Sergeants are stationed near the Penitent-Form, when penitents are expected in a Meeting.

3. The C.O. must impress upon the Penitent-Form workers the importance of a penitent being spoken to immediately he comes forward.

4. The C.O. must see that a Sergeant, or other duly-appointed Soldier, deals with each penitent.

5. The C.O. should see that the Penitent-Form Sergeants are carefully instructed in the best methods of dealing with penitents. The Sergeant should –

a) Discover whether the seeker is really in earnest. If he has come forward merely as a matter of form, or to satisfy some one who pressed him to do so, or because he thought it might do him some little good, or for any other reason apart from that of earnestly seeking and finding Salvation, the Penitent-Form Sergeant should at once set to work to bring him under true conviction. He should pray for him, reason with him, show him his danger, and endeavour him to bring him to repentance.

b) If convinced that the Penitent is in earnest, find out if he is willing to give up sin.

i. He should ask him plainly if he is willing to cease from everything which he knows to be displeasing to God.

ii. If he is not, nothing further can be done until he manifests his willingness to do so. It is useless going on to speak of the love or mercy of God, or the efficacy of the Blood, if a man is holding on to something which he knows God condemns.

Section 1. – Penitent-form Work in General

1. The penitent-form or mercy-seat (and in Holiness Meetings the holiness altar) occupies an important place in Salvation Army warfare.

a) No virtue attaches to the penitent-form itself as such, but coming there is a public confession of spiritual need, of desire after God, and of determination to seek Him. In short, it expresses decision, confession, seeking. Such an act is advantageous to the seeker in that it tests his sincerity, tends to bring him to that humble and submissive condition of soul in which God can deal with him, and assists him in breaking loose from worldly associations. Moreover, the penitent-form provides a place where spiritual guidance can suitably be given, and its use helps a leader to keep a definite aim before him in Meetings.

b) Certain dangers need to be guarded against in the use of the penitent-form; in particular:

i. Relying upon the act of going there, instead of upon the work which God does in the soul. This leads to the substitution of profession for actual experience.

ii. Regarding the penitent-form as a kind of 'confessional' for the easing of a guilty conscience, when there is no sincere determination to forsake sin.

iii. Going to the penitent-form without due thought, and thereby becoming so familiar with it that it loses its spiritual significance.

iv. Inefficient penitent-form dealing, which often results in seekers going away disappointed.

v. Failure to realize that what takes place at the penitent-form is only the beginning of God's work of grace, and should be followed by continual spiritual progress.

2. 'Seekers' include all who come to the penitent-form or holiness altar.

a) Salvation seekers are those seeking Salvation; they are also known as penitents. Backsliders needing restoration are dealt with as Salvation seekers.

b) Holiness seekers are those seeking Holiness.

c) A Salvation seeker who rises from the penitent-form having found Salvation is known as a Convert. One who leaves without being saved should still be spoken of as a seeker.

5. Various considerations show the supreme importance of helping seekers thoroughly.

a) Coming to the penitent-form is – or should be – the turning-point in the seeker's spiritual life, the step which leads to his new birth, and hence the outstanding event of his whole career. Coming to the holiness altar has similar importance.

b) The seeker at the penitent-form, owing to the conviction of sin and other emotions which have impelled him to decision, is then highly impressionable; in such a state he is more readily and lastingly influenced than at ordinary times. Consequently, the worker has a unique opportunity.

c) The true seeker expects to receive something definite from God, even though he may understand but dimly what he wants, and how to get it. If he does not find what he seeks his whole future will probably be affected; he may decide that 'there's nothing in it after all,' or that 'it's of no use for me to try,' and through discouragement stay away from The Army, so being for ever lost to its influences. In any case, if disappointed his Salvation (or Sanctification) will be indefinitely postponed.

O & R for Officers, 1950
Pt. VI]   Dealing with Seekers   [Chap. V, Sect. 1
Section 1. – Penitent Form Work in General
1. The Penitent Form or Mercy Seat (and in Holiness Meetings the Holiness Table) occupies an important place in Salvation Army warfare.

2. 'Seekers' include all who come to the Penitent Form or Holiness Table

a) Salvation seekers are those seeking Salvation; they are also known as penitents. Backsliders needing restoration are dealt with as Salvation seekers.

b) Holiness seekers are those seeking Holiness.

c) A Salvation seeker who rises from the Penitent Form having found Salvation is known as a Convert. One who leaves without being saved should still be spoken of as a seeker.

5. Various considerations show the supreme importance of helping seekers thoroughly.

a) Coming to the Penitent Form is – or should be – the turning-point in the seeker's spiritual life, the step which leads to his new birth, and hence the outstanding event of his whole career. Coming to the Holiness Table has similar importance.

O & R for Officers, 1960
Pt. VI]   Dealing with Seekers   [Chap. V, Sect. 1
Section 1. – Penitent Form Work in General
1. The Penitent-form or Mercy Seat (and in holiness meetings the holiness table) occupies an important place in Salvation Army warfare.

O & R for Officers, 1974
Pt. 3]   Counselling seekers   [Chap. IV
Chapter IV Counselling Seekers
1. The term 'seekers' includes all who come to the Penitent-form, Mercy Seat or holiness table.

O & R for Officers, 1987
Pt. 3]   Counselling seekers   [Chap. IV
Chapter IV Counselling Seekers
1. The term 'seekers' includes all who come to the mercy seat or holiness table.

O & R for Officers of The Salvation Army, 2003
Vol. 1 Pt. 2]   The Officer's Principal Responsibility   [Chap. IV
Chapter IV Counselling Seekers
Section 1. THE MERCY SEAT
1. The mercy seat or penitent form (and where used, the holiness table) is the central place in Salvation Army worship.

2. There is no virtue attached to either of these as such, but they provide a place for confession, repentance and consecration, as well as for spiritual guidance to be given to any seeker.

3. The ministry at a mercy seat is under the direction of the officer-in-charge who may be assisted by as many men and women counsellors as may be necessary. These should be Salvationists of recognised worth, warm in heart, sound in doctrine, and adequately trained for their duties. They will usually deal with persons of their own sex.

4. Counsellors should have a working knowledge of the chapter on salvation and sanctification in the *Handbook of Doctrine*, as well as the guidance for their duties provided in the *O & R for Local Officers*. In addition, the attention of counsellors should be drawn to other relevant literature published either internationally or within the territory. Counsellors should have a Bible with them and know key texts for spiritual needs. They should be competent to deal with emotional hurts which affect body and spirit.

5. Generally speaking, seekers should be spoken to, and listened to, without undue delay and helped to feel the warmth of the counsellor's personal concern.

6. Though counselling may at times be lengthy and difficult, it should never be hurried. Whether counselling is concluded at the mercy seat or in a quiet counselling room, the seeker should leave with the assurance of having entered into the desired experience.

7. In most cases only one counsellor will be required; however, where complex problems come to light, it may be necessary to enlist others to help, with the agreement of the seeker. Some seekers may not wish to have any assistance or counselling. This should be discovered at the outset and their wishes respected.

Chapter I General Statements
1. Every Salvation Army meeting should have as its primary purpose the worship of God leading to the salvation of the unconverted and/or the deepening of the spiritual life of God's people.

2. A mercy seat must be available for use in all Salvation Army meetings.

Chapter V The Mercy Seat
1. When inviting a congregation to make use of the mercy seat it should be made clear that the place itself has no virtue.
2. It should be emphasised that the act of coming to the mercy seat should be seen as an outward expression of an inward response to the Holy Spirit's leading.
3. The mercy seat provides a place where spiritual guidance can be given, although on occasion it may be more helpful to move the seeker to a counselling room where there is more privacy.

Chapter II Counselling Seekers
1. Those responsible for counselling in Army meetings should possess the following qualifications:
a) A sound spiritual experience that is evidenced by consistency in Christian life and witness;
b) A good knowledge of the Bible so that its important spiritual truths can be used to help and guide the seeker;
c) A clear understanding of Christian doctrine.
2. The counselling of seekers at the mercy seat should always be unhurried. If felt necessary and helpful, it should be continued elsewhere.
3. In principle, whatever confidences may be shared by the seeker with the counsellor must be regarded as sacred and not disclosed. However, counsellors will always bear in mind their legal and moral responsibilities to other parties who may be involved or at risk, and this may, in certain circumstances, necessitate the disclosure of information to others. Should a crime or some public misdemeanour be confessed, the counsellor should urge the penitent to inform the appropriate authority, and should offer personal help in every endeavour to make amends. In these

instances the counsellor should seek the guidance of his/her immediate leader.

4. To ensure suitable aftercare and discipling, the seeker's name and address must be recorded and entered into the seekers register as soon as possible.

5. An early opportunity for follow-up should be made.

Appendix H

Bibliography

Published by The Salvation Army
Arnold, Irena, *More Poems of a Salvationist*, 1945
Avery, Gordon, *Companion to the Song Book*, 1961
Baird, Catherine, *Reflections*, 1975
Barnes, Cyril, *Words of William Booth*, 1975
Begbie, Harold, *Life of William Booth*, 1919
Booth, Bramwell, *Echoes and Memories*, 1925
Booth, William, *Addresses to Staff Officers*, 1906
Booth, William, *In Darkest England and the Way Out*, 1890
Booth, William, *The Founder Speaks*, 1928
Brand, Will, *With Sword and Song*, 1975
Brengle, Samuel, *Ancient Prophets*, 1929
Brengle, Samuel, *Helps to Holiness*, 1896
Brengle, Samuel, *Love-Slaves*, 1923
Brengle, Samuel, *Resurrection Life and Power*, 1925
Burrows, William, *The Mercy Seat*, 1951
Burrows, William, *With Colours Waving*, 1957
Coutts, Frederick, *In Good Company*, 1980
Davey, Abram, *The Salvation War in the West*, c 1886
Gowans, John, *O Lord, Not More Verse!* 1999
Hall, Clarence, *Samuel Logan Brengle; Portrait of a Prophet*, 1933
Harris, Wesley, *Battle Lines*, 1984
Joy, Edward, *The Old Corps*, 1944
Kew, Clifford, *Closer Communion*, 1980
Larsson, John, *Spiritual Breakthrough*, 1983
Mingay, Albert, *My Day For Living*, 1970
Needham, Phil, *Community in Passion; a Salvationist Ecclesiology*, 1987

Railton, George Scott, *Captain Ted*, 1880
Street, Robert, *Called to be God's Soldier*, 1999
Taylor, Gordon, *Companion to the Song Book*, 1989
White, Arnold, *The Great Idea*, 1909

How to Counsel Seekers, 1985
Orders and Regulations for Field Officers, 1917, 1925
Orders and Regulations for Local Officers, 1991
Orders and Regulations for Officers, 1925, 1948, 1950, 1960, 1974, 1987, 2003
Salvationist
Salvation Story, 1998
The Field Officer
The Jubilant and Other Salvationist Verse, 1947
The Merchant of Heaven and Other Salvationist Verse, 1944
The Officer
The Sacraments: The Salvationist's Viewpoint, 1960
The Salvationist
The Salvation Army and the Body of Christ, 2008
The Salvation Army Handbook of Doctrine, 1881, 1969, 2010
The Salvation Army Song Book, 1899, 1930, 1953, 1986
The Salvation Army Year Book, 1907, 1942, 1993, 2010
The Salvation War, 1885
The War Cry
The War Cry, Australia
The War Cry, USA National
Twenty-one Years Salvation Army, c1886

Published by other publishers

Bennett, David, *The Altar Call: Its Origins and Present Usage*, University Press of America, New York, 2000
The Book of Common Prayer, Oxford University Press, London, 1928
Brewer E. Cobham, *Dictionary of Phrase and Fable*, Henry Altemus, Philadelphia, 1898

Carwardine, Richard, *Transatlantic Revivalism; Popular Evangelicalism in Britain and America 1790-1865*, Greenwood Press, Westport, Conn, 1978

Catechism of the Catholic Church, Continuum, London, 2006

Coleman, Robert, *The Origin of the Altar Call in American Methodism, The Asbury Seminarian*, Winter 1958

Colton, Calvin, *History and Character of American Revivals of Religion*, Frederick Westley and A. H. Davis, London, 1832

Costa, Ken, *God at Work*, Continuum, London and New York, 2007

Costello, Peter, *Dublin Churches*, Gill & MacMillan, Dublin, 1989

Doran, Susan and Durston Christopher, *Princes, Pastors, and People: The Church and Religion in England 1529-1689*, Routledge, London, 1991

Dow, Lorenzo, *History of Cosmopolite*, Joshua Martin, 1848

Dictionary of Christianity in America, IVP, Illinois, 1990

Ervine, St John, *God's Soldier: General William Booth*, William Heinemann Ltd, London & Toronto

Finney, Charles, *Lectures on Revivals of Religion*, Leavitt, Lord & Co, New York, 1835

Gesenius, Wilhelm, *Hebrew and Chaldee Lexicon to the Old Testament Scriptures* trs Samuel Prideaux Tregelles, Samuel Bagster and Sons, London, 1846

Hirsch, Samson, *The Pentateuch Translated and Explained*, London, 1956

Horridge, Glenn K., *The Salvation Army Origins and Early Days: 1865-1900*, Ammonite Books, Godalming, 1993

Jesus Life magazine, Jesus Fellowship Church, Northampton

Kent, John, *Holding the Fort*, Epworth Press, 1978

Kirk, Edward Norris, *Lectures on Revivals*, Congregational Publishing Society, Boston, 1875

Lothian, Murdoch, *The Cutty Stool*, Hughson Gallery, Glasgow, 1995

Mackay, Charles, *A Dictionary of Lowland Scotch*, Whittaker and Co. London, 1888

McGrath, Alister, *Mere Theology*, SPCK, London, 2010

McLendon, H. R., *The Mourner's Bench*. Thesis (Th.D.). Southern Baptist Theological Seminary, 1902

Newcastle Daily Chronicle, 21 May 1879

Oke, Norman, *We Have an Altar*, Nazarene Publishing House, Kansas City, Miss, 1954

O'Reilly, Sean, *Irish Churches and Monasteries*, The Collins Press, London, 1997

Parfitt, Tudor, *The Lost Ark of the Covenant*, HarperOne, New York, 2008

Pattison, Thomas Harwood, *The History of Christian Preaching*, American Baptist Publication Society, Philadelphia, 1903

Perry, J. R. and Struhbar L. M., *Evangelistic Preaching*, Moody Press, Chicago, 1979

Sandall, Robert, *The History of The Salvation Army*, Thomas Nelson and Son, London, Volume One 1947, Volume Two 1950

Streett, R. Alan, *The Effective Invitation*, Fleming H. Revell Company, 1984

The Christian Mission Magazine

The Encylopedia of World Methodism, United Methodist Publishing House, Nashville, Tn, 1974

The Rough Guide to Dublin, Rough Guides Ltd, 2002

Vine, W. E., *Expository Dictionary of New Testament Words*, MacDonald, Virginia

Wiggins, Arch, *The History of The Salvation Army*, Thomas Nelson and Son, Volume Four 1964,Volume Five 1968

Young, Robert, *Analytical Concordance to the Holy Bible*, Lutterworth Press, Guildford and London, 1977

Zodhiates, Spiros, *The Hebrew-Greek Key Study Bible*, Eyre and Spottiswoode, London, 1986

Officers responding to request in *The Officer*

Readers responding to request in *Salvationist*

International officer survey response

UK officer survey response

UK Divisional Commander survey response

UK Divisional Children's Officer survey response

UK Divisional Director for Personnel survey response

Index

24-7 prayer movement xvi

A

Addresses to Staff Officers 140
Aelfric, Abbot 181
Afghanistan 57
Alaska 77
Alexandria, Virginia (USA) 92
All Saints' Church, Wittenberg 15
Alpha International 219
Altar Call: Its Origins and Present Usage, The 19
Altars in the Street 126
'An Open Letter to a Young Man Seeking Spiritual Help' 62
Ancient Prophets 59
Anderson, Lindsay 190
Andersson, Helena 81
Angels Guard the Mercy-Seat 108
Antony of Padua 14
Anxious seat 20, 27, 28, 29, 30, 31, 85, 168, 174, 175, 215, 216, 217
Arabia 206
Argentina 78, 93
Ark of Care, The 108
'Army's Stance on the Sacraments, The' 196
Arnold, Irena 108
Asbury, Francis 26
Atlanta, Georgia (USA) 56, 76
Augustine of Hippo 185, 196
Australia 62, 83, 84, 89
Australia Southern Territory 149

B

Baird, Bram 141, 142
Baird, Catherine 114, 145

Barnes, Cyril 33, 45
Barrow-in-Furness 53
Battle Lines 64, 66
Benge, Janet and Geoff 35
Bennett, David 19, 21, 22, 23, 25, 26
Berlin 44
Bernard of Clairvaux 14
Beside the Mercy Seat 113
Bishop, Dale 141
Blackfriars 44
Blackwall 19
Blurton, Geoff 142
Boehm, Henry 24
Bolton 48, 86
Bond, Linda 68
Bonhoeffer, Dietrich 170
Book of Common Prayer, The 173, 182, 190
Booth, Bramwell 45, 46, 55, 66
Booth, Catherine 35, 36, 39, 40, 52
Booth, Catherine Bramwell 145
Booth, Evangeline 104, 175, 176, 186, 188
Booth, Florence 54
Booth, William (the Founder, the General) xv, xvi, 33, 34, 35, 36, 37, 38, 39, 40, 41, 42, 43, 44, 45, 46, 47, 58, 61, 62, 125, 140, 155, 183, 185, 192, 195, 217
Booth-Tucker, Frederick 217
Boston, Massachusetts (USA) 62
Bourne, Hugh 26
Bouziges, Sonia 78, 93
Bovey, Ken 90
Bovey, Laurie 55
Bovey, Margaret 163
Bovey, Nigel ix, x, 115
Bradford 47
Bradford, William 15
Bradshaw, Mrs Elsie 86